Rebuilding the News

REBUILDING THE NEWS

Metropolitan Journalism in the Digital Age

C. W. Anderson

TEMPLE UNIVERSITY PRESS
Philadelphia

TEMPLE UNIVERSITY PRESS
Philadelphia, Pennsylvania 19122
www.temple.edu/tempress

Copyright © 2013 by Temple University
All rights reserved
Published 2013

Library of Congress Cataloging-in-Publication Data

Anderson, C. W. (Christopher William), 1977–
    Rebuilding the news : metropolitan journalism in the digital age / C. W. Anderson.
        p.   cm.
    Includes bibliographical references and index.
    ISBN 978-1-4399-0933-1 (hardback : alk. paper)
    ISBN 978-1-4399-0934-8 (paper : alk. paper)
    ISBN 978-1-4399-0935-5 (e-book)
    1. Journalism—Technological innovations.   2. Journalism—Social aspects.   I. Title.
    PN4784.T34A83 2013
      070.4'3—dc23   2012015511

♾ The paper used in this publication meets the requirements of the American National Standard
for Information Sciences—Permanence of Paper for Printed Library Materials, ANSI Z39.48-1992

Printed in the United States of America

2 4 6 8 9 7 5 3 1

To my parents

Contents

Acknowledgments

R*ebuilding the News* is a bridge between two academic lifetimes: the first as a doctoral student in communications at the Columbia University Graduate School of Journalism, and the second as an assistant professor at the College of Staten Island (City University of New York). Consequently, during the writing of this book, I have accumulated a large number of debts.

The project began under the guidance of the late Professor James Carey and continued under the equally wonderful guidance of Todd Gitlin and Michael Schudson. Along with Andrea Tucher, Gil Eyal, and Jay Rosen, these mentors could not have provided better support and direction. Each taught me in his or her own way, and their example greatly enhanced my understanding of the deeper purposes of writing and scholarship. Also at Columbia, I was lucky enough to be surrounded by a most wonderful collection of doctoral students, and I owe special thanks to (in no particular order) Joe Cutbirth, Jefferson Pooley, Rasmus Kleis Nielsen, Ruth Palmer, Ben Peters, Tom Glaiyser, Katherine Brown, Jonah Bossewitch, Julia Sonnevend, Laura Forlano, Olivier Sylvain, and Joost van Dreunen. Lucas Graves first mentioned the words "actor-network theory" to me (a decision that, having since heard me babble on about it incessantly, he may now regret). John Kelly was instrumental in helping me think through the larger nuances of social network analysis, and the network maps in this book are as much a product of his labor as of mine. Members of a larger community of scholars have read parts of this manuscript and provided welcome feedback, including Christina Dunbar-Hester, Dave Karpf, Rasmus Kleis Nielsen, Lucas Graves, Siva Vaidhyanathan, Pablo Boczkowski, Rodney Benson, Geneva Overholser, Fred Turner, Phil Napoli, Clay Shirky, Seth Lewis, Nikki Usher, and Steve Reese. Daniel Kreiss performed a particularly heroic act by reading the entire book and offering wonderfully detailed input.

Aspects of this work have been presented at far too many conferences to name, but over the course of its transformation from dissertation to book, I have drawn sustenance from five intellectual homes in particular. The first is the College of Staten Island, where my fellow faculty has touched me with their kindness; I am grateful to them for providing me with a place to both teach and think. The second is the Yale Information Society Project, where I served as a visiting fellow from 2010 to 2011; in particular, I thank Jack Balkin and Laura DeNardis for their support. The third is the New America Foundation; I thank Steve Coll for the chance to think hard about media policy and Tom Glaiyser for the direction he provided when I served as a visiting fellow from 2009 to 2010. The fourth is the virtual community of the Nieman Journalism Lab; I am grateful to Josh Benton, who took the risk of allowing an unknown blogger to think in public, and to all of the lab editors, but particularly Megan Garber, whose help greatly improved that public thinking. The last is the Tow Center at Columbia University, whose first director, Emily Bell, gave me the opportunity to continue my public policy work in a meaningful way and provided me with a steady supply of Britishisms.

The road from doctoral thesis (whose audience is a committee of five) to academic monograph (whose audience is, with luck, slightly larger) can be filled with land mines and uncertainty. Working with Temple University Press, however, I have experienced no detonations of any kind. Much of the credit for that goes to my editor, Mick Gusinde-Duffy, who has skillfully guided a first-time author through the labyrinth of twenty-first-century publishing. I also owe a debt of gratitude to the two anonymous readers for Temple University Press, whose feedback greatly enriched the final manuscript.

An earlier version of Chapter 4 was published as C. W. Anderson, "Journalistic Networks and the Diffusion of Local News: The Brief, Happy News Life of the 'Francisville Four,'" *Political Communication* 27, no. 3 (2010): 289–309. Small portions of Chapter 6 were originally published in C. W. Anderson, "Web Production, News Judgment, and Emerging Categories of Online Newswork in Metropolitan Journalism," *Journalism: Theory, Practice, Criticism* 12, no. 5 (2011): 630–646, and will be published in C. W. Anderson, "What the Aggregators Do: Toward a Networked Concept of Journalistic Expertise," *Journalism: Theory, Practice, Criticism* (forthcoming). As much of my thinking about this project has occurred "in public," scattered thoughts contained in this book appear in different form on Twitter, in a variety of blog posts, and on the Nieman Journalism Lab.

Two sets of people and one individual deserve a special note of thanks. The first pair is my mother and father, whose lifetime of encouraging me to read and think as much as I could, combined with their own respect for education and knowledge, helped set me on this road. They even tolerated my reading every local newspaper I could find during our many road trips when I was a teenager. I dedicate this book to them.

The second thank-you goes to my wife, Jessica. She has been with me through every single step of this long intellectual process, and she has always reminded me that what is happening in the world is at least as important as what is happening in my head. Without her love, support, and patience, this book would not exist, and I would not even be able to muster the happiness to care. I thank Jess for everything.

Finally, I offer my heartfelt gratitude to the many, many journalists and bloggers whose thoughts are chronicled in these pages. I am grateful to them for letting me into their world and allowing me to chronicle a very difficult time in their professional lives. I can only hope that the final product repays the trust they have shown me and the time they have given to what probably often seemed like a very abstract effort. Special thanks go to Will Bunch, Chris Krewson, Karl Martino, Amy Z. Quinn, and Wendy Warren; with all of them manning the news barricades in one way or another, the future of journalism will surely be bright.

Timeline of Digital News

Developments in Philadelphia
and Nationally

1982 **Philadelphia**
- The *Philadelphia Evening Bulletin* closes, part of a wave of consolidation in the news industry. Philadelphia now has two daily newspapers owned by a single national chain, Knight-Ridder.

1995 **Philadelphia**
- The *New York Times* reports on threats to turn Philadelphia into a "one newspaper town" by closing the tabloid the *Philadelphia Daily News*. Various iterations of this threat are repeated, under different circumstances, over the next fifteen years.
- Phillylife.com—an entertainment-only version of the Philadelphia newspapers—is launched. It is later renamed Philadelphiaonline.com.
- The *City Paper,* a local alternative weekly, launches City Paper City Net. Modeled after Prodigy and AOL, the site supplies news, e-mail, usenet, and bulletin-board (BBS) access.

1996 **Philadelphia**
- The website GrooveLingo is launched by a self-described "bored college student." The website is designed to cover the Philadelphia music scene.

Nationally
- The *New York Times* goes online.

1997 **Philadelphia**
- Philadelphiaonline.com launches Blackhawk Down, a massive experiment in collaborative, long-form digital storytelling.

1999   Philadelphia

- Philadelphiaonline.com is renamed Philly.com. It begins using a content management system for the first time, replacing its earlier flat-file system.
- In December, Karl Martino launches the "collaborative blog" Philly Future. Originally hosted at EditThisPage.com, the site invites Philadelphians to register as either editors or contributors.

Nationally

- Blogger is released by PyraLabs. The software is designed to make online self-publishing—later known as "blogging"—easy and ubiquitous.
- The first Independent Media Center (IMC) opens its doors in Seattle. The IMC is founded to provide grassroots coverage of demonstrations against the World Trade Organization. It is one of the first digital media websites to emphasize participant-powered journalistic coverage of breaking news.

2000   Philadelphia

- The Independent Media Center of Philadelphia, a branch of the larger IMC network, opens in the summer to cover the Republican National Convention in Philadelphia.

Nationally

- Knight-Ridder centralizes control of its local newspaper properties through Knight-Ridder Digital, which launches with thirty-three websites. As part of this change, operations and website management are consolidated.
- Knight-Ridder begins to rethink the role of its online local media properties, attempting to brand them as local portals that not only contain news but also are gateways to an entire geographic region.
- The dot-com bubble bursts.

2002   Philadelphia

- Philly.com redesigns its website, with a look and a content management system that is now part of a Knight-Ridder standard.
- The small, personal blog Mere Cat is founded by a web developer who has dabbled in programming. The site is entirely personal and covers topics such as lobster rolls and artisan beer.
- A technology staff member with the *Philadelphia Daily News* travels to San Jose to hear a lecture by Dan Gilmor. He returns to Philadelphia advocating that the paper embrace "blogging." Later that year, the first *Daily News* blog, Bark's Bytes, launches. It covers the Philadelphia Eagles but is discontinued after the season ends.

2004   **Philadelphia**
- The journalist Amy Z. Quinn launches the blog Tales of a Feminist Housewife. In 2005, it is renamed Citizen Mom and becomes an important blog in Philadelphia.
- Joey Sweeney, sometime music critic with the *City Paper* and *Philadelphia Weekly,* launches Philebrity, a website designed to integrate an alternative weekly attitude with an interactive digital presence.
- A *Reading Eagle* staff member launches Berks Phillies Fans, a website chronicling the Philadelphia Phillies, originally as a way to make group e-mails about the trials of the baseball team more public and permanent. The site is later renamed Beerleaguer.
- The *Daily News* launches the special blog Campaign Extra to cover the presidential race of 2004. In 2005, the blog is renamed Attytood and is maintained by Will Bunch.
- Karl Martino relaunches Philly Future, moving away from the idea of a "group blog" and toward a site that is powered by aggregating RSS feeds and the best content of other local blogs.

2005   **Philadelphia**
- Philly.com and the *Daily News* launch the Next Mayor, an attempt to combine public and networked journalism to report on the mayoral race.

Nationally
- Knight-Ridder, owner of the Philadelphia newspapers, announces plans to break up and sell its assets.

2006   **Philadelphia**
- A variety of Philadelphia journalists gather for the first and only Norgs Unconference to discuss building a networked news organization in the city.
- The Pew Foundation discusses creating a website nicknamed the Phly, which would rely heavily on user-generated content and citizen journalism. The site is never launched.

2008   **Philadelphia**
- The *Philadelphia Inquirer* begins to staff a breaking news desk.
- Pew again considers launching a journalism project in Philadelphia, this time under the informal moniker the Y-Factor. Once again, the site does not launch.

Nationally
- Newspapers suffer one of their worst financial years on record, partly because of pressure from the solidifying digital information environment and partly because of the onset of the recession.

2009 Philadelphia
- Philadelphia Media Holdings files for bankruptcy.
- Three young journalism entrepreneurs, graduates of Temple University, found Technically Philly, designed to actively chronicle Philadelphia's startup scene.

2010 Philadelphia
- The Philadelphia newspapers are auctioned off in bankruptcy proceedings. Attempts by the owners to retain control of the properties fail, and the papers come under the control of Philadelphia Media Network, a consortium of banks and hedge funds.
- The local public radio station WHYY launches Newsworks, a local news website that combines original digital reporting, aggregation, and content from the radio news team.
- The William Penn Foundation commissions a report on the Philadelphia media ecosystem and draws up plans to create a "network news" hub online.
- The *Daily News* begins staffing a breaking news desk.
- The new chief executive of Philadelphia Media Network, which owns the local newspapers, announces a number of initiatives, including launching a startup incubator at the newspapers and placing some content behind a partial pay wall.

2011 Philadelphia
- The Philadelphia newspapers begin to sell digital subscriptions as part of an all-inclusive tablet.

Nationally
- The *New York Times* launches its website's pay wall.

2012 Philadelphia
- The Philadelphia newspapers leave behind their iconic home at 200 North Broad Street and move to a location downtown, at Eighth and Market streets.
- The Philadelphia Media Network is once again placed on the market. It is revealed that ownership has been interfering with the paper's coverage of its own sale and that one of the bidders consists of a large group of locally connected political insiders.
- A chief executive is hired for the Philadelphia Public Interest News Network, the network news hub based at Temple University and funded in part by the William Penn Foundation.
- A group of six local investors purchase Philadelphia Media Network amid fears these connected insiders will use the papers to advance their own interests. The sale gives the Philadelphia newspapers their fifth owner in six years.

Rebuilding the News

Local Journalism on the Brink

The Crossroads

In August of 2000, a hoary political institution—the Republican National Convention, assembling in Philadelphia—confronted a new kind of media network. As the national Republican Party descended on the city in the summer of 2000, its delegates were met by hundreds of convention protesters carrying cell phones, videocameras, and old-fashioned pencils and paper notebooks, all calling themselves reporters and all networked into a website that displayed reports from the street protests as news broke. Growing out of the World Trade Organization protests in Seattle in 1999 and expanding to several other American and European cities in the months that followed, these Philadelphia protester-reporters identified themselves as members of the Independent Media Center of Philadelphia (also known as the Philly IMC) and promised their readers overtly biased political reporting, by amateurs, directly from the scene of anti–Republican National Convention protests. As the political protesters clashed with Philadelphia police on the convention's second day—"thousands of roving demonstrators and helmeted police faced off in intersections around the city yesterday afternoon," the *Pittsburgh Post-Gazette* wrote, "trading blows at some junctures, while in Center City several delegate hotels locked their doors . . . as the two sides sparred for control of the streets"—amateur Indymedia journalists did more than simply comment on the drama as it unfolded. They were instrumental in documenting it online for a mass audience.[1] These Independent Media Center volunteers were among the first group of digital activists to directly pose the question of who counted as a legitimate journalist in an era of low-cost, digital information gathering and distribution.

Six years later, at the Annenberg School for Communication at the University of Pennsylvania, a few of the radical reporters who had first stormed the journalistic barricades during the Republican Convention in 2000 sat down with local bloggers, newspaper editors, cable television executives, and new-media thinkers to plot a future for local news. The pace of the changes buffeting journalism, changes that first announced themselves in dramatic fashion during coverage of the 2000 convention, had only accelerated in the intervening half-decade since the Republican National Convention. "Do-it-yourself journalism" was no longer a practice confined to political radicals and anarchists. It had manifested itself as part of a "war-blogging" revolution, a "mommy-blogging" revolution, a YouTube revolution, a MySpace revolution, a flash mob revolution, a "hyperlocal citizens' media" revolution, and in hundreds of other trends that lacked only a catchy moniker. Perhaps more ominously, the first signs of deep economic distress inside the news industry had begun to filter out of Philadelphia; in late 2005, the Knight-Ridder news chain, which owned both daily newspapers in Philadelphia (and had, for decades, posted double-digit profit margins), announced it was breaking itself up and selling its multiple media assets. In the face of the citizen media explosion and these distant economic rumblings, the Annenberg meeting was nothing like the occupational uprising in 2000 that saw radical journalists eviscerate the "lackeys of the corporate press" and professional journalists snidely dismiss their scruffy, decidedly non-objective challengers. Instead, participants in the oddly titled Norgs [new news organizations] Unconference" came together, in their words, "in a spirit of cooperation . . . to save local news in Philadelphia."[2] The Norgs Unconference was one of the first meetings explicitly to raise the question: could traditional journalists and the new breed of professional-amateur hybrids work together to improve local journalism?[3]

On February 22, 2009, three years after the Norgs Conference, a decade after the earliest meetings to plan a global Indymedia news network, and twelve years since the first newspapers in Philadelphia went online, the journalistic center finally collapsed. Philadelphia Media Holdings, the local ownership group that had purchased the city's two leading news institutions—the *Philadelphia Inquirer* and the *Philadelphia Daily News*—amid much hope, goodwill, and optimism, filed for Chapter 11 bankruptcy. The news was first broken by a local blog, analyzed breathlessly on Twitter, and reported (hours later) in lengthy, accurate depth by the bankrupt papers themselves.[4] For more than a year, the newspapers labored in a kind of Chapter 11 twilight zone, as local ownership fought a desperate rearguard action to maintain their financial control over their ailing media properties. In April 2010, these efforts were finally thwarted, with the newspapers becoming one of several media outlets across the United States controlled by banks and post-bankruptcy hedge funds. Yet even as the newspapers labored under the weight of their debts, journalistic networks at the edges of traditional media institutions continued to organize and experiment. The weekend before the bankruptcy auction, technology geeks from across the country descended on Philadelphia to brainstorm the future of news.[5] The very month the newspapers were bought by distant banks, a local foundation announced plans to fund a collaborative news network outside the walls of Philadelphia's legacy media organizations.[6] If 2008 was a year of uncertainty for Philadelphia journalism, and 2009 was a year of bankruptcy-addled stasis, 2010 seemed like a moment when innovation and energy would outpace the general economic gloom enveloping the news industry. In 2011, continued hopes for a rebirth—the new Philadelphia Media Network announced new revenue plans and launched an in-house "startup incubator"—sat uneasily alongside fears that large news organizations were incapable of making the kind of transition needed to survive in the digital twenty-first century. These fears—fears that the journey to a new world of local news would fail before it could really even begin—only increased as word arose in early 2012 that the Philadelphia newspapers were again on the verge of being sold.

Rebuilding the News: Metropolitan Journalism in the Digital Age narrates these journalistic moments of confrontation, collaboration, and collapse, filtering them through the lens of a single American city. Written and researched during a period of tremendous upheaval in the news industry, *Rebuilding the News* argues that, in the face of the chaos pressing in on them from all sides, local news organizations made particular choices about how best to adapt to emerging economic, social, and technological realities. The book analyzes the economic, organizational, and cultural factors that helped shape and direct these choices. In particular, local journalism's occupational self-image, its vision of itself as an autonomous workforce conducting original reporting on behalf of a unitary public, blocked the kind of cross-institutional collaboration that might have helped journalism thrive in an era of fractured communication. This failure, in turn, highlights the central normative problem at the heart of this book. Local journalism's vision of itself—as an institutionally grounded profession that empirically informs (and even, perhaps, "assembles") the public—is a noble vision of tremendous democratic importance. But the unreflexive commitment to a particular and historically contingent version of this self-image now undermines these larger democratic aspirations. The story of how journalism's vision of its unified public unraveled, how long taken-for-granted practices of news reporting were suddenly rendered problematic, and how news organizations struggled to rebuild local journalism—to network the news—is the story of this book.

Journalism as Ecosystem and Assemblage

The impetus for this book began with a series of questions that grew out of developments in the news industry itself. Given the tremendous technological, economic, political, cultural, and organizational changes that appear to be pummeling the journalistic sphere, how is metropolitan journalism changing? What kind of work do local journalists do? How do they collaborate and work with other institutions? And how are changes in work and working together also changing the professional authority of local journalism? For better or worse, many books have been written about the "future of journalism" in the United States, and this is not one of them. Rather, it is an in-depth analysis of how metropolitan journalism is practiced today and the economic, cultural, and philosophical challenges these current modes and practices pose for democracy and public life. To the degree that journalism has a future, the shape of that future will be determined by journalists themselves as they struggle within a web of institutional, economic, and cultural constraints. *Rebuilding the News* is, I would like to think, a history of the present.

The primary method used to research these questions was qualitative and ethnographic, although it was ethnography of a rather unusual kind. After narrowing my analytical object to local, metropolitan journalism in the United States, and after picking Philadelphia as the city whose news I wanted to understand, it quickly became clear to me that simply studying traditional Philadelphia newsrooms was not enough to get a sense of the real state of journalism in the early twenty-first century. Rather than understanding Philadelphia newsrooms, I wanted to understand the Philadelphia *news ecosystem*: I wanted to look not simply at professional journalists working for traditional news outlets but also at bloggers, radical media producers, foundations, computer hackers, and social media experts. To that end, these pages generally practice what Phil Howard calls the *network ethnography,* the practice of using network analysis to help determine relevant field sites and places of qualitative study.[7] In 2005, the decision to look at the news ecosystem rather than simply at news institutions might have seemed like an unusual impulse. Today, as the fragmentation of news continues to accelerate, I would argue that it was prescient. *Rebuilding the News* thus provides a narrative that moves easily from the *Philadelphia Inquirer* newsroom to bars in Northern Liberties and Fishtown and the large houses and activist spaces of West Philadelphia. A detailed account of my ethnographic method can is in the Appendix to this book.

A commitment to the ecosystemic analysis of Philadelphia news was accompanied by a second decision with theoretical, methodological, and philosophical implications. Throughout this book, I conceive of the practice of journalism as the practice of *assemblage*: assemblage of news products, institutions, and networks. What do I mean when I say that journalism can be thought of as assemblage? Journalism is in the business of drawing together of a variety of objects, big and small, social and technological, human and non-human. Through this work, journalists produce a remarkable variety of public-oriented products, from news stories and streams of tweets to entire news organizations. For working journalists and bloggers, that statement will most likely appear mundane. As reporters hustle to track down documents and struggle to secure interviews with recalcitrant human beings, it is obvious (to them, at least) that there is no a priori "difference between hard kernels of objective reality and wispy fumes of social force"—between quotes, texts, and technologies.[8] Readers interested in a more detailed elaboration of these theories and how they apply to the study of journalism might once again wish to skip ahead to the Appendix. For everyone else, suffice it to say that assemblage theory thus cuts across the methodological, empirical, institutional, and normative aspects of *Rebuilding the News.*[9]

The twin notions of assemblage and ecosystem also inform the primary empirical conclusions of *Rebuilding the News*—conclusions reached only after many years of ethnographic research. To state them plainly: first, local journalism has long rested its authority on the twin pillars of original reporting and a particular vision of the journalistic public. Second, both the nature of reporting and concepts of the public have been problematized in the digital era. Third, a variety of organizational, economic, and cultural factors have made navigating this transition extraordinarily difficult. Fourth, these factors cannot be analyzed simply as failures of management or misguided traditionalism; rather, the very cultural orientations that provide journalists with meaning to their work lives have also blocked newsroom evolution. To push that evolution forward, journalists must begin the hard process of rethinking who they are, what they do, and who their work is actually for.

Rebuilding the News is thus both an empirical analysis and a narrative about journalism in a particular place at a particularly dramatic time. Having briefly outlined my method and conclusions, I now summarize that narrative. I also describe the larger themes that snake through the story.

Themes of *Rebuilding the News*

What happened to journalism in the last years of the twentieth century and the first years of the twenty-first? What did it feel like to be a reporter or editor in Philadelphia as newspaper companies were sold, bankruptcies were filed, and an audience that was assumed to be mute and passive suddenly began to talk back? How did these systemic shocks ricochet through the institutions and daily work routines of journalists, bloggers, and media activists? What can these local events in one city teach us about the future of news in general? What do these on-the-ground developments teach us about the fate of journalism, one of America's most vital democratic institutions? And how does this particular *story*—the development of a specific media ecosystem at a specific moment in time—intersect with the more theoretical claims made above? As *Rebuilding the News* unfolds, four major narrative themes emerge that connect this local study to larger questions about the evolution of news and point toward problems and opportunities that will continue to affect the news industry.

First, *Rebuilding the News* chronicles how journalists' conception of the local public began to unravel. Second, the book describes the importance of reporting within the journalistic imagination, as well as the ways that bloggers and aggregators challenged this notion of "original reporting." Third, the book discusses the "non-diffusion" of innovation within news organizations and the non-diffusion of collaboration between news organizations. I take seriously the idea that the future of journalism lies partly in networked collaboration but conclude that the creation of networks is not inherently a networked property. Deinstitutionalized organizations have a complex relationship with institutions; in many ways, they are dependent on the stability and organizational heft of the very institutional structures they scorn. Fourth, and finally, *Rebuilding the News* describes the slow-motion collapse of the industrial work model on which much of journalistic content production is based, as well as attempts to rebuild that model on firmer ground. In sum, this book is the study of the legacy systems that made the news organizations I studied behave in deeply irrational ways. It is also a study of the attempts by individuals and organizations to overcome these often debilitating, locked-in processes, usually under situations in which they had few resources and little institutional support. This tension between stasis and change is the driving force behind the narrative that propels this book.

The first thematic development chronicled in this study of the Philadelphia news ecosystem is the *fracturing of the idea and image of the metropolitan public.* Over the course of my research, I became conscious of the degree to which "the public" occupied a particular pride of place in the journalistic imaginary. Philadelphia journalists were quick to invoke the way their daily newswork informed the local public. On a deeper level, they often talk about the manner in which their newswork called that very public *into being.* And the importance of this public was not just affirmed by status-conscious traditional journalists at the major Philadelphia newspapers. It was a claim echoed by radical citizen reporters and even by some bloggers. It was in part this unexpected rhetorical overlap that helped me first recognize the importance of the local public in the journalistic consciousness. One of the arguments of this book is that the idea and the materiality of the local public have come unbundled in the age of the Internet. Over the course of my research, the notion that "the public" was capable of being captured by any single set of work practices or institutions seemed increasingly difficult for many journalists to honestly believe. Nevertheless, it was a belief that many of them continued to voice, often in increasingly desperate tones. This gap between this rhetoric of the local public, informed and embodied by journalism, and the dawning realization that this public was breaking the communicative shell traditionally designed to house it is one of the stories of this book.

A second narrative thread analyzes the work practices of local journalism. Over the course of my time in Philadelphia, I was struck by the degree to which the act of simply "reporting the news" continued to loom large in journalists' rhetoric about who they were and what they did. When journalists wanted to validate themselves and their profession, they noted that reporting was what distinguished true journalism from other activities. When they wished, on the other hand, to denigrate themselves, many of my informants would sheepishly admit that they "didn't do reporting," and were therefore less valuable than "real" journalists. In reality, however, my research demonstrated that the practice of original reporting was far from being either pure or unproblematic. The kind of work that constituted "original reporting" seemed increasingly difficult for journalists to define. Reporting existed side by side with other forms of newswork such as blogging and aggregation, often within news organizations that heaped rhetorical scorn on these so-called lesser practices. At the same time, these traditional institutions would reappropriate newswork practices such as blogging and news aggregation and shape them to reportorial ends. All of these complexities are described in the pages that follow. For now, I simply want to highlight this important pairing: acts of reporting and images of the public. These linked concepts encapsulate much of the narrative that follows.

A third thread, which is also concerned with newswork practices but from an ecosystemic and institutional perspective, revolves around the strange persistence of the industrial work model of traditional journalism, along with emerging challenges to that model from the edges of journalistic space. In his newsroom ethnographies from the 1970s, Herbert Gans quoted one executive saying that daily news routines are "like screwing nuts on a bolt."[10] No metaphor that I am aware of better captures the industrial processes most associated with traditional journalism. Indeed, these practices remained dominant in most Philadelphia newsrooms I studied. Reporters and editors still worked to build news stories in an assembly line-like fashion, and news organizations struggled to collaborate with people and groups outside their formal institutional walls. Around the edges of these industrial-era practices, however, there was increasing decay. Technological artifacts and communications practices pressed in on static workflows. Economic challenges made it harder and harder for news organizations to maintain the staffing levels necessary to manage the complex process of gathering the news. Insurgent news organizations harnessed digital technologies and new employment regimes in ways that allowed them to open up their work routines to outside institutions, volunteers, and loosely affiliated freelancers. The industrial-era ecosystem of news assemblage that I observed in Philadelphia appeared simultaneously solid and on the verge of collapse.

A final theme of this book, then, might be labeled the "non-diffusion of collaboration." Each of the threads above—the fragmenting of the image local public, the continued centrality of reporting, and the decay of industrial production models—would seem to point to a scenario in which journalistic innovation and cross-organizational collaboration were not only rhetorically praised but also institutionally optimal. In other words, developments in the local Philadelphia news ecosystem seemed to be creating a situation in which it made rational sense to "network the news" through institutional collaboration, hypertext linking, and formal and informal partnerships. In the first round of my ethnographic research, such collaboration and innovation not only did not occur; it seemed to be purposefully thwarted. In the second round of my research, from 2009 through 2011, the situation had changed somewhat, and active attempts at building a local news hub and news network were under way. In all, however, these networked developments were slow in coming and did not rest on particularly firm ground. Many of them seemed fragile, as if they might disappear at any time. Ultimately, I conclude that the difficulties in networking the news stem as much from journalistic culture—journalism's vision of "its" public and the importance of the act of reporting in the journalistic imaginary—as they do from logistical or transaction-cost difficulties that can be easily remedied through managerial solutions.

Readers may note that this overview has not discussed a fifth theme: audience reception and media consumption. In one sense, questions about how consumers reacted to the changes sweeping the Philadelphia media ecosystem lie outside the scope of this analysis. Indeed, one of the analytical starting points of *Rebuilding the News* is that this very line between "producer" and "consumer" of media is more difficult to draw in an age of participatory content creation and "citizen journalism." At the same time, the book does adopt what Joseph Turow has called the "industrial construction" of audiences perspective,[11] "the ways that the people who create [media] materials think of" the people who consume that media, which in turn has "important implications for the texts that viewers and readers receive in the first place." The consumers of media are analyzed from the point of view of the producers.

Narrative Overview

Rebuilding the News unfolds as follows. Chapters 1 and 2 chronicle the emergence and growth of the online media ecosystem in Philadelphia, from the first local bulletin board system (BBS) users in the early 1990s to the early online efforts of the Philadelphia newspapers in 1997, and from the explosion of citizen journalism efforts at the turn of the century to more recent attempts by newspapers and other online media outlets to manage the implications of this transition. These chapters chronicle how the foundation of journalistic work—original reporting—became problematized in the early days of the World Wide Web. These chapters also trace what I call the expansion and fragmentation of the local news public and discuss early attempts to come to terms with the exponential explosion of "local publics" that now populated Philadelphia's communicative space. I map the networked threads that linked the Philadelphia's online ecosystem in 2008 and trace the connections that tied various nodes, institutions, and individuals together online. I also briefly examine the clustering of various micro-publics in different geographical spaces across the city. In these chapters, we see the professionally internalized notion of journalism as something that "assembles the public" first begin to fray.

Once Chapters 1 and 2 place Philadelphia news organizations in their historical context, readers might want to think about the remaining chapters as a spool of thread that slowly unwinds in parallel to the overall narrative arc of the story. I begin with micro-interactions—the way workers at news organizations reported a single news item, along with the changing definitions of news that were implicated in a close analysis of this reporting process. I then move on to describe the manner by which a news story moved out into the world, leaping over the walls of journalism organizations and diffusing across the entire local media ecosystem. From discussing the diffusion of a single story, I move on to consider how the elements of the entire local media ecosystem linked—or failed to link—the organizations and stories into a larger, collaborative news ecosystem. Following the thread even further, I finally leave traditional journalism institutions behind and examine outside institutions and forces that are affecting the news. On the one hand, this narrative journey can be seen as the analytical equivalent of moving from "interaction to structure," or from "micro-level" to "macro-level." However, I prefer to think about it as the methodological equivalent to following a single thread, from its starting pace in the heart of the Philadelphia journalism industry out toward wherever it happens to end up.

In this spirit, Chapters 3 and 4 draw heavily on my newsroom fieldwork in 2008, tracing the simultaneous disintegration and stability of the legacy model of industrial newswork. Through an analysis of work practices at the *Philadelphia Inquirer*, Philly.com, the *Philadelphia Daily News*, the Philly IMC, Philly Future, and dozens of local area blogs, Chapter 3 describes two dominant forms of newswork in the digital age: reporting and aggregation. It looks at the impact of mobile devices on the reporting of news and the increasing role of social media in newsroom decision making. Chapter 4 provides a newsroom-based overview of the diffusion of one news story across the entire local media ecosystem. In Chapter 3, the tension between reporting and aggregation alluded to in Chapter 2 is elaborated, as are the oddly paired strains and durabilities of the assembly-line newswork model. Chapter 4, in its overview of the diffusion of the story of the so-called Francisville Four, analyzes the local news ecosystem in action. These chapters describe the day-to-day processes by which news is networked together in the twenty-first century.

Zooming back from the newsroom, Chapter 5 chronicles the inability of local Philadelphia institutions, networks, and bloggers to create significant collaborative networks in the years between 2005 and 2008. It is here that I take assemblage theory up on its promise to help analyze networking the news on an *inter*-organizational as well as an *intra*-organizational level. Although all of the social, cultural, technological, and economic trends in journalism seemed to be pointing in a particular direction—toward newsrooms' increasingly "working together" to report the news—these collaborative networks were not built in Philadelphia, at least not during my first fieldwork period. Between 2005 and 2008, I witnessed cross-institutional innovation at the edges of news space and occasional attempts by network entrepreneurs to build new collaborative forums. For the most part, however, I observed fading institutions that were slow to change and organizations—even newer, more digitally native ones—whose rationalized structures enabled the production of valuable journalism but also erected high barriers around a variety of networked collaborative possibilities. Although Chapter 5 opens with two small collaborative successes—the so-called Norgs Unconference of 2005 and the Next Mayor project in 2005–2006—it quickly demonstrates that the temporary successes masked larger, more systemic collaborative failures. I discuss the eventual decay and disintegration of the "norgs group," as well as the early difficulties faced by two very different news institutions—Philly.com and the Philly IMC—when they attempted to formalize their commitment to digital hyperlinking. All the while, the ultimate "network failure"—the bankruptcy of the major Philadelphia newspapers—looms on the horizon.

If you had told journalists working at the *Philadelphia Inquirer* and the *Philadelphia Daily News* in 2005 that their newspapers would be bankrupt in less than five years, they would have scoffed. Journalism was in a precarious state in 2005—the Internet had disrupted many certainties and professional models—but the financial collapse of solid, profitable organizations like the companies that owned the Philadelphia newspapers was hard to imagine. Even the Philly IMC reporters who pioneered the original acts of citizen journalism in 2000—who told everyday citizens "not to hate the media but to be the media"—would have found it hard to imagine a Philadelphia in which the *Inquirer* and *Daily News* were bankrupt. The opening pages of Chapter 6 describe some of the darkest days of Philadelphia journalism. It shows how the act of reporting the news had become an increasingly precarious enterprise in 2008 and how many of the digital news organizations were highly fragile enterprises, driven by love and sweat equity more than money and prone to collapse at any moment. The chapter also sheds more light on changing journalistic visions of "the public," particularly how this public comes to be increasingly segmented and quantified by various digital measurement procedures inside newsrooms.

The story, however, does not end in wreckage, with the collapse of Philadelphia journalism. The second half of Chapter 6 chronicles the bankruptcy's aftermath, from 2009 to 2011, when a new group of innovators struggled to network the Philadelphia media ecosystem on their own terms and a reborn "Philadelphia Media Network" attempted to retrofit its legacy newspapers for the Internet era. It shows how local institutions, including several area foundations, started to push for a more collaborative journalistic environment. The chapter concludes with a discussion of a group of young technology entrepreneurs who sought to rethink journalism's core reporting practices in light of the emergence of data-driven technologies and analytical systems and briefly analyzes the changes that loomed on the horizon for the Philadelphia newspapers as they were sold yet again.

In Chapter 7, finally, I draw my research together to discuss the broader lessons that Philadelphia's attempts to "network the news" might hold for other news organizations and for concepts of digital culture and public life more generally. I consider the role that institutions, reporting, and journalists' visions of "the public" played in the story I recount here and the manner in which these concepts will continue to shape the future of metropolitan news.

Conclusion

Over the past decade, practices of newsgathering in America have been transformed. Just as the 1830s saw the invention of the penny press and the 1960s saw the rise of an aggressive form of national investigative journalism, the last years of the twentieth century and the early years of the twenty-first century constitute an equally important moment in the history of news production. During the time period studied here, some news organizations in Philadelphia thrived, while others literally struggled to survive. This book focuses on the slow-motion collapse of a major urban institution—Philadelphia's local newspapers—and the many attempts to reform and rebuild the larger news ecosystem in which they are embedded.

Rebuilding the News describes the emergence of citizen journalism in Philadelphia in 2000. It describes how the local news "went online" between 1997 and 2010. It describes some attempts at collaboration between journalistic amateurs and their corporate counterparts. It zooms in on local news practices and describes how, exactly, local news gets made in 2013, as well as how that news circulates on- and offline. And it chronicles how Philadelphia's newspapers slid into bankruptcy and how other institutions, individuals, and journalists struggled to rebuild Philadelphia's media ecosystem—to "network the news"—at a moment when the odds seemed decidedly against them. The book spends time inside the newsrooms and editorial suites of Philadelphia's major news organizations. It travels to gentrifying neighborhoods with names such as Fishtown and Northern Liberties to see how ordinary citizens are creating their own, quasi-journalistic practices of digital communication. It looks to Philadelphia's suburbs to chronicle how a new breed of bloggers is rewiring the production of sports journalism. And it lingers in the neighborhoods of West Philadelphia, where the first citizen journalism organizations rose up in opposition to the "corporate media," never honestly expecting that, ten years later, the mainstream media organizations would themselves be struggling to survive. These varied thematic threads—of individuals, institutions, collaboration, competition, and collapse—weave the narrative of this book together. Together, they tell the story of local journalism at the dawn of the digital age.

I

How Local Journalism Went Online

1

Philadelphia's Newspapers Go Online (1997–2008)

In 1997, Jennifer Musser-Metz, a web producer at Philly.com, sat at her desk turning piles of raw interview tape into RealAudio files, preparing them for uploading to the World Wide Web. The interviews were by the *Philadelphia Inquirer*'s foreign correspondent Mark Bowden, and the subject was the American military adventure in Somalia of 1993, one of the defining episodes of the early Clinton presidency. Bowden had not yet published the book that would bear the title *Black Hawk Down,* and the Ridley Scott film was four years away. But as Bowden and his editors at the newspaper prepared to run a staggering twenty-nine-part series based on his reporting from Somalia, the idea was broached for a digital component that would supplement the narrative. As Bowden later recalled, "[Jennifer] stopped by my desk to ask me what sort of research material and documentation I had for the project. I had been working on it for years at that point, and had piles of audiotapes, notes, documents, radio transcripts, photos, etc. 'Could you bring them in?' she asked. I brought in bags of stuff, and Jennifer and the other folks at Philly.com put together a Web site."[1] Out of this pile of primary documentation, which included notes, radio transcripts, and photos, Musser-Metz—who had been granted leave from Philly.com to work with the *Inquirer,* which did not have an online staff—created an interactive storytelling experience, one of the first newsroom projects to tap into the digital potential of the Internet.

The Blackhawk Down Internet project was something of a "one-off," however; an exceptional project that proves the digital rule. Although Philly.com's digital technology team did create remarkable special projects in the early days of the web, the company as a whole spent most of the 1990s and early 2000s formulating a variety of strategies to secure its online footprint, stopping the implementation of these strategies halfway, and then trying new ones. I argue in this chapter that, while some of the difficulties in figuring out what to do online were logistical and organizational, just as important (though less obvious) were changing definitions of what "the journalistic public" meant during a moment of widespread digitization. For most journalists in the early online era, "the public" was a simple concept—a large collection of locally based readers who would be informed and enlightened by journalistic reportage. The key challenge of the web for news executives, editors, and journalists was to figure out how to "move" this public online in as unified a fashion as possible. The difficulty in doing so, and the manner by which the Internet started to problematize this notion of the unified journalistic public, is a key theme of this chapter. All of the various attempts to "build a newspaper website" discussed in Chapter 2 can be seen, in part, as an attempt to bring the unproblematized public online.

Assembling Local News Infrastructures

In *Making Local News,* her overview of local news production in Philadelphia, Phyllis Kaniss ties the development of local metropolitan journalism to the growth of the American city, a link that she argues has been overlooked in the majority of media research, which focuses instead on the relationship of news, national political developments, and social history.[2] The transition from urban mercantile to manufacturing economies, population diversification, and geographic suburbanization each played a role in the growth of the penny press, the mass-circulation daily, and the zoned newspaper, as well as in the emergence of local radio and television. Just as Kaniss links changes in local news production to changes in the infrastructure of urban America, Chapter 2 charts the development of Philadelphia's digital news sphere against the backdrop of changes in online technology and the growth of the Internet. By placing media changes in their digital context, we can gain one angle on the tumultuous recent history of local news production in Philadelphia.[3] An analysis of the transformation of the local online news in that city can shed light on similar transformations in other American cities, where long-dominant newspapers—themselves having consolidated their monopoly positions in the aftermath of a first wave of newspaper extinctions in the 1970s—faced dozens of new entrants in the emerging digital universe.

There are few serious histories of the metropolitan media and local journalism in any American city. Chapters 2 and 3 limit their chronology to the past two decades and focus primarily on digital developments at a few select websites and news organizations. The component parts of the analysis in those chapters might be defined as *assemblages, controversy,* and *code.* By *assemblages,* I mean the structures, political beliefs, and organizational goals of media project managers. Is a media project run by labor organizers allied with anarchists? Has the chain management of a local newspaper recently centralized its web operations in Silicon Valley? By *assemblage,* I also mean the individuals or social groups that news organizations imagine as making up their audiences, as well as the members of that audience who elect to participate in digital content creation as "readers-producers." Do they primarily see website visitors as lazy suburbanites looking for the day's traffic and weather reports, as political protesters wanting to contribute photos about their latest mass action, or as generic "news consumers"? All media projects have a tacit vision of who their readers are and of what their audiences look like, and this shapes their organizational behavior. By *controversy*, I mean particular moments in which taken-for-granted assumptions about the definition of a technology or the proper role for a journalist are opened up for dispute, usually accompanied by a particular set of rhetorical arguments or fights about the meaning of objects and processes. By *code*, I mean the existence and level of diffusion of various technologies and technological affordances—the accessibility of certain programming languages, or content management systems, for instance. As one activist-programmer has written, "each technological design or set of features creates a particular publishing structure, and, as a result, empowers users to 'be their own media' in an equally particular way."[4]

To construct this historical overview, Chapters 2 and 3 identify seven Philadelphia websites as subjects for analysis: the Independent Media Center of Philadelphia (http://www.phillyimc.org); Philly Future (http://www.phillyfuture.org); Philebrity (http://www.philebrity.com); Beerleaguer (http://beerleaguer.typepad .com), Citizen Mom (http://quinnchannel.typepad.com); Mere Cat (http://mere cat.org); and Philly.com (http://www.philly.com). (In later chapters, I draw on interviews with, and observations of, these news projects, as well as other local websites and projects.) Table 1.1 provides an overview of some of the organizations analyzed in this and subsequent chapters. Why were these particular organizations chosen? I have already alluded to the "networked" perspective that guides this book, as well as to my desire to analyze the entire media *ecosystem* of Philadelphia, as opposed to a few key news institutions. Through a process of digital network mapping, snowball ethnographic legwork, and simply "following the actors" across the city and beyond, I selected these organizations for special focus, although I refer to many other organizations and actors briefly throughout the text. Obviously, issues of access also guided my focus: occasionally, institutions that seemed important to draw into the narrative simply were inaccessible for one reason or another. More detail about these choices is found in the Appendix; for now, I simply want to argue that the organizations chosen for study represent a fairly representative swath of the local media ecosystem in Philadelphia.

Philly.com is the joint website of Philadelphia's two major newspapers, the broadsheet *Philadelphia Inquirer* and tabloid *Philadelphia Daily News*, both of which are currently owned by Philadelphia Media Network, a consortium of local owners. Philly Future and the Philly IMC are locally oriented collaborative news websites. Mere Cat, Citizen Mom, Beerleaguer, and Philebrity are weblogs that vary in their level of local focus, personalization, and professionalism. As I described in the Introduction, the seven sites were part of a larger cluster of network sites that I identified through early fieldwork and social network mapping of the key nodes in Philadelphia's digital media sphere. To collect data on each site, I conducted at least one (and usually more than one) in-depth,

semi-structured interview with its founder or chief technological officer and analyzed the current architecture of its web page. I have also relied on public e-mail
archives describing the histories of many of the projects and the redesigns of
their websites. I have made extensive use of the Internet Archive (http://www
.archive.org), a public library service that collects versions of websites going as
far back as 1996. I also gained access to an in-depth PowerPoint presentation
describing the history of Philly.com that was compiled by a Jennifer Musser-
Metz, a member of the information technology staff who has worked for Philadelphia newspapers since 1996; I have drawn extensively on her collection of
screen captures and on the lengthy interview I conducted with her in the summer of 2008. As background, finally, I consulted Philly Internet History Week
oral history archive maintained by the Philebrity weblog.[5] While not a traditional
history archive by any stretch, the Philebrity project nonetheless did collect useful reminiscences about the early days of bulletin board systems and World Wide
Web use in Philadelphia.

Before I begin the narrative history of local digital-era journalism, however,
I will take a quick step backward to discuss the prehistory of Philadelphia newspapers: the road that led from a resource-flush "golden age" to a moment, twenty-
five years later, in which the entire future of journalism in Philadelphia seemed
up for grabs.

The Early Ecosystem

By almost any measure, the journalism industry limped toward the second
decade of the twenty-first century in a state of profound crisis. According to
many business analysts, 2008 was the worst year for newspapers since the Great
Depression, and the situation of the news media in general in that year, according to the annual report on the state of the news media by the Project on Excellence in Journalism (PEJ)" was more troubled than [it had been] a year ago [and]
2009 looked worse." The PEJ was blunt: "Newspapers are still far from dead, but
the language of obituary is creeping in." And although total newspaper reach
and readership were holding steady (if the Internet was taken into account), and
might even have grown from 2006 and 2008, advertisers continued to desert
print in droves. "The biggest problem facing traditional print media has less to
do with where people get information than how to pay for it," the report stated.
"The crisis in journalism, in other words, may not strictly be loss of audience. It
may be, more fundamentally, the decoupling of news and advertising."[6]

Locally in Philadelphia, the so-called rise and fall of the metropolitan paper
that won 17 Pulitzer Prizes in 18 years has become something of a dramatic narrative stand-in for the travails of the newspaper industry in general (see Table
1.1). The recent history of newspapers in Philadelphia began in 1982, with the
demise of the *Inquirer*'s primary rival, the *Philadelphia Evening Bulletin*;[7] the
emergence of Gene Roberts, editor of the *Inquirer,* as the undisputed genius of
Philadelphia newspaper publishing; and the implementation of what Michael

TABLE 1.1 Overview of Media Organizations Discussed in the Book

	Year	Organization Size	Background of Staff	Career Arc	Traffic Rank	Inbound Links	Funding
Attytood	2004	1	Professional reporter	Remains a "straight news reporter" as well as blogger	n/a (part of Philly.com)	n/a (part of Philly.com)	Paid to blog, but also must balance blogging and reporting
Beerleaguer	2004	1	Newspaper background but on marketing side	Continues to manage Beerleaguer	>300,000	98	Advertising, some donated time and labor
Citizen Mom	2004	1	Professional reporter for daily paper prior to starting blog	Continues Citizen Mom blog; freelances for paying journalism projects, particularly the new WHYY project Newsworks.	>3,300,00	61	From advertising, but time and labor primarily donated
Mere Cat	2002	1	Techie and web designer	Continues to manage Mere Cat	>3,800,000	51	Donated time and labor
Philebrity	2004	1–3	Professional columnist for alternative weekly	The editor continues to manage Philebrity	>250,000	359	From advertising; paid non-volunteer
Philly.com	1997	30–40*	Professional reporters and editors, techies	Website has hired a substantial number of former newspaper reporters to run the editorial side	>3500	13,338	Primarily commercial and advertising-based
Philly Future	2000	1–3	Technologist and software engineer	The editor has largely left the project behind; still updates his personal blog and works for a Philadelphia media company	>500,000	355	From advertising, but time and labor primarily donated
Philly IMC	2000	>10	Activists, techies, "alternative" and (a few) professional journalists	Website has undergone numerous organizational splits; some volunteer reporters have gone into professional reporting, and others have created a spin-off project, called the Media Mobilizing Project (MM)	>136,000	478	Entirely noncommercial; founded by personal contributions and a few grants

* The editorial staff of Philly.com consists of fewer than ten people; counting the editorial staff from the contributing newspapers, the editorial staff would number about two hundred people.

Shapiro has called the *Inquirer*'s "Alpha Plan," the plan to use the death of the *Bulletin* as a way to assert the *Inquirer*'s dominance in Philadelphia. The shuttering of the *Evening Bulletin,* part of a nationwide trend of disappearing afternoon papers and the growth of "one newspaper towns,"[8] consolidated the *Inquirer*'s position as the "official" Philadelphia newspaper (with its tabloid cousin, the *Daily News,* which was also owned by Knight-Ridder at the time, seemingly relegated to the role of court jester). Michael Shapiro describes the developments at the *Inquirer* after the *Bulletin*'s demise this way:

> The death of the *Bulletin,* [Roberts] reasoned, offered his paper's corporate owners their one chance to prove to Philadelphia that they were serious about producing a paper of the highest quality. . . . The *Bulletin* folded on January 29, 1982, and that day Roberts, who almost never held staff meetings, stood in the middle of the newsroom and announced that the *Inquirer* would immediately hire seventeen reporters from the *Bulletin* and would double its number of foreign and national bureaus.[9]

"I started at the paper literally the week the *Philadelphia Bulletin* folded and the *Philadelphia Inquirer* launched its expansion with national and foreign correspondents," one national editor at the *Inquirer* told me in 2008. "From that point forward, we had about half a dozen people or so [covering national and foreign news]."[10] From a staff of a little more than four hundred in the early 1980s, the newsroom reached a peak with 721 staff members in 1989, the next-to-last year of the so-called Roberts era. Even as late as 2000, the newsroom staff stood at more than six hundred employees.[11]

Although the *Inquirer*'s rebirth under Roberts in 1982 might have driven up circulation numbers in the medium term, the trends for the second half of the 1980s through today document a steady decline in circulation for both the *Inquirer* and the *Philadelphia Daily News.* Once again, industry reports tend to emphasize changes from quarter to quarter (or from year to year), but a longer-term look at the data is telling. In 1984, the *Inquirer*'s daily circulation stood at 535,205; nine years later, it was 455,000. After a bump in 1996, circulation dropped again throughout the second half of the 1990s, standing at 392,438 in 2001 and at 330,662 in 2005—or at 60 percent of its 1984 total. The *Daily News* lacked even the *Inquirer*'s brief uptick in 1996, dropping from a circulation of 293,931 in 1984 to 118,822 two decades later (down to a mere 40 percent of its 1984 total). These numbers are broadly consistent with national trends, although they are slightly more extreme.

For its part, the *Daily News* never had a resource-flush golden age to speak of. At least in 1995, and possibly earlier, threats to close the tabloid were being wielded in negotiations with the local union, the Newspaper Guild. After grave public statements throughout the fall of 1995, the *New York Times* reported that Knight-Ridder management had begun to consider turning Philadelphia into a one-newspaper town by killing the *Daily News.* The *Daily News* has always been financially weaker than the *Inquirer,* which is one of the country's fifteen largest newspapers.[12] While the *Daily News* would be spared the ax in 1995, predictions of its "imminent death" would continue to be made periodically over the next thirteen years. In the interim, the paper was gutted—with a staff of 215 in 1984 standing at a mere 106 in 2007.

Participation and Place:
Early Online Media in Philadelphia

It was against this backdrop of consolidation, complacency, and journalistic success that the two major Philadelphia newspapers ventured onto the wild world of the mid-1990s Internet with the launch of the entertainment website Phillylife.com in 1995. The URL was changed to Philadelphiaonline.com in 1996, with the content of the newspapers appearing online shortly thereafter. (Philadelphia Online changed its name to Philly.com in 1999; for our purposes, the sites are functionally equivalent.) According to an overview of design changes made at Philly.com by Musser-Metz, the 1997 version of Philly.com (see Figure 1.1) was "minimalist for the modem-based user. Design iconography was very small—we called this our 'chiclet era.'"[13] She added that the technology at the time dictated what the site was able to do: "The site was obviously optimized for

FIGURE 1.1　Screen capture of the original Philly.com website from 1997. *(Source: http://archive.org.)*

the majority of our readers at the time, who were [using] 56.6 [kilobits per second] modems. . . . The way we designed the layout of the site was a very simple table structure before XHMTL and CSS,"[14] which made it difficult to format the site for all web browsers and computer screens. Archaic-looking chiclets and stripped-down design aside, an analysis of the content featured on this early version of Philly.com demonstrates the complex organizational relationship between the *Inquirer,* the *Daily News,* and Philly.com, all of which were owned by Knight-Ridder. The *Inquirer* and *Daily News,* despite their common ownership, maintain separate newsrooms and compete fiercely for stories; Philly.com syndicates the content of both papers. This arrangement has created an extraordinarily complex news management system.

A few points about the structure of the 1997 site (see Figure 1.1) provide a glimpse into the difficulties of managing the relationship between the *Inquirer* and the *Daily News.* Musser-Metz remembered how the lead story shown in Figure 1.1—that of a local rabbi accused of murdering his family—was chosen by the Philly.com staff. "The main part of the page really focused on the news people were actually reading," she said, "which was more organized around the Philly.com production team's gut feeling and statistics from our tracking systems on what our readers were actually interested in [rather than what the *Inquirer* thought was important]. So when this story [about the rabbi] broke, . . . it was a huge deal. That was the kind of thing that might not have made [the front page of] the *Inquirer.* It was definitely on the cover of the *Daily News.* But it was something that our readers were definitely interested in."[15] Even at this early point in its history, Philly.com was attempting to establish itself as a somewhat unique media entity, separate from the papers that provided nearly all of its content. This relationship has waxed and waned over the history of Philly.com right up to the present day; at times, Philly.com has served as little more than the digital arm of the *Inquirer,* and at others, it has striven to establish its own identity. These complex organizational relationships are also inscribed in the digital content of Philly.com. The story of the murderous rabbi contained at least three links, according to Musser-Metz. The first was to the *Daily News;* the second was to "either a sidebar or a story in the *Philadelphia Inquirer;* and the third was . . . where we package[d] together all of the content for the *Philadelphia Inquirer* and the *Philadelphia Daily News* on a given subject."[16] Since its inception, Philly.com has generated little or no original content of its own; it has been concerned almost entirely with aggregation, content partnerships, user interaction, and marketing. And yet Philly.com's network in the early years consisted almost entirely of the newspapers from which it was syndicating most of its material. The simultaneous demand for a "separate identity" and the dependence on highly institutionalized and cultural capital–rich organizations has been a paradox of Philly.com from its inception.

The apex of Philly.com's early attempts to establish its own digital persona, apart from the newspapers it more or less syndicated, came in 1998, when it briefly adopted the "one-screen homepage design" then being used by America Online. No screen captures of that design remain, but it was described by a trade publication at the time as "a compact, one-screen design that better serves the reading habits of Web users. . . . The new home page fits on a single screen, no scrolling required (unless you're viewing it on a laptop or small screen), and features a dominant news story or feature of the day—often from the newspapers, with links to coverage from both the *Philadelphia Daily News* and the *Philadelphia Inquirer*."[17] Musser-Metz wryly remarked, "We followed the *Zeitgeist* of AOL . . . because at the time . . . one of their biggest digital markets was Philadelphia. So we knew our readership was interested in that kind of an experience. Of course, our stories are hugely long, and they never fit on one screen, so going with a one-screen design was kind of insane."[18] Reporters and editors "complained that their stories [were] getting less play on the Web, now that they no longer ha[d] headlines, text blurbs and direct links on Philadelphia Online's home page."[19] They complained further that the newspapers were being marginalized by what they called "this online thing." The one-page redesign was shelved after only a few months.

What lessons might we take away from this brief sketch of the early days of Philly.com? In the early years of "dot-com" mania, Philly.com was struggling to come to an understanding of why it was online in the first place. What "added value" does a stand-alone website provide to a series of well-established, institutionally powerful newspapers? During Philly.com's early years, it was actually the Blackhawk Down project that marked the most successful integration of long-form newspaper journalism and the new possibilities of digital content production (see Figure 1.2). As Bowden remembered, "We had some discussions about presenting the story at the same time on the paper's Web site. At the time, it seemed like a fairly simple task. To the extent I thought about it at all, I figured it meant we would just display the text of the story each day online, along with the rest of the paper's offerings." That was when Jennifer Musser-Metz asked Bowden for his background material, as recounted at the beginning of this chapter. "I can brag about this Web site because, other than writing the story and supplying the background material, I had nothing to do with creating it," Bowden continued. "It blew me away. When I started in the newspaper business, I learned to work on a typewriter with carbon paper, paste pot and scissors. Jennifer's creation combined text, video, audio, documents, maps, illustrations and a sprawling [question-and-answer] feature into something that was more than an amazing presentation—it was a glimpse of journalism's future. It demonstrated the clear superiority of the Internet over the printing press."[20]

Blackhawk Down debuted with technology that was crude compared with that of today. Multimedia was done with the WAV audio file format and the VDO video file format, and much of the HTML was coded manually. Apart from the technological razzle-dazzle, however, Bowden's most lasting memories of the Blackhawk Down project were of the twenty-part question-and-answer session in which he engaged with readers, a global dialogue that "included men who had fought in the battle." Every week, Bowden discussed aspects of the story with *Inquirer* readers, an arrangement that long preceded the days of regular

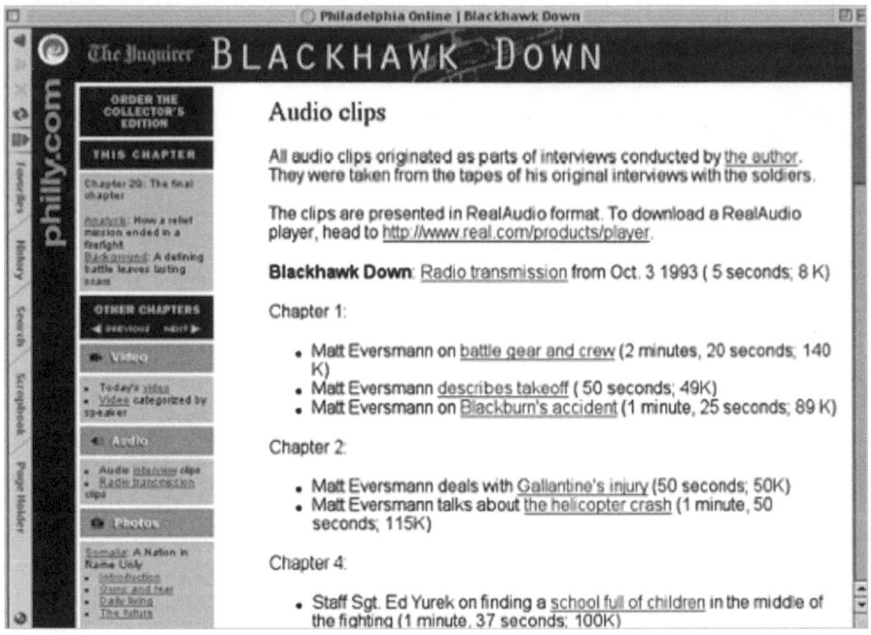

FIGURE 1.2 Screen capture of the special digital journalism project Blackhawk Down. *(Source: Jennifer Musser-Metz.)*

newspaper "web chats." Readers "corrected my mistakes, pointed me to better information, and offered to be interviewed," he recalled, "allowing me to improve greatly on the story before it was published as a book in 1999."[21]

In large part because of this dialogue, almost everyone who worked on it recalls the Blackhawk Down project fondly and views it as an early example of the technological and dialogical potential of the web. Bowden contends that it remained "in the vanguard of Internet story presentation" more a decade later. Nevertheless, Philly.com staff members also emphasized that Blackhawk Down was a "special project" and that as such it was a "separate stand-alone [site] during this time period," with entirely different labor allocations and management structures.[22] And while web producers from Philly.com would go on to lead similar "blow-out" online projects (including Killing Pablo, the follow-up to Blackhawk Down, as well as Faces of Pennsylvania Voters and Down with Crime), it is important to remember that while Blackhawk Down may have represented an unusual, groundbreaking fusion of long-form newspaper journalism, digital media, and reader-journalist dialogue, it was not the day-to-day focus of regular work at the *Inquirer,* the *Daily News,* or Philly.com. Instead, in 1999–2000, Philly.com was trying to move beyond what was possible in the papers' print editions but was doing so primarily through content-sharing partnerships with local media providers and through efforts to become a regional "portal"—not through narrative-focused projects like Blackhawk Down.

Centralization and Localization:
Philly.com's Relationship with Knight-Ridder

By the spring of 1999, attempts were being made at Knight-Ridder, the owner of the *Inquirer* and *Daily News* (as well as of dozens of other newspapers and websites around the country), to articulate a new understanding of what it meant to be a Philadelphia-based media project operating in digital space. The strategy the company ultimately embraced was "location-based": management sought to transform Philadelphia's digital properties from online newspapers into regional websites, which would feature not just traditional news but also a variety of information about where to go and what to do in Philadelphia. Announcing this strategic shift, the general manager of Philly.com told the trade journal *Editor and Publisher,* "We want Philly.com to be recognized as the place to go on the Web to find out anything and everything about our region."[23] Knight-Ridder was not the only so-called mass-media company to see the portal as a potential solution to the more fragmented nature of the web. In 2000, radio websites were also "trying to be local portals, where we would provide everything that someone would need while on the web," Mel Taylor, a former disc jockey and regional sales manager for Clear Channel Communications, told the Philebrity Internet History Week project.[24] By 2001, according to Dan Finnigan, who had been hired as president of Knight-Ridder Digital Media, "every local business . . . is going to have a Web site. It's going to be like a telephone number." He added:

> Aggregating the local eyeballs needed for those kinds of businesses is going to require consumer products that go beyond what an online newspaper does. The goal here is, over time, to build a super-regional brand that drives traffic to local newspaper sites, local radio station sites, local TV sites, but is essentially the first stop one goes to for local information in the Bay Area, or in Miami, or in the Twin Cities. It is my ultimate goal that we are the "go local" buttons all across the Net—across vertical sites and national portal sites.[25]

Philly.com's regionalization strategy saw place—or, rather, the place-based collections of eyeballs—as an already existing revenue stream that simply needed to be moved online in as whole a form as possible. After all, the *Inquirer* and *Daily News* had always been local newspapers. For these companies, the questions raised by the web seemed less about how to ground themselves in a community (they were already in a community and had been for decades) or how to begin a community conversation (the conversation, as far as they knew, occurred through them) than about how to maintain regional advertising revenues that had always depended on the mass delivery of eyeballs to advertisers (see Figure 1.3). As a programmer at Philly.com recalled, Knight-Ridder's portal strategy encouraged the site to secure an Internet radio deal; to enter into a short-lived content-sharing partnership with the *Philadelphia City Paper* and Channel 6's Action News;[26] to create its own regional search engine, called Philly

FIGURE 1.3   Screen capture of the Philly.com website from 2000, at the height of its stand-alone independence from Knight-Ridder. *(Source: http://archive.org.)*

Finder;[27] to develop a community calendar; and to launch a variety of other local partnerships. The technology and design of the site also evolved. A tab-driven home page and long, scrolling pages of multimedia content replaced the single-page, or "chiclet oriented," websites of an earlier era. By 1999, Philly.com had also started using a content management system with a database-driven back end replacing the simpler, flat-file system used in the site's early days.[28]

As part of these changes, "we also let the newspapers have their own identities," Musser-Metz remembers. "So we ran with that and [basically told them] that they could have their own part of the site to do what they wanted to do." The same content could be accessed from all three sites, housed in different packages. "You could access all those *Philadelphia Inquirer* stories from Philly.com and get a Philly.com experience," she said, "or you could come in through the *Philadelphia Inquirer* and get a *Philadelphia Inquirer* experience."[29]

By the peak of the dot-com boom, in early 2000, Philly.com had evolved into an awkward (though functional) hybrid. It aggregated content from both newspapers (though primarily the *Inquirer*). It pursued partnerships with local media outlets. It occasionally (though less frequently than in the early years) created large-scale multimedia news projects. And along the way, its vision of its users shifted from, initially, a technologically limited early adapter primarily concerned with reading newspaper content online to, next, an active multimedia consumer of in-depth reporting, including reporting of the global variety (such as the Blackhawk Down project) to, finally, a regionally based consumer of information of all kinds, not simply *news,* who was looking for a "one-stop location" to find out what was happening in the community. Most important, Philly.com's early years were marked by a combination of national ownership and local control. "What we were able to do with our website in those days wasn't just a product of our technology," says Musser-Metz. "It had to do with our ownership and what we were able to do freedom-wise, in terms of our ability to run things on our own."[30] In 2000, however, the dot-com economy collapsed. "Most of our vendors went bankrupt," according to Musser-Metz, and the dominant groups within the Philly.com assemblage moved from Philadelphia to San Jose, California. The shift westward inaugurated a profound change in the operating philosophy of Philly.com and would affect both its sense of place and its notion of what was possible on the World Wide Web.

The move to create regional portals out of what had once been newspaper websites was one of the earliest ownership-driven decisions of the Internet era. "Before 1999 or so," a Philly.com staff member recalls, "nobody cared much what we did. Nobody in corporate headquarters was paying much attention to the Internet."[31] But as "we got into the 2000s," Musser-Metz remembered, "what happened here is that Knight-Ridder decided that it was too expensive for all of its local properties to run their own websites. So [they decided] to centralize everything. The first thing they did was take the online divisions at all of the newspapers and break them off into what they called Knightridder.com. It later became Knight-Ridder Digital."[32] The collapse of the online economy accelerated this centralization process. To make digital publishing and advertising across its network more cost-effective, Musser-Metz said, Knight-Ridder decided "to run one ad platform for the classifieds, one ad platform for the display ads, and one publishing platform from the editorial side. That way it could standardize the operation and have one tech team, one design team. . . . [Knight-Ridder] had thirty-three newspaper sites when we went live around 2000. There were probably twenty different staffs. Within a year, we were down to thirteen. There were various iterations. For a while, I worked on Philly.com, the Wilkes-Barre site, and the State College site, too."[33]

Centralization also mandated a single design that could serve all of the company's thirty sites. One Philly.com designer remembers the new website, which launched in the spring of 2002, as "a cookie cutter approach. We were allowed to pick our color scheme within a range that was preset by corporate, and we could put our logo on. That was pretty much it. They did almost everything else" (see Figure 1.4).[34] At some local Knight-Ridder newspapers, reaction was fiercely negative. Tom Pellegrene Jr., supervisor of web operations at the *Fort Wayne* (Ind.) *Journal Gazette,* even went as far as to post a public apology on his newspaper's website in April 2002:

> We know many of you don't like the redesign. More than 200 of you have been kind enough to e-mail us or phone us to tell us so. (Eight of you have

FIGURE 1.4   Screen capture of Philly.com from 2004, after the centralized Knight-Ridder redesign. *(Source: http://archive.org.)*

said you like the change.) What you may not know is that we don't like it, either. The new site loads more slowly on your computer than the old one did. It's harder to find what you want. . . . And our ability to make changes to what you see is very limited and time-consuming. So, currently, we're stuck with Knight-Ridder Digital, and it's stuck with us.[35]

After enduring withering criticism during its first few months, Knight-Ridder Digital ended up re-ceding some control of its regional websites back to their local operators,[36] and most staff members of Philly.com and the other Philadelphia web teams agreed that the system improved over time. Even as operations improved, however, by 2006 the websites of the *Daily News* and of *Inquirer* and Philly.com were largely identical. What was more, according to Musser-Metz, the papers "were limited in terms of what we could do locally, especially in terms of partnerships. If we wanted to make a deal with WHYY, the public radio station, or 88.5 (XPN), which is the one at Penn that has a cult following, we couldn't make a deal with them if we wanted to."[37] It would take a dramatic development—the self-liquidation of the Knight-Ridder chain and the return of the two newspapers and Philly.com to local ownership—for Philly.com to re-embrace some of the deeply local practices it had largely abandoned in 2000.

Community Conversation and "User-Centered" Design

The primary forces shaping Philly.com between 2006 and 2009 were less technological than they were managerial and economic; specifically, their roots could be found in the sale and dismemberment of Knight-Ridder in 2006. The eventual purchase of the *Inquirer,* the *Daily News,* and Philly.com by a group of local investors opened the door for Philly.com to re-embark on some of the local strategies it been pursuing in 2000—strategies that had been interrupted by the dot-com crash and the move toward centralization at Knight-Ridder. As a member of the Philly.com staff ruefully remarked in 2008, "The stuff we started doing [after we were bought by Brian Tierney and Philadelphia Media Holdings] was like déjà vu all over again because it was so similar in a way to the stuff that we were doing in 2000. . . . [H]aving local ownership has been a huge boon because we're back there, because we can decide what fits our local market."[38] As in 2000, the "new" Philly.com began pursuing content partnerships with outside organizations and re-engaged with the local music scene. Along with the sale, and the loss of Knight-Ridder's centralized content management system, came the task—or, for many, the opportunity—to redesign Philly.com with a local, more web-savvy audience in mind (see Figure 1.5).

Figure 1.5 shows the fruits of the website redesign in 2008—a redesign seen by many of those involved as a chance for Philly.com to "reawaken" itself after six stultifying years of centralized control in San Jose. "The Knight-Ridder design—that was obviously a cookie-cutter template that didn't resonate at all with the city's personality," the director of the website redesign company Avenue A Razorfish told me.[39] And although the design was criticized by many journalists for "not looking like a traditional newspaper website"—the most common complaint was the lack of so-called stacked headlines in favor of a layout with fewer points of entry—members of the redesign team informed me during interviews that this was "exactly the point. We didn't want to look like a newspaper. We wanted to look like something new."[40]

As Boczkowski and others in the domain of media and technology studies remind us, moreover, a website redesign is never *just* a redesign. It contains within it not only changes in computer code but also a changing vision of its user. For the first time, in fact, Philly.com's "vision of its user" was no longer guided by guesswork, or even by journalistic values; instead, the outside design firm hired by Philadelphia Media Holdings (the new local ownership group) to lead the relaunch devoted extensive attention to the composition, dynamics, and desires of the Philly.com audience. "They were talking about [the website] in a very news sense," leaders of the redesign team told me. "But we came in and said, 'There's a brand here.' It's the quality of the experience the user will feel. You had a brand at one time and it atrophied. And we're going to create, going to do this reawakening; we're going to rethink all that stuff. Philly.com is a brand." Once it

FIGURE 1.5 Screen capture of Philly.com from 2008, after the Avenue A Razorfish redesign and the return to local ownership. *(Source: http://archive.org.)*

identified what it called its user community, the Razorfish team was also interested in "embracing and engaging with the user community in a playful way. The people who use Philly.com are soccer moms, not newspaper nerds," I was told, "and these are the groups that are 'underserved' by the classic news organization. Philly.com's real competition and model isn't another newspaper; it is [the social networking site] Dig Philly. . . . Information is a bigger thing than news, and news, to the degree that it's the focus of Philly.com at all, doesn't have to be boring."[41]

For the first time, the Philly.com website was designed with the interactive features of the web firmly in mind—features that, as we will see in Chapter 2, had been part of the basic DNA of the Internet for more than a decade. Interestingly, this interactive capacity was usually expressed by the Razorfish team in terms of branding metaphors. "We wanted the new Philly.com to do something that only the web can do," Avenue A's executive creative director said. "It is a place where you can talk to people like you about things you care about. . . . Remember, brands as a whole have changed. Users need to have control. You can't push from the mountaintop anymore."

In its promotional literature, website managers would echo this language of interactive capacity. "Throughout [our new] website you now have opportunities to react and to interact with our content and each other," stated an online announcement welcoming readers to the new Philly.com product. "Wherever you see a yellow box, you'll have discovered a place to share your opinion, read others' thoughts, add your own photos or videos and see those posed by other readers. We've provided you with this service because we know that when it comes to life in and around Philadelphia, no one is a better expert then you are. Additionally, we wanted you to be able to communicate more easily with the newspapers' reporters and columnists."[42] Philly.com staff members I talked to were excited to emphasize that each piece of front-page content they posted was mandated to have an accompanying piece of "user-generated content"— often a poll or a section for readers' comments. For almost all articles posted on Philly.com, user comments were "default on," meaning they were open for instantaneous reader commentary—long a feature of most weblogs and an element that recalled the "question and answer" of the 1997 Blackhawk Down project fully into the twenty-first century.

"Your traditional newspaper website," a former Philly.com executive in charge of the website redesign summed up,

> sort of assumes that all people care about is a whole pile of headlines. I think news people care about a whole pile of headlines, but I think that what we were trying to get was what would help people plan their lives in Philadelphia? I mean, that's what we were going for, how do you create something that is more of, to use a word that has kind of become a dirty word in the Internet business, a portal into life in Philadelphia. Life in Philadelphia doesn't *just* include news. . . . [S]even or 8 years ago everyone wanted to build a portal; it turned out that portals were really hard to build in news ways, so it fell out of favor. But I think its still kind of interesting and valid, just because we couldn't do them right doesn't mean it was a bad idea. . . . News is good for building the sustaining interest, but for building utility, you have to throw all the other stuff in.[43]

So just who was Philly.com's user community? Philadelphia journalists "thought they knew who their users were," designers at Avenue A Razorfish told me, "but it was more of a pastiche notion of what that meant. We asked them, 'What's your product?' 'Philadelphia,' they said. 'Who is your audience?' 'It's anyone who lives in Philly, as well as people in the suburbs.' It was just too much initially; it was too big. . . . So we did online surveys and focus interviews to figure out who the users *actually* were." According to the team leading the redesign of the website, Philly.com users consisted of three primary groups, each with its own brand identification: they were "foodies" (Philadelphians who were interested in food and dining out), "skyboxes" (sports fans), and "planners and doers." In remembering this notion of the Philly.com readership, based on the latest audience research, one website staff member recalled:

> The new designers were trying to increase our audience's engagement with our site. They wanted to help our readers plan, discover, engage. They called them the skyboxes, planners and doers. Discover, plan and take action, something like that. Sorry, it's pathetic. I should know this inside out, but I have amnesia. It was very, very stressful trying to get that done.[44]

The undercurrent of discomfort at the root of this interview is an important clue in our attempts to understand the dynamics of news production in 2009. While difficult to convey on the written page, the words quoted here were expressed in a voice laden with sarcasm and skepticism. It is hard to imagine that many of the veteran journalists chronicled in these pages would woken up in the morning exclaiming, "I'm here to serve the skybox community!" Remember, too, Philadelphia journalists' original, "pastiche" version of their user: it was a vision built on mass appeal, of being able to speak to and about an entire city. "'What's your product?' the question went. "Philadelphia," came the answer. "Who's your audience?" "Anyone who lives in Philly, as well as people in the suburbs." After a new, more nuanced, and avowedly accurate image of their "user community" was offered up to them, what was Philly.com's rebranded tag line? It was "Anything and Everything Philly," a slogan that deliberately an executive's comments to *Editor and Publisher* magazine quoted earlier: "We want Philly.com to be recognized as the place to go on the Web to find out anything and everything about our region." Indeed, this uncertainty toward the notion of audience goes beyond Philly.com. Questions about the online "user community"—who is it? how can we create it? is it "universal" in some meaningful sense?—have been tensions encountered throughout this chapter.

Conclusion: Thinking about the Local Public during the First Wave of Online Journalism

In this chapter, I have examined the various instantiations of traditional Philadelphia journalism as they moved online over the course of the web era. The analysis has been carried out primarily through archival research and a qualitative reconstruction of Philly.com's digital presence. It is obvious that a number of macro-level factors were at work in determining the "form of news" in the early web era,[45] among them organizational influences, changes in corporate structure, and technological capacity. Also playing a role in these debates, however, was local journalism's "vision of itself": what it was for and who its audience was. The idea of the web-savvy user of the earliest Philadelphiaonline.com was replaced by the one-stop-shopping, portal-seeking Philadelphian, which in turn was replaced by the notion of the generic digital information seeker and, finally, by the market-research-profiled consumer. Even more profound than debates about the online audience, however, was the question of the makeup of the digital journalistic public as it was envisioned and imagined by working professional journalists. In only a few cases—during the assemblage of the digital

Blackhawk Down project, for instance—was the public viewed as an entity that wanted to interact deeply with the news. Even less often was the public seen as anything other than a homogeneous mass that simply and unproblematically needed to be moved online and monetized. The vision of the public embraced by most working journalists in the early years of the digital transformation of the news, in short, was not much different from the one that had operated in the years prior to the Internet. The practices of *assembling* this public—of reporting the news—had also changed little in the first years of the web, a fact that is explored much more deeply in Chapter 2.

During these years of transition, however, an overlooked category of online media organizations were embracing a far more radical vision of what online journalism could become. Some, like the Philly IMC, had dreams of throwing open the doors of traditional reporting practices to anyone with who had witnessed an event or who had a political ax to grind. Others, like Philly Future, wanted to use digital media as a way to foster conversations about the direction of the city. A third cluster of sites, which grew into some of the earliest local blogs, ignored journalistic conventions and political events and focused on establishing a diverse set of "communities of interest" clustered around particular topics.

Each of these digital sites—though operating, chronologically, at the same as Philly.com—went far beyond the primary newspaper website in terms of their ability to rethink the fundamentals of journalistic work. They also were beginning to articulate a different understanding of the journalistic public. In Chapter 2, I discuss this "second wave" of online journalism—one that emerged not at the center of journalism, but at the margins.

2

Alternate Paths in the Transition to Online Journalism (2000–2008)

The Philly IMC, Philly Future, and the "Second Wave" of Online Journalism

The Philadelphia branch of the Independent Media Center (IMC) movement, a network of more than 150 participatory media projects around the world, opened its doors in 2000 to cover protests at the Republican National Convention. One irony of the Philly IMC's early journalistic success is that the organization was originally conceived as a limited, "tactical" media intervention documenting a rolling series of political protests. It was not originally seen as a permanent "citizen journalism" project per se.[1] While it would be a mistake to identify the establishment of the Philly IMC with the "birth" of participatory journalism in Philadelphia, the questions raised by the Indymedia project are an unavoidable narrative thread that runs throughout my history of digital journalism in Philadelphia.

Indeed, it might be useful to ask at this point: why study or discuss the Philly IMC at all in a book on digital journalism in Philadelphia? By the time this book was written, the Indymedia project of "being the media" and radical citizen journalism had largely been overtaken by new organizations at the center of the journalistic field. Organizationally, too, the Philly IMC was in disarray when I began to visit in the fall of 2007, and the project seemed as if it had ended by 2010. While many of the journalists I talked to remembered Indymedia, it was certainly not an organization they used as an source of information or spent much time thinking about. Why, then, is the history of the Philly IMC included in this tale?

There are, I think, at least three reasons. The first is methodological: my project of following the actors across the local Philadelphia news network continually led me back to the assemblage of people, technology, and institutions that made up the original Independent Media Center of Philadelphia. The Norgs Unconference of 2006 at the Annenberg School for Communication at the University of Pennsylvania (discussed in Chapter 5), one of my first days of on-the-ground fieldwork, surprised me in its inclusion of members of the Philly IMC. The news stories I analyze here also intersected with news projects related to Indymedia, including the story of the Francisville Four that I trace in Chapter 4.

A second reason for including the Philly IMC in this story is more substantive. Over time, it became clear to me that many of the transformations in journalistic work I was documenting could find their antecedents in practices and processes of the larger Indymedia movement of which the Philly IMC was a part. It is important to emphasize: *this diffusion of newswork was not intentional or even a conscious process.* Journalists working at the *Philadelphia Inquirer*'s breaking news desk did not deliberately model their reporting practices on those pioneered by radical journalists a few years earlier. But the strategies found precedents in earlier eras.

A final point: the recent renewal of interest in activist technology use and digitally based "protest journalism," spurred by the Arab Spring, Occupy Wall Street, and other such events, provides further evidence that the worlds of journalism, digital production, and social-movement protest are deeply enmeshed. The line here between the Philly IMC, Philly Future, blogs, and the Philly.com newsroom is not one of linear evolution or progressive descent, of course. Rather, it is a genealogical transformation full of breaks, stops, unexpected developments, and oblique movements. But there is movement, and only by including all of the relevant actors can that movement become clear.

As has been documented extensively elsewhere,[2] the Indymedia movement first leapt into public consciousness during anti–World Trade Organization (WTO) protests in Seattle in 1999, part of a growing wave of protests in the late 1990s against "corporate globalization." According to its internal history, "The Indymedia project was started in late November of 1999, to allow participants in the anti-globalization movement to *report* on the protests against the WTO meeting that took place in Seattle, Washington, and to *act as an alternative media source.*"[3] As the *Christian Science Monitor* noted in December 1999, the original IMC was "was sending hundreds of accounts from the riotous streets and orderly seminars to thousands tuning in around the globe. . . . [Indymedia] reporters are part-activist, part-journalist, and say their coverage will . . . serve as a role model for a kind of democratic reporting made possible by new and emerging technologies."[4]

Despite the activist mythology that has grown up around the so-called Battle of Seattle,[5] the actual details of IMC operation during these protests have been obscured both by the passage of time and the lack of widely available digital documentation concerning the processes and procedures of the original Seattle media center. Most of the descriptions we have—including Indymedia's own remembered origin myths and the occasional on-scene newspaper report—are generally accurate but post hoc. Perhaps the most useful document surrounding the early days of the Seattle IMC are notes from a pre-WTO media planning meeting held in October 1999. Activists gathered in Austin, Texas, to prepare their coverage of the protests and to formulate their operational logistics. "The news of actions coming out of the 'Indy Media Center' in Seattle will be abstractly converted into print, audio, video, graphics and photography," meeting notes recounted:

> The available methods for distributing these media include web, e-mail, list-serve, realaudio, realvideo, MP3, satellite, audio and videotape, disk, paper, mail, phone, fax, events and gatherings, and word of mouth. A one-stop-shopping web site, to be mirrored on decentralized URLs and servers, was proposed to connect people outside of Seattle with the available news. *The site would allow media activists on the ground in Seattle to upload their particular offerings through a web based interface,* and also allow any community or media group outside of Seattle to download whatever they would like to pass on.[6]

Indymedia's vision of its hybrid producer-consumer community, in other words, can be glimpsed through its description of its hypothetical users ("media activists on the ground in Seattle" who would "upload their particular offerings through a web based interface") and the people who would consume its media ("any community or media group outside of Seattle"). Indymedia's contributors were on-the-ground protesters; its readers were a likeminded local and international diaspora of activists and media organizations.

Along with its imagined community of users, Indymedia's founding coalition can be reconstructed by looking at the groups that participated in the planning meeting in Austin: the Seattle Independent Media Coalition, anarchist programmers with the Community Activist Technology collective (Catalyst) in Sydney, anti-WTO organizers, the Direct Action Media Network (DAMN), Free Speech TV, Paper Tiger Television, and others. The IMC organizing assemblage that first emerged in Seattle thus included at least three clusterings: dissident alternative media makers, many coming out of the alternative newspaper, video art, and public-access TV movements of the 1980s; a group of less media-focused technical web developers affiliated with Catalyst who had developed the Active content management system and who would collaborate with tech-minded members of Free Speech TV to import the code that powered the back end of the Seattle IMC website; and, finally, a loose collective of anti-WTO organizers affiliated with the burgeoning "anti-globalization movement" who quickly embraced the IMC model as a way to "break through the information blockade" imposed on radical protest events by what they called the "corporate media."[7]

What, then, was Indymedia's rather unusual intersection of assemblage and (in particular) code? Unlike much of the web-publishing software available at the time, publishing with what became known as the Active-IMC codebase would entail no need for an editorial approval process. "Items submitted [by activists] over the web show up immediately on the web pages," its developer wrote. Other features of the original IMC content management software that were unusual enough at the time to warrant specific documentation included the ability of "users [to] add their own multi-media news articles, the basic ability for readers to add comments underneath stories," and the option for "related stories [to] be linked so that they are grouped together in the summary display, e.g. a picture with a text story; a modem quality real audio sound piece with a high quality MP3 for reuse by radio stations; a collection of pictures of the same event [or] a video with a freeze frame image, [as well as] a management page for editing, linking and removing news."[8] None of these features was inevitable or particularly native to the web at the time; indeed, as the documenting programmer jokingly noted, the lack of a need for editorial approval before publication could be considered either a feature or a bug.

A key to Indymedia's basic model was this "open publishing" concept embedded in the Active code. As defined by its inventor, Matthew Arnison, "open publishing" drew its inspiration from the free-software movement:

> [It is] a process of creating news [that] is transparent to the readers. They can contribute a story and see it instantly appear in the pool of stories publicly available. Those stories are filtered as little as possible to help the readers find the stories they want. Readers can see editorial decisions being made by others. They can see how to get involved and help make editorial decisions.[9]

By the summer of 2000, Indymedia's unique hybrid of new and veteran media producers, community groups, and a radically flat open publishing system—its assemblage, community, and code—were well on their way to becoming the default mode of "guerrilla journalism" practiced by activist journalists during the rolling series of creative anti-globalization protests then sweeping the globe.[10] This explosion of protest helped power the simultaneous explosion of Indymedia, which had launched thirty-three websites in its first ten months of existence, mostly in cities that hosted particularly protest-worthy summits.[11] Indymedia was following in the wake of the social movement that had inspired it, and Philadelphia—the scene of the Republican National Convention in 2000— was considered a logical start-up city for this growing do-it-yourself media coalition (see Figure 2.1).

The IMC's on-the-ground coverage of activist protests outside the Philadelphia convention center took on a shape and structure similar to that of the original IMC in Seattle:

> IMC-Philly's participatory web site (www.phillyimc.org) served as [the coverage] hub [for the convention]. Over a million visitors from 58 countries logged on to find articles, editorials, photos and videos about the week of protests and critiques of the US political system. A live web radio station (dubbed WR2K) reported directly from the streets, and community radio stations across the country downloaded and rebroadcast their summaries. IMC-Philly

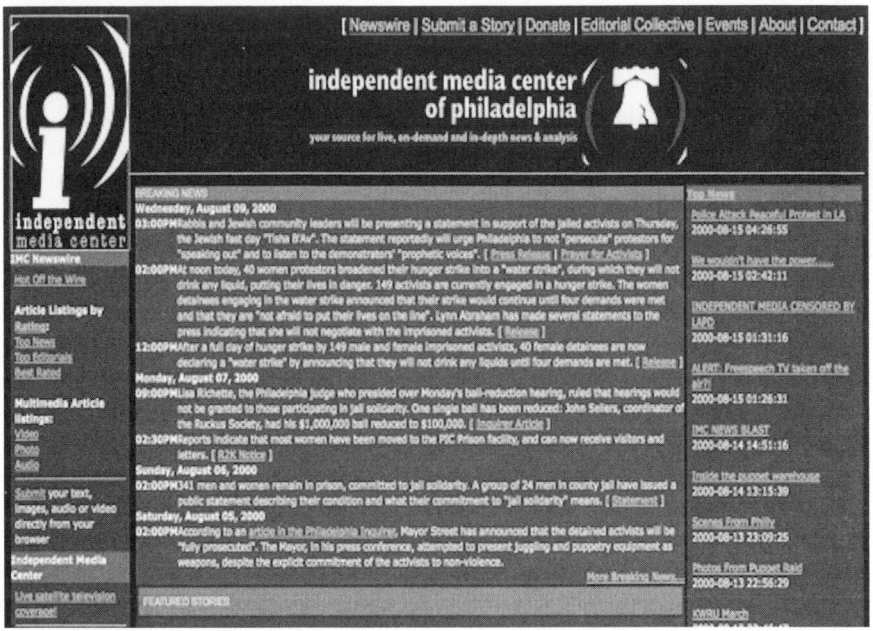

FIGURE 2.1 Screen capture of the Independent Media Center of Philadelphia (Philly IMC) from 2000. *(Source: http://archive.org.)*

was the first Independent Media Center to attempt live television, broadcast via satellite to dish subscribers and public television stations across the country, including DUTV and WYBE in Philadelphia.[12]

Figure 2.1 shows the Philly IMC website in the summer of 2000. The center of the page is dominated by a long list of breaking news updates and links to activist press releases, user-submitted reports, and stories from the *Philadelphia Inquirer* and *Daily News*. In the right-hand column is a running series of user-submitted reports, almost all of which concerned protests in Philadelphia and Los Angeles (the site of the Democratic National Convention, which was also the scene of radical protests). The left-hand column makes use of the Philly IMC's unique, Slash-based ratings system, which allowed readers to vote articles "up" or "down," highlights locally produced multimedia work, and asks users to "submit their text, images, audio or video directly from their browser." The website is aimed at highly politicized individuals who have most likely witnessed or encountered some act of political or social protest. It emphasizes radio, audio, and print journalism, in addition to online media, an emphasis that most likely stemmed from the presence of veteran multimedia makers in the original IMC coalition. Finally, the site highlights Indymedia's participatory, "one-click" submission policy in text that asks users to "submit their news." An emphasis on participation is also inscribed in the page's highly simplified (if, by today's standards, awkward and clunky) submission form.

The vision of the participatory journalist that emerges from this overview is of an eyewitness who is temporarily participating in a tactical media project.[13] This journalist is using the IMC website as a one-stop "bulletin board" for the consumption, production, and dissemination of radical political news. The emphasis of the IMC, as can be seen from its website architecture and its coverage plan, was quite clearly on *protest news* and *on-scene reporting*.

Before the anti-WTO protests, there were no formal plans to create any permanent IMCs. All previous incarnations of similar protest-media–making groups had quickly disbanded after the events they were covering ended. The Chicago "Counter Media" coalition, for instance, never formally institutionalized on a local level after the Democratic National Convention protests of 1996, though it did go on to help found the more dispersed Direct Action Media Network. "We really thought [the original Indymedia] would be a one-time event," a Seattle organizer told me. "But after the protests, it was not just a decision like 'Let's stay together or not.' Life basically swept us up into a certain organizational role."[14] Much of the difference, the organizer recalled, was political (i.e., there was now a larger movement for media makers to attach themselves to). Other changes were technological: the costs of dispersed digital connectivity had declined dramatically since 1996. But although they were founded in a wave of transnational movement building, most IMCs made a decision to remain in the cities in which they were founded; there were always local political struggles to be chronicled, organizers' logic went, and this emphasis on localism meshed easily with a more general anarchist valorization of local, small-scale politics.

Indymedia could have chosen to remain a tactical media project, but it did not. In light of the desire to institutionalize, the Philly IMC was beginning to try to come to terms with what it meant to be a *Philadelphia* IMC. As its website noted in 2001, "We hope that [our] site will serve as a forum for grassroots reporters to disseminate stories on a day-to-day basis on topics ranging from Philadelphia zoning politics to the [Republican National Convention in 2000] felony trials. Our vision is to build a shared dispatch center for grassroots news that is located in physical, not just virtual space."[15] How, in other words, did Indymedia's online, activist-oriented media production translate into a world of permanence? What was its *place*? How did it actually relate to the people and groups in the city in which it operated? There were tensions here—between the Philly IMC's founding coalition (a locally based cluster of media workers and a more diasporic collection of activists), its assemblage of users and readers (already committed activists and so-called ordinary Philadelphians), and its code (which was entirely open to participation by all yet geared toward promoting a certain deeply political point of view). Indymedia's struggles with the universalistic pretensions of its open publishing model, and its need to discover and admit to the fragmentary nature of its user community, can be seen as an early example of a struggle that would plague a number of online media organizations in the years ahead: how might the "political public" be captured or brought into existence as a meaningful entity within virtual space? What did it mean to be a news organization in a crowded, fragmented media universe? In a world of theoretically endless digital content, how could claims of journalistic universality or comprehensiveness be grounded? For the Philly IMC, the answer was to embrace the rhetoric of openness and the code base of open publishing. To obtain a universal perspective, Indymedia argued, everyone must be allowed not only to speak but also to produce journalistic content. By speaking, ordinary people could challenge the dominance of traditional media outlets in reporting the news.

Indymedia was not the only participatory online media project in Philadelphia to push the potential of online journalism beyond Philly.com's early, professionally driven experiments. Another local project was the community blog Philly Future, which was only several months old when it linked to the IMC for the first time on July 28, 2000, during a discussion about the upcoming Republican National Convention. Both before and after posts about the impending protests, however, Philly Future blogged about an F-14 Tomcat crash near Philadelphia after an air show, the impact of suburban sprawl, what it meant to be a "real Philadelphian," sports, culture, and dozens of other topics unrelated to politics. Karl Martino, the site's founder, described the origin and purposes of his website this way:

> The site began as a blog I published at EditThisPage.com [and] launched in December 1999. The potential of tools to empower people to communicate and connect always has inspired me. Dave Winer [chief executive of the software company UserLand] would post daily back then about the "read-write" web. He was on to something. And the last, but most important reason— I already had my own personal site—and had a difficult time growing up (a long story for another day), so I wanted to give something back to the city. I focused this new effort on Philadelphia, on its growth and health as a city— hence its name.[16]

To build the original version of Philly Future, Martino solicited other Philadelphia residents, asking them join him as either officially registered contributors or as website editors. "Joining Philly Future is free and easy," he wrote on the blog. "After [you register with your e-mail address], you can post some news right away. News posts appear right on the home page. Not as a discussion board, buried someplace. . . . People who contribute regularly will be made Managing Editors and given access to the whole shebang." Martino emphasized that the posts were "subject to approval by a small group of managing editors (me)," but noted that he planned "to accept damn near everything that is topical here. I may just turn off the approval process and let the floodgates open! That may be truly interesting in a crazy way." As Philly Future (see Figure 2.2) succeeded in

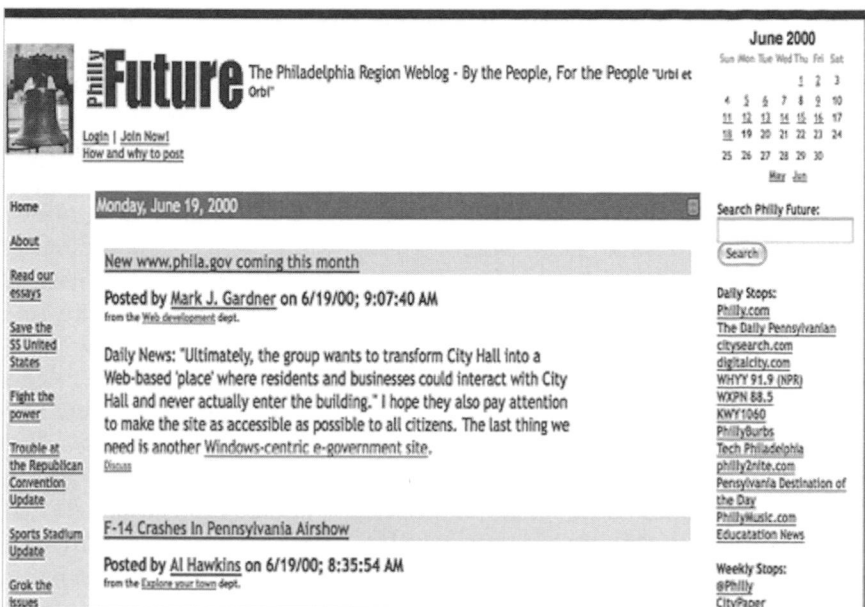

FIGURE 2.2   Screen capture of Philly Future from 2000. *(Source: http://archive.org.)*

attracting a small stable of guest contributors, Martino expressed obvious pride. "What really made these past two days special [on Philly Future]," Martino wrote on June 15, 2000, were "the contributions of others. Yesterday I didn't even post. We are becoming a real community web."[17]

Like the Philly IMC, Philly Future viewed itself as a participatory, multi editor project. Also like the Philly IMC, Philly Future was based on the offerings provided by a particular code—in this case, Manila, a content-management system developed by Dave Winer's UserLand. While the term had not yet widely come into popular use, Manila's basic function—the relatively unproblematic hosting and editing of online content—would eventually become known as "blogging." Writing about the birth of Philly Future, Martino tells an origin story that, despite its brevity, spans software, corporate structures, and personal history:

> I wanted to experiment with EditThisPage.com, a Manila hosting service. Manila . . . is a content management system with terrific blogging functionality. I had already used another [UserLand] product . . . (Frontier) to manage my personal blog. Dan Gillmor, a columnist from the *San Jose Mercury News,* was running his eJournal with Manila. I was a software engineer for the *Philadelphia Inquirer* and *Philadelphia Daily News,* but being the only known blogger in Knight-Ridder Newspapers at the time, and having experience with UserLand software, Dan contacted me for various questions. I wanted to be as familiar as I could with Manila.[18]

The Philly IMC's code base, tied closely to the development of Active by a group of politicized transnational programmers for use in documenting political protest, was seen as both radically open and focused on the act of reporting the news. Philly Future, by contrast, was grounded in a "mainstream" web-development community centered in Silicon Valley, with its own code-based offerings geared more toward ideas of user conversation than toward reporting.

Philly Future also saw its consumer and producer communities in specifically geographic terms. "Philly Future is a *regional* weblog," early versions of the site explained, "covering issues related to making *Philadelphia* and it's [*sic*] region a better place to live. . . . There are a million stories to tell in the city. And *Philadelphia is one hell of a city.*"[19] Combined with this explicit focus on Philadelphia was open comfort with the process of linking to outside sources; indeed, linking was the primary purpose of the site. The early pages of Philly Future consisted largely of links to *Philadelphia Inquirer,* the *Philadelphia Daily News,* the *City Paper,* and *Philadelphia Weekly* news stories posted in "weblog" fashion. "During the early months," Martino recalled, "I would scour morning newspapers on the train to work for interesting bits. When I got to work (early, very early in the day), I would hunt down their URLs and then post. It was, oh, so manual."[20] Philly Future's vision of its user was thus largely *geographical*—its readers (and contributors) were presumed to have an interest in the city of Philadelphia and likely were current or former residents. Its center column was a series of links to news stories about Philadelphia, and the websites included as part of the site's blogroll ("Daily Stops") were almost entirely regional. Also embracing Philly Future's vision of a tightly net digital community, but focused more on the particular (and peculiar) interests of members of that community, was a third marginal form of early digital journalism: early home pages and weblogs. These early websites were among the first to begin to understand the journalistic public not as a mass but, rather, as an interlinked series of micro-publics. With them, the fragmentation of the news network began in earnest.

Being the Media: Individualization, Institutionalization, and the Emergence of Weblogs

Recollections of the early Internet communities in Philadelphia archived as part of Philebrity's Internet History Week project waxed nostalgic for the days of City Paper City Net (CPCN), the local BBS and electronic newspaper started and maintained by the *City Paper,* one of Philadelphia's two alternative weeklies. A BBS is "a computer or an application dedicated to the sharing or exchange of messages or other files on a network. Originally an electronic version of the type of bulletin board found on the wall in many kitchens and work places, the BBS was used to post simple messages between users."[21] One of the unique aspects of early BBS communities was their "forced localization": logging into a BBS system usually entailed dialing a local number to avoid paying long-distance charges, meaning that almost all users were from the same geographical location. This *localized* Internet experience can be seen in descriptions of CPCN as "one of the first Philly-based online communities," a description that also provides a taste of the anarchic and technologically primitive flavor of the early bulletin board systems:

> I wasted many hours (and a shitload of money in long-distance charges) telnetting to the BBS from Rutgers in Camden [New Jersey]. The site was extremely bare bones. There were no photos, no search function, no fancy hyperlinks, or user profiles. There were only a few commands: press "W" to see Who was online, "C" for Chat, and so on. There was access to Usenet Groups and other locally stored newsgroups/bulletin boards. What was most striking to me, though, was how unpopular the site was, even though [the *City Paper*] took out full-page ads beckoning people to the site. At any given time, there were never more than maybe 15 people online.[22]

Between 1992 and 1995, the standardization of Hypertext Transfer Protocol (HTTP) and Hypertext Markup Language (HTML), along with the invention of the graphic browser interface (Mosaic, in 1993), transformed the experience of "being online," with the visual, graphic-heavy environment of the "World Wide Web" becoming ubiquitous. Websites like GrooveLingo, launched in 1996 and described as "Philly's Premiere Local Music Proto-Blog," were part of the early days of the Internet as a visual webspace. Founded in 1996 by a self-described "bored college graduate living with her parents in the suburbs," GrooveLingo was designed to keep track of the Philadelphia music scene—itself a strategy, according to Trishy Gdowik, to "make new friends who went out and did interesting things":

> I scoured the *City Paper* and *Welcomat/Weekly* listings for interesting shows and made notes. I religiously collected the Khyber and Grape Street Pub calendars and kept them in my purse at all times in the hopes of rejoining some kind of arts scene where things were happening. But while there were many bands playing around town, and reviews of different bands each week . . . [w]here were the archives when we needed them? I wanted to look everything up in Alta Vista (later Google) and have all the answers at my fingertips! Other people must have felt the same. Groove Lingo started as a way for me to document which bands were good, which ones would be worth watching again, and which ones to never, ever, spend any more money on.[23]

This description of the origins of GrooveLingo (see Figure 2.3) nicely parallels W. Caleb McDaniel's discussion of weblogs as the latest example of a centuries-old process of "journalization": the attempt to cope with an explosion of printed (and now digital) matter though regular references to a personalized selection of these items, first, in journals, and now on websites.[24] These websites—consisting of a fairly slapdash mixture of hyperlinks, cultural criticism, and political rumination—would soon include a category of online artifact now known as the "weblog."

FIGURE 2.3 Screen capture of the popular local blog Groovelingo from 1997.
(Source: http://archive.org.)

In the winter of 1999, one popular website would list a grand total of the twenty-three "weblogs"—defined simply as websites that consisted of a series of written entries displayed in reverse chronological order—then known to exist.[25] Between 2000 and March 2003, when the blog-tracking website Technorati began preparing its regular reports on the state of what it was calling "the blogosphere," the number of weblogs had increased from 136,000 to an estimated 4 million.[26] As Rebecca Blood summarizes in her classic essay on the early history of blogging, "[In early 1999] the blogging bandwagon jumping began. . . . [R]apid growth continued steadily until July 1999 when Pitas, the first free build-your-own-weblog tool, launched, and suddenly there were hundreds. In August, Pyra released Blogger, and Groksoup launched, and with the ease that these web-based tools provided, the bandwagon-jumping turned into an explosion."[27]

To summarize a complex history,[28] the exponential growth of blogging practices should be traced to a complex confluence of social, cultural, economic, and political factors: the release of Blogger, Moveable Type, and EditThisPage as free and easy-to-use blogging services in 1999; the dot-com collapse, which, ironically, left some of the earliest Internet adopters with enormous amounts of disposable time, insofar as they were out of work; the enormous political upheavals stirred by the terrorist attacks of September 11, 2011, and the Iraq War; and

FIGURE 2.4　Four representative local blogs.

finally, the rise of Google, whose search engine's idiosyncrasies, purchase of the software company Blogger, and blogging ad services increased both the visibility and the (potential) profitability of web journaling.[29] By 2004, when enflamed political passions found an outlet in America's first post-9/11 presidential election, blogging began to be embraced by more traditional journalists and mainstream culture producers. In April 2006, an analysis by Technorati noted that the blogosphere, which by then consisted of more than 35 million blogs, was more than sixty times larger than it had been in 2003.[30]

Three of the four so-called traditional blogs (see Figure 2.4) reviewed in this chapter—the for-profit gossip site Philebrity (http://www.philebrity.com), founded by Joey Sweeney; Beerleaguer (http://beerleaguer.typepad.com), a weblog started under the title "Berks Phillies Fans" by a member of the *Reading Eagle*'s marketing staff; and Citizen Mom (http://quinnchannel.typepad.com), launched by the professional reporter Amy Z. Quinn as Tales of the Feminist Housewife—began in the summer or fall of 2004. Mere Cat, launched in 2002, is the exception that proves the rule; its founder was an "early adopter" who had worked as a web developer and had dabbled in programming. The other three sites were each the side projects of current or former "traditional" journalists. During the two years between 2002 and 2004, the blogger demographic slowly moved from those with a technology background to more conventional print journalists looking to expand their horizons.

Despite the fact that their launch dates overlap, each of the four blogs began for a different purpose (although, as already pointed out, three of the four were launched by former or current journalists). Quinn, the founder Citizen Mom, began by guest writing on various websites in Washington, DC, and originally saw blogging as a way "to share things with people without the intrusion of e-mail." Later, she added, blogging became a writing exercise. She had worked as a reporter for the *Asbury Park Press* in Asbury Park, New Jersey, and freelanced for the *Philadelphia Inquirer*; when she started Tales of the Feminist Housewife in 2004, she was raising a son and had been out of journalism for a while. "I was ready to write again," she said. "I needed to write. I was also ready to sort of take myself seriously as a journalist again."[31] Tales of the Feminist Housewife largely acted as a personal journal, but by the time she adopted the moniker Citizen Mom in 2005, Quinn said, she was ready for a change. Her decision, as described in her renamed blog, was made as she began to take blogging seriously as a (temporary, at least) substitute for more traditional journalistic expression.

Current and former journalists also began Berks Phillies Fans and Philebrity. Describing itself as a "a weblog that acts as a media filter and gossip/tipsheet for discerning livers of life in the Philadelphia area,"[32] Philebrity began as an explicitly for-profit enterprise, rather than a hobby, and was the brainchild of Joey Sweeney, a former music critic for the *Philadelphia Weekly* and *City Paper*. In 2004, "no newspaper in the city had a blog," Sweeney remembered. "Basically, there were all just regurgitating the print product. Weeklies, my chosen profession, were dying on the vine."[33] In its content (primarily, though not entirely, related to arts and culture) and its tone (snarky to the point of self-parody), Philebrity, not surprisingly, resembles the alternative weekly universe from which it emerged. Berks's Phillies Fans, started by a *Reading Eagle* staff member, began after the founder read a story about blogging in the *New York Times Magazine* in 2003. "I'd heard the word blog before," he recalled. "Then, Google started offering a free service, called Blogger, and I helped put up a site for a friend. One day I found myself writing a long e-mail about the Phillies, and I thought, maybe, instead of just sending this e-mail to one person, or forwarding it around, I should just make an online home for this stuff."[34] At first, he added, "I was just writing for myself. But then somebody links to you, and your stats go from three to six to fifteen. I felt like I need[ed] to make a move, an upgrade, so I moved to Typepad in May 2005. From there it just really grew." The site later changed its name to Beerleaguer, and in 2008, *Philadelphia Magazine* named the blogger the "Best Sports Reporter in Philadelphia."

Mere Cat (http://merecat.org), in contrast, started with modest business ambitions but turned into an entirely personal endeavor. After describing his original web page, launched in 2000, as a chance to expand his work portfolio into web design, Mere Cat's founder Tony Green, recalled: "[I] never felt confident enough with my efforts to create a site that would convince customers that I could build their websites. . . . Eventually I realized that I was just procrastinating . . . so I created a simple template using Dreamweaver 3 and started writing about one of my favorite subjects: lobster rolls. That effort dates from early 2002. Later that year, I revised the design and starting 'blogging.'"[35]

This description of the reasons that Green maintains Mere Cat capture the thoughts and feelings of the vast majority of bloggers, in Philadelphia and elsewhere.[36] His ambitions, as he happily admitted, are modest:

> What guides me when working on this site is simply my notion of the kind of site I would like to visit myself. For example, when I visit other people's sites (photographers, musicians, or programmers, for example), I find the glimpse into their lives they sometimes provide as interesting as their work. I also see websites as a form of self-expression, if not an outright art form (not this [website], mind you), so I find it satisfying and creatively fulfilling. I expect the site will be interesting to a tiny (OK, microscopic) audience of like-minded individuals [who are] also obsessed with computers and photography.[37]

Despite their different authors and diverging ambitions, the four blogs selected for analysis share a number of basic traits. They are usually three columns wide, with a center column consisting primarily of featured material and two sidebars. The entries in the center column are arranged chronologically, with the most recent material first. Usually, the center column consists of text and a series of links. On the surface, all four of the blogs appear structurally similar to the Philly IMC and Philly Future, but there are major differences. A single person usually writes nearly all of the content on all four of the weblogs; indeed, all but Philebrity are one-person operations. One author generates material, manages content, and maintains any limited business operations that may be required. In particular, all of the new material, which is always posted to the center column, seems to be generated by one person. Even Philebrity, which has a staff, produces its individual blog posts *as if* they had a single author. This differs dramatically from the Philly IMC, for example, which relies primarily on volunteers to submit content to its newswire and uses a committee of longer-term volunteers to select content worthy of featuring. While Philly Future closely resembled a traditional blog in its early days (most of the items in its center column were posted by its founder, Karl Martino), its ambitions were always, in Martino's words, to act as a "participatory group project." In other words, the Philly IMC was an organization, and Philly Future had organizational ambitions. The four blogs, by contrast, were largely individualized projects. Their content, too, was often dramatically personal—in the case of Mere Cat, explicitly so. In its founder's self-deprecating allusion to the "microscopic audience of like-minded individuals also obsessed with computers and photography," it is possible to hear an echo of the communitarian sentiments of the individuals who first logged into the early bulletin board systems. The graphics may be slicker and the tools to connect more advanced, but the impulse to congregate in digital groups with the likeminded remains.

Despite the personal nature of these blogs, in other words—and this is the paradox of blogging—none of the websites just mentioned should be seen as a solitary, hermeneutically sealed affair. All of them supplement their idiosyncratic takes on various aspects of the web world with links to other sites. As Joseph Turow and Lokman Tsui note, weblinks are the deep structure of the Internet, online "associative trails [that] not only [are] ubiquitous . . . [but also] are the basic forces that relate creative works together for fun, fame, or fortune. Through links, individuals and organizations nominate what ideas and actors should be heard and with what priority. They also indicate to audiences which associations among topics are worthwhile and which are not."[38] Practices of linking, as carried out by bloggers at Citizen Mom, Beerleaguer, Philebrity, and Mere Cat, are combined with the more individualized practice of personal reflection and expression to create the basic DNA of the blog. While the blogs examined in this chapter differ in terms of their subject matter, the background of their authors, and their levels of "journalistic" practice, they share this basic hybrid of individualization and linking.

The four blogs also can be seen as locally representative of larger shifts in the online ecology of participatory media making that occurred between 2001 and 2005. Blogs were fundamentally individualized affairs; while the Philly IMC assemblage consisted of a series of multimedia working groups and community activists with an elaborate decision-making structure to ensure democracy transparency, and Philly Future (although traditionally blog-like in many ways) saw itself as a collaborative community portal, the Philadelphia blogs were deeply individualized. This shift toward the "one-person printing press" was itself driven partly by changes in code, particularly the emergence of Blogger, and other easy-to-use and well-marketed blogging software. The Citizen Mom, Beerleaguer, Philebrity, and Mere Cat bloggers had different visions of their readerships, finally, but each saw her or his readers as members of a particular community of interest (e.g., fans of the Phillies or lovers of lobster rolls). The communities were seen largely as *readers* rather than as content producers; in a world where anyone might theoretically start her or his own blog, there was little interest in opening the doors of existing blogs to large-scale reader participation.

Blogging Goes Mainstream: From "Would We Lie?" to Attytood

Even as the blogosphere began its explosive growth, and just as managers of Philly.com were negotiating their complex relationship with Knight-Ridder Digital (as described earlier), reporters and editors at the *Philadelphia Inquirer* and *Philadelphia Daily News* were also coming to an improvised division of labor regarding their use of new technology, especially their understanding of the technology and culture of blogging. As Philly.com focused on its mandate to act as a regional portal, the *Inquirer* began to organize "an online desk focused on breaking news . . . providing the breaking news throughout the day."[39] Interestingly,

Would We Lie?

January 07, 2005

Hard job, but ... you know the rest

And finally:

A Florida worker has received a workers' comp settlement after complaining that her job caused her to develop carpal tunnel syndrome.

Her job? Phone sex operator.

Business   Our sources say the woman told officials that she developed the condition after masturbating several times a day as part of her job.

Her lawyer, who asked someone that he and his client not be identified (other than by the two wrist braces the woman will have to wear for a while), said the woman had to hold the phone with one hand and take notes and masturbate with the other.

The lawyer said the Fort Lauderdale woman was told "to do whatever it takes to keep the person on the phone as long as possible."

Which makes "Would We Lie?" wonder: Wouldn't pleasant conversation have sufficed?

And with this entry, we'll say ta-ta for now.

"Would We Lie?" has decided to beat it.

Posted at **11:33 AM**

December 22, 2004

Let's give Santa a hand -- in the chops

FIGURE 2.5   Screen capture of Would We Lie?—one of the first *Philadelphia Daily News* journalism blogs, from 2005. *(Source: http://archive.org.)*

the *Inquirer*'s decision to launch an "online news desk" did not originate with Knight-Ridder's management in San Jose, California. It was a local initiative by the manager of the *Inquirer*'s TechLife section, who said he "wanted to compete with the 6 ABC [local news], and the KYW news radio [news]. It [was] a way for the newsroom to be competitive in a way that it hadn't been able to because extra editions are so costly and no one does an afternoon edition anymore."[40]

As the *Inquirer* focused on breaking news, the *Daily News* was starting to experiment with blogging. In 2002, an employee in the paper's technology department attended a conference in Los Angeles on "the next wave of technological innovation in news production." At the conference, San Jose Mercury News technology columnist and blogging pioneer Dan Gilmor talked about newspapers' starting blogs. "So I went back to headquarters," the *Daily News* employee said, "and I told the managing editor that we should get some blogging going."[41] In the fall of 2002, the *Daily News* launched Bark's Bytes, a blog about the Philadelphia Eagles; once the Eagles' season ended, the blog was discontinued. Other blogs followed, including Girlfriend's Guide to Getting Fit, Would We Lie? (which featured pithy "news of the weird" blurbs and cartoons; see Figure 2.5), and, perhaps most important, Campaign Extra in 2004, which was run primarily by the reporter Will Bunch and became the direct ancestor of his pathbreaking *Daily News* blog Attytood. As Bunch recalls, his experience with online conversation began after he wrote the column "Why War?" in January 2003. Although the article made the front page of the *Daily News,* he said, "It obviously got no play nationally, as we were a second tier regional paper that most people outside Philadelphia ha[d] never heard of. So I emailed it around to some of the blogs that I'd been reading, and they liked it and linked to it, and the emails I got went through the roof. This was the kind of national attention I'd been looking for!"[42] By the summer of 2004, he said, "I wanted to try some new things and proposed blogging. At the same time, [the online editor for the *Daily News*] was pushing for a blog that would focus on the election. It all came together amazingly quickly, in the form of Campaign Extra." Campaign Extra continued as Attytood in 2005, and Bunch began to split his time between reporting and blogging.

Although the *Inquirer* began its first blog, Blinq, a year later, most of the people I spoke to in Philadelphia echoed this statement by a top Philly.com editor: "For the first few years, we had a pretty functional division of labor. The *Philadelphia Inquirer* handled breaking news. The *Philadelphia Daily News,* which was all about voice and attitude anyway, handled blogging."[43] Whatever the details, the key point is this: by 2005, the blogosphere was not the province solely of hobby enthusiasts, entrepreneurial former journalists, or even stay-at-home reporters. It had been embraced by the management of Philadelphia's largest media properties.

The Philadelphia online media sphere in 2005 was dramatically different from what it had been in 2000: vastly larger, more personalized, and increasingly fragmented. The importance of organizational infrastructure and collaboration seemed to have declined relative to the possibilities of individualization. In addition, some of the hyper-communitarian tendencies present even in the earliest days of the Internet re-emerged with the blogging explosion. For those websites that came early to the online media revolution, many of which had the ambition to become participatory media hubs, the growth of the fragmented, personalized blogosphere posed particular challenges. As one member of the Philly IMC noted at a meeting in 2005, "Blogging has changed the face of the media landscape. Independent voices are now getting a voice previously reserved for corporate media. How does the emergence of blogging affect the goals and focus of Indymedia?"[44] In Chapter 5, I examine more closely how the earliest digital news websites began to grapple with the mainstreaming and popularization of their participatory practices.

Conclusion

In this chapter and Chapter 1, I chronicled the emergence and development of the media ecosystem in Philadelphia between 1997 and 2008. Drawing on extensive digital archives, I examined the history of representative websites in Philadelphia to understand how journalism in the city "went online" and argued that, to grasp this history, we need to look at the values embedded in these organizations' website design and the manner in which they inscribed visions of their producers and consumers in their digital architecture. Early "citizen journalism" websites such as the Philly IMC and Philly Future pioneered the practices of collaborative journalism and do-it-yourself reporting; they had strongly defined missions that emphasized their vision of a radical restructuring of journalistic practice. Although it went online in 1997, Philly.com seemed uncertain about what its purpose on the Internet actually was, moving through a number of design, organizational, and mission changes over the course of its digital lifetime.

For most of its history, the most forward-looking aspects of Philly.com actually turned out to be embedded in a series of special projects, some launched as early as 1998. The dot-com crash of 2000, along with perpetual managerial interference from Knight-Ridder executives, wiped out many of the gains made by Philadelphia's traditional media, creating a new round of more cautious reinvention in the mid-2000s. During this period, area bloggers also began to develop their own understanding of what it meant to create a communicative community online. Overall, these two chapters foreshadow many of the themes encountered later in this book: the difficulty of capturing the essence of the local public online, the problems caused by news organizations' management structures in adapting to the web, and the surprising way concepts such as "community-decentralized reporting" and "audience participation in journalism" moved (and did not move) from the fringes of journalistic discourse to the center of the reshaped profession.

The central themes of Chapters 1 and 2 are their discussions of how notions of journalistic community, of audience, and even of "the public" have become problematic in the digital era, as well as their documentation of the growth and eventual mixing of a number of journalistic publications and work practices. These chapters chronicle the problematization of the public, for as we have seen, the content explosion of 1999–2009 created an endless number of online communities, at once individualistic and networked. What sort of public might be formed in this bloggy universe? Online media organizations with pretensions toward institutionalization also faced questions about communities and publics. The Philly IMC was founded on the back of its political commitments and its open-publishing software. Was its audience a universal public, as its technologists and revolutionary anarchist users imagined? Philly Future, by contrast, adopted a resolutely geographical notion of its audience. How, then, could it bring that audience together in dialogue? The more traditional newspapers in Philadelphia, finally, grappled with questions of community, wondering how to transfer their imagined monopoly of mass-audience eyeballs to the more individualized web while gaining ever more nuanced information about the *actual,* far more fragmentary, composition of that audience. For all participants in the online media sphere, in short, previously simple notions of community, readership, and public suddenly became problematic.

In addition to the "problem of the public" and the simultaneous fragmentation and crowding of digital space, these chapters have documented the growth and hybridization of a number of journalistic publications and work practices. Online media demonstrated an increasing tendency toward overlap and institutional hybridity. Professional reporters worked with radical activists on projects that eventually produced a new crop of journalistic professionals. Columnists at alternative weeklies started independent blogs, while traditional newspapers paid in-house bloggers. Reporters moved from professional space to volunteer space back to quasi-professional space. Consider, for example, the many mutations in the concept of "citizen journalism" discussed in this chapter: the differences between the Philly IMC's "open newswire," in which a large button asks users to contribute content directly to the front page of the site and the options for participation available through most blogs (where a small "comment" link allows readers to share their thoughts on material already produced by the organizers of a particular weblog on a page at least one link deep).[45] As I have already argued, the rise of online interactivity, citizen journalism, and user-generated content are not straight-line, technologically determined affairs. They are, instead, abstract terms and developments that have been enacted in strikingly different ways, each representing different visions of journalism, political participation, and the public. As Nietzsche remarked in another context, only if we empty the phrase "citizen journalism" of its history can it be easily defined.

Part I has this placed the organizations chronicled by this book inside history. Part II turns to a study of micro-level practices, analyzing the day-to-day editorial and journalistic procedures and routines embedded within this local news ecosystem.

II

Local Newswork in the Digital Age

3

A Day in the Life of Twenty-First-Century Journalism (July 16, 2008)

Twenty-First-Century Newswork: Reporters and Aggregators

On Wednesday, July 16, 2008, an early-morning news story broke inside the *Philadelphia Inquirer* newsroom. It was not a dramatic tale; nor did it shape city politics and culture for years or even days to come. Indeed, it some ways it was the kind of story that even journalists themselves shudder to admit they take seriously: it was a report of a car crash, a multiple-fatality accident on Roosevelt Boulevard in Northeast Philadelphia. What turned this story from a run-of-the-mill crash piece into a story worth devoting news resources to, in the minds of the reporters and editors at the *Inquirer*, was the fact that early reports of the accident stressed that a high-speed car chase between a pair of former lovers was the cause of the crash and that a baby had been gravely injured. By 7:30 A.M., one of the online desk reporters had completed a first draft of the story largely based on conversations with the police department and had posted it online. A second reporter, the young amateur photographer and journalistic jack-of-all-trades Bob Moran, had gone to the crash scene and was calling back to the online news editor with additional information. A third reporter, Sam Wood—a journalist with the air of a newsroom veteran trying to find inspiration in the world of online news—ended up taking dictation from the reporter in the field. His notes, the joint product of the field reporter's observations and his own transcription, read like this: "Accident occurred just Northeast of Adams Ave in the Westbound lanes of the Roosevelt Blvd. It was right at the adams avenue exit. In front of the Northeast Tower Shopping center (there's a walmart and homedepot there) . . . Accident is close to the old navy and raymour and flanigan. . . . There's nobody around except for TV people"—and so on for another page.[1]

Chapters 3 and 4 leave the digital space of the online world behind to focus on the daily practices and routines of everyday journalism in Philadelphia. Given the digital developments outlined in Chapters 1 and 2—the emergence of a wide variety of online individuals and organizations making and sharing the news, the financial pressures buffeting traditional newsrooms—what was an average day of newswork like in Philadelphia in the summer of 2008, and how was this average day being shaped by pressures from outside the newsroom? Given the changes in the Philadelphia news ecosystem, how was the circulation of news in the city changing? The time period chronicled in these pages was only a few months before the major Philadelphia newspapers filed for bankruptcy, though one would not have known it by watching journalists take part in their daily news-room routines. The tensions between the routine work practices described in this chapter and the dramatic developments chronicled in the chapters that follow amount to something of a puzzle.

Building on a the lengthy period of time I spent at the *Inquirer,* Philly.com, the *Philadelphia Daily News,* the Philly IMC, Philly Future, and dozens of local area blogs, watching workers do their jobs in a radically restructuring industry, this chapter argues that two dominant forms of newswork now exist in the digi-tal age: "news reporting" and "news aggregation." The activities involved in the twenty-first-century *reporting* of the news should be roughly familiar to any reader who has ever seen a film or television show about journalism. While the processes of reporting were changing to the degree that reportorial work inter-sected with shifting economic, technological, and organizational imperatives, the underlying practices and structures were not all that different from those observed by earlier generations of newsroom researchers. Acts of journalistic aggregation, however, seemed to represent a quantitatively emergent form of journalistic labor, even though, as I note below, what I have called this "second-order newswork" has always been a part of the job description of a newspaper editor, designer, and layout coordinator. But while the basic work of news aggre-gation has not changed, the rhetorical tension and conflict inspired by that term *has* changed. What has also changed is the sheer quantity of resources devoted to the practice of aggregating external news sources, as well as the role of "blogging" in the new journalistic ecosystem.

Historically, blogging has been the bête noir of the twenty-first-century jour-nalistic imaginary, and nowhere is the complex dynamic surrounding the inter-section between news reporting and news aggregation clearer than in the history of "blogging" as a journalistic practice. Blogging has migrated from the edges of the news ecosystem to a place of centrality within major news organizations. Once primarily a practice of news aggregation and conversation, blogging had been transformed, within the news institutions I studied, into a largely reporting-based practice. So-called traditional bloggers were a rarity in the Philadelphia newsrooms during my research. (They have since become more common.) At the same time, newspapers repurposed the title of blogger and the work of blog-ging to serve reportorial ends. In this complex reimagining of what blogging was and what it has become, we can see evidence of the malleability of journalistic definitions and the ultimate importance of the idea of "reporting" for journalists.

But we can also see that the rhetoric surrounding the differences between aggregation and reporting draws far sharper lines between these forms of newswork than these practices themselves actually permit. The rhetoric of journalism purges the border zone between "aggregating the news" and "reporting the news" of its complexity, even while these journalistic activities are increasingly tangled in practice.

The tension between entanglement of practice and the purging nature of rhetoric is one of the central themes of this chapter. A second and related theme is the simultaneous crackup and stability of journalism's industrial-era model of "assembly-line" newswork. There is little doubt that a multitude of external factors are impinging on journalism's traditional, often century-old news routines. At the same time, the dominant feeling I gathered from my research in Philadelphia's newsrooms was one of business as usual. How could the Philadelphia news ecosystem be simultaneously flying apart and carrying on as if nothing strange was happening to journalism? While I do not begin to tackle this question seriously until later in the book, this chapter and the next contain the most detailed exploration of the puzzling dynamic between stabilization and fracture in the Philadelphia news ecosystem.

A third theme of Chapters 3 and 4 connects the discussions of the journalistic public (which feature prominently in Chapters 1 and 2) with the analysis of reporting practices found in this chapter and the next. Recall that I have argued that the major change in twenty-first-century digital journalism involves journalists' understanding of the empirical techniques by which a public assembled, as well as the nature of that public itself. Discussions about change in reporting practices inevitably affect journalism's conceptions of the public to which it addresses is reported information. While this third theme is only alluded to here, the relationship between reporting and public will become clear in Part III.

Reporting

For five intense months in the spring and summer of 2008, and on and off for a period of five years, I observed the daily work practices of journalists in Philadelphia. On first glance as I watched journalists work, little about their daily routines seemed to have changed. This apparent stasis, however, was an illusion. While the reporting process appeared "timeless" in many offline newsrooms, reporters working in positions more connected to the demands of the Internet were constructing dramatically different news-gathering routines. The *Daily News* did not fully institutionalize an online news desk until 2010, and the daily reportorial routines remained largely static. Reporters gathered story ideas through the routine of working their beat and receiving a tip (usually by landline phone), or "checking their traps." These reporters would then run the story by their immediate superior on the newsroom chain of command, asking specifically about its newsworthiness and possible reporting angles. If possible, the reporter would collect a photographer, gather the relevant data (including photos), return to the newsroom, submit the written draft, edit the story, and go home for the day. At the *Inquirer,* however, which had launched a fully staffed online news department in January 2008, this placid process was changing rapidly. While the overall *role* of the online news reporter remained basically intact, the emphasis on speed—and, thus, on the mechanics of reporting—was shifting. "Your deadline is every minute [on the web]," noted Hai Do, photography editor at the *Inquirer.* "There has been a breakdown in people's daily schedules. Reporters no longer work from 10 in the morning until 7 or 8 at night; they also usually submit more than a single public draft of each story." Reporters, videographers, or photographers often began their reporting process by submitting a breaking news blurb, a single photo or video that could quickly be posted online. They followed this blurb with a short but developed story. Later in the day, they submitted a full story, which often was also used in the paper. Finally, if possible, new information was added to "tweak" the story, rendering it "fresh" after the traditional deadline for story submission had passed. Five versions of a single story might now get posted online, one after the other, each a more "complete" version than the previous one.

Before January 2008, the *Inquirer'*s online desk consisted of one reporter and one photographer; now, the online editor Julie Busby told me, the online desk was fully staffed, and most of the reporters on all of the desks "kn[e]w it [was] their job to break a story online and explain it in print."[2] Busby—a friendly, energetic woman who for many years had worked at the *Inquirer'*s South Jersey bureau—told me, "We are part of the electronic media now," with a peculiar mixture of excitement and resignation. A second reporter, working on the online desk, noted:

> For a lot of journalists, this is not something new. TV people have to rush out and get something really fast, and wire services have always done that, but for newspaper reporters, before ten or fifteen years ago, you had the luxury of having a whole day to report something. You do that, it makes for better stories, but you know, that's for a story that goes in the newspaper tomorrow. Now we have to put up a story now.[3]

Many reporters in Philadelphia accepted these changing filing patterns, and some enjoyed the excitement of the new, fast-paced era. Others, however, expressed skepticism. A second veteran reporter compared the Internet news cycle to the time and filing pressures as the Associated Press, where he had worked for most of the 1970s. This longtime journalist, one of the leading reporters at the *Daily News,* was not happy about the change. "In the old days," he said, "we would have worked on a story all day and gotten something error-free for the next day's paper." A scoop, he added, would have been an exclusive, finished story that would have advanced the news cycle by an entire day rather than what amounted now to a "signal flare," in which the time frame of organizational competition was measured in minutes rather than hours or days.[4] A third reporter made the obvious point that "if you spend 20 percent of your day filing stories online, that's 20 percent of the day you can't spend doing something else."[5]

The combination of this shifting notion of news time—a need to break news online "like TV people"; the notion of the scoop as a kind of signal flare (often a single piece of information or even a video or photograph); and the desire for multiple, increasingly detailed versions of the same story over the course of the day; along with the emergence of portable, digital, "anytime, anywhere" technology (BlackBerries, laptops, wireless broadband)—has created a paradoxical situation in which old journalistic practices are being repurposed for a new media era. In locations where wireless Internet access is readily available and reporters are equipped with a portable device they feel comfortable using, breaking news stories can be reported remotely and e-mailed to editors. During my fieldwork in Philadelphia, several stories were written and transmitted this way. The appointment of Pennsylvania's Governor Ed Rendell to head the National Governors Association was written by the *Inquirer* reporter Tom Fitzgerald on his Black-Berry,[6] as was the first draft of a story on the resignation of the controversial head of the State Gaming Board, written by Angela Couloumbis.[7] In situations in which reporters lacked the access to necessary technology, however, or where wireless Internet was not available or mobile communications devices were off-limits, reporting practices more common to the early newspaper era were repurposed to fulfill an *institutional need* to get stories filed quickly. One of these repurposings—what I call the return of the "rewrite desk"—not only is an example of the more widespread demands on reporters' time in the Internet era but also marks a moment in which an early form of citizen's journalism, the Philly IMC's street reporting from the scene of activist protests in 2000 and 2001, prefigured the routines that later came to be adopted at more mainstream papers.

One particularly humorous moment highlighted the fact that reporters simply cannot write breaking news "anytime, anywhere." On June 5, 2008, Jocelyn Kirsch, the celebrated college student turned identity-scam artist (whom the *Daily News* nicknamed "Bonnie," after Bonnie and Clyde) attended her pretrial hearing. Kirsch had been a tabloid celebrity since the spring, and stories about her were guaranteed to draw heavy traffic. Because of the high level of interest among readers in Kirsch's fate, the *Inquirer* decided to "live-blog" her hearing. However, barely two posts into the trial, the on-scene reporter was booted from the courthouse for violating electronic media rules. Even as late as 2008, some places were simply off-limits to communications technology, digital or otherwise. In addition, economic circumstances prevented the *Inquirer* and *Daily News* from supplying many of their reporters with BlackBerries and laptops, although the situation changed when new management took over the papers in 2010. Finally, not every reporter felt comfortable using devices. When faced with these conditions, an editor at the *Inquirer* noted, he might end up in a situation in which a reporter first phones a story into the newsroom, then runs to her or his bureau to write a second version, which, in turn, is expanded over multiple online drafts until it is used in the next day's paper.[8]

An *Inquirer* reporter drew an interesting parallel between current breaking-news practices and the days of the newspaper "rewrite desk." In earlier eras of newspaper journalism, he said, a reporter would call a phone bank of "rewrite journalists," who would take dictation and write his story for him. For a long time, many good reporters could not actually write very well, this journalist told me, but they were experts in gathering information. The gradual standardization, professionalization, and education of reporters; the proliferation of journalism schools; and the elimination of multiple daily editions of the same newspaper gradually eliminated the need for a rewrite desk—until recently. "There's a lot of calling in and dictation [now]," a second reporter said. "I always wondered what happened to the old rewrite guys, but I guess I know now: it's us. We're kind of doing it out of necessity. If you have people calling in fragments of statements, you need rewrite. And rewrite also makes stories more interesting; it gives them more pop."[9]

One example of the rewrite process demonstrates how complex the reporting process has become in an era of remote technology and multiple deadlines. In mid-July, the Dalai Lama visited Philadelphia for the first time since 1990; the story of his trip was a fairly standard "dignitary visits the city" tale, with plenty of advance presswork filling in the biographical details long before he arrived. The *Inquirer*'s religion reporter, David O'Reilly, reported the story, calling in to the online news desk at the conclusion of the Dalai Lama's first public appearance, at 10:26 A.M. Sam Wood served in the rewrite role. Wood did more than simply type fragments of dictation; he typed entire sentences. A back and forth of aggregation can provide an example of the joint process at work:

> *Wood:* OK, can we call the crowd "well-wishers"?
> *O'Reilly:* It's important to note that they're mostly of Mongolian descent.

Meanwhile, on Wood's computer screen I saw this rapidly changing sentence:

> He spoke to a crowd of about 100 people. →
>
> He spoke to a crowd of about 100 ~~people~~ well-wishers. →
>
> He spoke to a crowd of about 100 ~~well-wishers~~ people, mostly of Mongolian descent.

Barely ten minutes after the phone call began, Wood reread O'Reilly the first sentence of the story over the phone, and the aggregation was done. For the next fifteen minutes, Wood continued with his own editing of the story. At 10:43, Wood returned to the 6:40 advance story that was already online. He then cut and pasted details from the online story into his open Microsoft Word document; the last two paragraphs at the bottom of the 6:40 advance became the next-to-last paragraphs in the newer version. "Are you going to need more time, Sam?" shouted the online editor from across the room. "I'm done," Wood shouted back. At 10:50, the editor did another quick rewrite and posted the story, and barely an hour later, the story moved on to Philly.com.

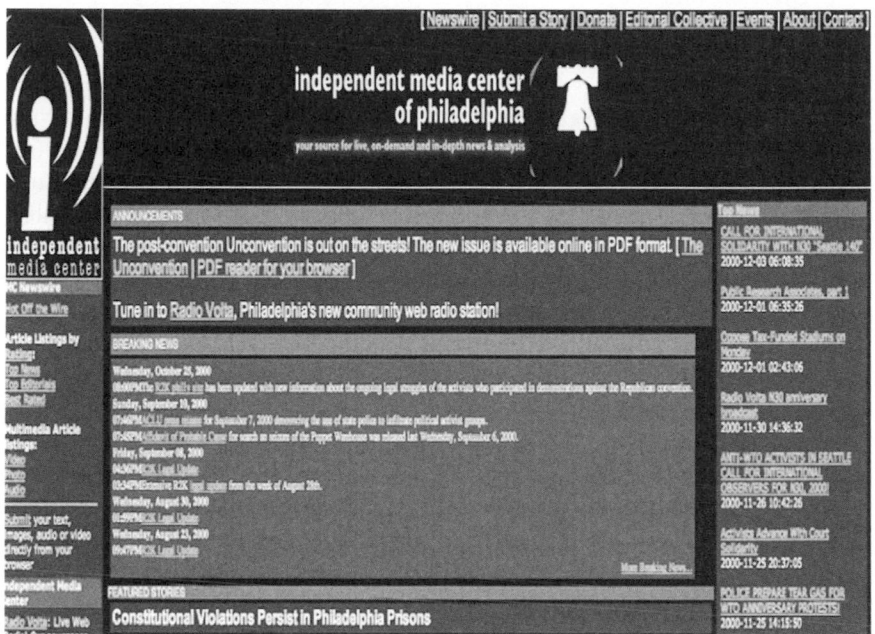

FIGURE 3.1   Screen capture of the Philly IMC breaking newswire from 2000, emphasizing the similarity between its own breaking news display and those eventually adopted by more traditional news organizations. *(Source: http://archive.org.)*

For reporters who are not familiar with the old days of the rewrite desk, this procedure can be disorienting. Unknown to most journalists, however, is that the process of observation to phone call to rewrite was prefigured in Philadelphia by the Philly IMC at least as early as the Republican National Convention in 2000. There, it took on the following structure: citizen reporters, who often were also protesters, gathered observations and, occasionally, interviews from the protests; they periodically called the material in to the Philly IMC headquarters, which acted like a bank of rewrite journalists; and a second group of IMC volunteers posted the observations to the "breaking newswire" in real time (see Figure 3.1).

Working from the information provided by the breaking news reporters (the large center column in Figure 3.1), along with information from the IMC's open newswire (the right-hand column), a final group of volunteers packaged the information into individual "feature stories," rewriting the news for a second or third time and attempting to provide a more holistic, big-picture look at the protests.

This iterative rewrite method, pioneered by Indymedia journalists during the "anti-globalization" protests of 1999 and 2000, remained the standard procedure for covering breaking news throughout the history of the IMC.[10] By 2008, the process had been repurposed again, this time by institutionalized journalists at the *Inquirer,* themselves drawing on the older culture of the rewrite desk. In these instances, new technological developments (and the new institutionalized expectations the technology made possible) helped to create a series of reporting practices that would transcend occasional technological failures (e.g., not having wireless Internet). Digital technology is not the sole driver of changes in news practices; rather, the Internet is creating a journalistic culture in which frequent filing is the norm, even when it is technologically unfeasible or even impossible, as well as a culture in which a strict notion of "authorship" is once again dissolving under the pressures of new work routines.

The roles, routines, and news judgments of local reporters working offline in the early twenty-first century have changed little since most of the classic news ethnographies were written more than a quarter-century ago. But for reporters more tied to the rhythms of the online digital world, fact-gathering routines are beginning to shift in important ways. Notions of news time have become compressed, with a new focus on speed and continuously rewritten copy. A culture of frequent filing, in part spurred by shifts in technology that emphasize the ability to transmit news from a distance rather than simply record it (processes I observed at both the Philly IMC and the *Inquirer*), have led to the emergence of news routines that occasionally appear paradoxical or needlessly complex—for instance, the return of the rewrite desk. This focus on speed seems to result in more reactive than proactive reporting. Indeed, the reactivity seems to make reporters more reliant on the most basic forms of news judgment; the culture of speed fostered by the Internet may be leading reporters toward dispensing with nuance and considered thought, which in turn may be honing their reliance on basic news values.

Building the Everyday News: A Car Crash

Let us return to the story of the Roosevelt Boulevard car crash, introduced above, to see how these changing reportorial practices unfold in real time over the course of a single story. I left off as Sam Wood was transcribing notes from the scene of the crash. Following the transcription, Wood proceeded to craft a second draft of the story for rapid online submission. Editors and reporters discussed the story's lead and the need for it to balance several conflicting imperatives—first, the emerging information that that the crash had been caused by road rage; second, the number of injuries sustained; and third, the amount of time that the road was shut down—all without making the opening paragraph too long. "There's also conflicting reports regarding the make of the cars and the number of injuries," one reporter noted, "but all in all, it looks like we have a fairly complete story." "And," the online news editor noted in triumph, "we have one photo from the scene, Bob Moran—he took it with his iPhone and e-mailed it to me. I love that iPhone photograph. I appreciate it. Ah, technology." Julie Busby, convinced that on-the-scene reporting had uncovered all of the information it was going to—"There's no one to talk to, we haven't gotten any names, and the victims have gone to four different hospitals," she said[11]—called the reporter back to the office. By 9:50 A.M., Moran had returned to the newsroom and was uploading a second, higher-quality photo to the computer system, and a far more complete version of the story had been submitted to the *Inquirer*'s website and to Philly.com.

Moran later described being dispatched to the scene of the early-morning crash:

> I just got this new iPhone yesterday, so this has been consuming my brain. [*Takes out the iPhone.*] And so I came in, and they told me, "Oh, there's been this big crash on Roosevelt Boulevard, up in Northeast Philadelphia. We want you to go out there." OK. The only information that was out there was, I guess, it was on TV, but I wasn't watching TV. I checked the Channel 10 website, and . . . the location was on there. So I got the location and wrote down some of the basics on this page [*shows notebook*], off of that thing [the TV]. So I went up to the scene. And it was so minimal, I only got three pages of notes. Most of it was just me standing there, ultimately, just telling the onlines what I saw.

Moran then described the process that led him to snap his iPhone photo:

> Then I used the [*stops and holds up a camera*]. I always carry this with me, even on my own personal time; it's a really great camera, and it also has a video function, even though I have two videocameras that I own. But I don't like carrying them around. I have a camera that's about this big [*gestures*]. I'm not going to carry that around. This is pretty cool; just put it in your pocket. So I took some pictures with this. And then I thought, "Let's try this [*takes out iPhone*]." And I can also e-mail right from it. So I took a picture [*goes to the desktop computer and loads up his story*]. Let's see if this is going to work; I don't know if they swapped it out already. [*Pause*] No, there it is [*points at the screen, which shows the Philly.com home page*]; that's my iPhone photo. I just e-mailed it to them. It looks OK there [on the screen], but it's really bright. . . . I sent them another one, too; there's some police tape in the background of that one.

Busby praised Moran for taking the photo at the crash scene:

> He [Moran] really is sort of the role model for this newsroom in terms of the new journalism, when it comes to being a one-man band. . . . His pictures and video may not be as good as the professional photographers', but [they're] good enough for the web. It's essential that we move in the direction of one journalist being able to do it all. It's partly a resources thing. Why send two or three people to a scene when you can send one?[12]

Moran himself summed it up this way:

> I used to take pictures when they used to have rules and wouldn't allow it. We were all separate. Its funny how things have changed in such a short period. In 2006, I was doing a lot of stories on the surge of urban violence. I took

pictures and remember one occasion when I took out the camera and there was a photographer from the staff there. I was just taking some pictures, and she comes up to me and she goes, "What are you doing?" She was really up in my face and being kind of . . . "You're not allowed to take pictures." And I'm like, "This is for me, not for the paper." Now that whole wall is just torn down. . . . The other way is nice and cushy and gives . . . more people more work. But this . . . way is for efficiency. If somebody is available to do it, and do it faster, they're going to do it. The one thing you lose is obviously [that] the professional photographers can take much better photographs than I can. But you can't have them everywhere, so you need to have people that can do stuff when they're not around.[13]

Although the online news desk felt comfortable with its version of the Roosevelt Boulevard crash story by mid-morning on July 16, the reporting work devoted to it was far from complete. At 10:30 A.M., word went around the online news desk that the regular police reporter, Barbara Boyer, was taking over the story. "She's there at the roundhouse, talking to cops and getting new information," one reporter said. "She's going to rewrite it thoroughly, her own version, and put it up online." Indeed, at 12:06 P.M., a radically changed version of the crash story appeared, first on the *Inquirer* website, and then, at 12:13, in the breaking news section of Philly.com. When I asked one of the online reporters about the change, the response was less irritated than I had anticipated. "Am I upset that I lost the story?" he said. "No. I have so much to do and so many stories to work on, if someone takes something off my hands, it is kind of a relief. This story could follow us for days, and then how would I have time to do anything else?"[14] The handover "was handled skillfully," said Busby. "When the online desk started, I checked in with the key beats to see how they wanted to handle this sort of situation. . . . Do you want to be called at 3:00 A.M. to do breaking news? [I asked them]. Most of them were comfortable with online taking the first stab at the story and then picking it up on their own."[15] This, then, marks the re-emergence of an *older* news cycle—the daily print newspaper beat cycle—*culturally prior* and *chronologically anterior* to the new, faster online news cycle. To some degree these, cycles sit uneasily on top of each other, particularly in the late morning, which is the traditional starting time for many print journalists. Had there been no Internet and had there been no online news desk, reporting on the Roosevelt Boulevard car crash would have begun with Boyer's appearance at police headquarters. But the reporting process *did not* begin then. It began several hours earlier. In a broader sense, this example reinforces the general feeling of watching journalistic processes in transition. The duplication of labor is inefficient from a managerial, mechanistic standpoint; from a standpoint that is concerned with the preservation of particular journalistic values, the first-round reporting of this story is a bastardization of traditional journalistic work. The primary driver of these changes is a shifting conception of news time.

Aggregation

Individual articles produced by reporters and journalists have always been collected in some fashion: first in newspapers and later on radio shows, newscasts, and websites. More than just the creation of individual articles, publishing the news usually involves an additional, labor-intensive process in which individual news stories are pieced together in a coherent fashion and turned into the packaged news of the day. I distinguish here between "first-level" news processes (which involves turning news facts into news stories) from "second-level" processes (putting stories together into a larger whole). It is at this second level that the editor—along with the designer, the layout coordinator, and, later, the web producer—plays a key role in the construction of news. Editorial work consisted of more than simply "editing" a news story: newspaper editors used their sense of what news was to help guide the work of reporters under them, managed both subordinate personnel and time, helped construct a *newspaper* out of *news stories,* and interfaced between Philly.com and their own online news websites.

Editors were responsible for helping reporters uncover the "angle" of a particular news story—providing assistance in determining exactly what about a series of potentially disconnected facts made them newsworthy. Gar Joseph, an editor at the *Daily News,* noted that there was a mental formula for assembling a story, knowing how good a story it was, and knowing when the story was complete. "A lot of this is instinct," he told me. "It's the kind of thing that can mature [in a reporter], but it can't be taught. Not really." For reporters whose news sense was either lacking or undeveloped, it was the editor's job to supplement it. Editors were also responsible for the personnel management that was necessary to realize the news potential of a story. "Good editor[s] needs to ask themselves, OK, so what are the pieces I need to do this story?" said Barbara Laker, an editor and Pulitzer Prize–winning reporter at the *Daily News.* "You should think about what you need to get in order to re-create the entire scene and then divide up what you need to re-create it among who you've got on your team."

The changes in the pace of the news cycle discussed in the previous section also affected the editorial process, particularly the speed at which stories were edited. On a random day in the middle of July, for instance, an assignment editor at the online news desk of the *Inquirer* had shepherded nine stories through the complete production process. Breaking online news stories included the robbery of a local 7-Eleven; the closing of a South Jersey Starbucks (related to an announcement by Starbucks that it was closing multiple stores nationwide); a large package of stories on the final days of the Spectrum Sports Arena; a concert review of the Eagles at the Wachovia Center (filed at 2:30 A.M., after the conclusion of the concert); the story of a Burlington County Bike Race (from an advance press release); and a report on diabetes rates among Hispanics from an embargoed National Institutes of Health report. Differences in the management of news time stemmed from the material constraints of each story—for example, one story was based on a press release, another required travel to South Jersey, and so on. As a whole, however, the sped-up news cycle imposed a new sense of news time not only on reporters, but also on editors. "We move quickly because we see, online, that if something has a time stamp people will read it," an online assignment editor told me. "But we've got a lot less time to think through the bigger news implications of the stories we're pursuing." The basic elements of a story—documents, sources, direct observations—are exactly the same, the editor told me. There was just less time to gather each one.[16]

Editors use news sense to guide them in the networking of *news stories* into a *newspaper*—what I call the second-level construction of news facts. Twice a day at both Philadelphia newspapers, the section and photography editors gathered together to plan the layout of the next day's paper. At both meetings, various members of the editorial staff sat around a large conference table. At the morning meeting, the assistant managing editor led the discussion, calling on individual editors, who responded with the stories their reporters were working on for the next day's paper. Although seemingly random, the dialogue had a highly ritualized quality. "Editor X!" the assistant managing editor would bark out, usually drawing a response like the following: "Well, Reporter Y is going to put together the big politics story by relying on reported copy from Reporter A, along with wire copy about stuff that Clinton and Obama do outside the region. Hillary Clinton is going to be having a 10:00 P.M. event, which is late, and that will only make it into the local edition." Slowly, working from editors' memories, production documents, and an internalized sense of how a newspaper should "hang together," editors built the record of the day's news, climaxing with the choice of cover stories. Formal cover decisions were made (usually by an executive editor) in separate afternoon meetings at both the *Inquirer* and the *Daily News.* For the tabloid *Daily News,* the format (one large story on the front page) and distribution strategy (more than 75 percent of the paper's circulation was through newsstand sales) placed a particular premium on the choice of a front-page story. These meetings demonstrated the interplay between news sense, the material conditions surrounding the construction of a news story, and time constraints— this time with the editor rather than the reporter occupying a central node in the heterogeneous network of story construction.[17]

With the growth of the Internet and, in particular, the emergence of Philly.com as an autonomous news website drawing heavily on the content produced by the *Inquirer* and *Daily News,* a few newspaper editors have taken on the additional role of interfacing with the web production staff of Philly.com. Their work, in this sense, involves both coordination (managing the shifting demands of online news time in as rational a way as possible) and logistics (physically moving content from one institutional system to another). Usually, these editors were the online managers of their respective newspaper websites, a position that allowed them to occupy a middle point between the dedicated print staff and the digital web producers. "Once a morning, I will have a phone call with Philly.com," the struck by an allegedly drunk driver.

LATEST HEADLINES

Bad news brewing; S.J. Starbucks to close - 8:36am

• **Kardashian girl new reality: jail** - 6:10am

Police shoot suspect who held up 7-Eleven with fake gun - 7:47am

Review: The Eagles at Wachovia Center - 6:36am

2 docs hurt when scooter, SUV collide

More headlines | News page »

Spectrum to close after 2008-09 season

Comcast-Spectacor chairman Ed Snider announced this morning that this "will be the final year of the Spectrum."

What's your best memory of the Spectrum?

FIGURE 3.2   Screen capture of a typical breaking news headline container from Philly.com, once again emphasizing cross-website overlap. *(Source: http://www.philly.com.)*

Inquirer's online editor said, "but the rest of the communication with Phlly.com is part of a daily running e-mail conversation."

Online editors at both papers were responsible for pushing their newspaper content over to Philly.com. The generation and posting of almost all digital content rested with members of the newspaper staff rather than with employees of Philly.com; because of this, some action was necessary to move that content from newspaper websites to Philly.com. In its most schematic form, the process, repeated many times over the course of a single news day, went this way: reporters filed stories via the their own internal content management system. An online editor looked it over and give it a final edit, if necessary. The editor would then submit the story by pressing a specific combination of keys on the computer keyboard. A menu titled "Export/Destinations," along with a list of possible websites, would then appear. After clicking on "Post stories to Philly.com," one of the options in the drop-down menu, the story appeared on the Philly.com website, initially under the content container "Latest Headlines" (see Figure 3.2).

At the moment that a newspaper editor hits "Post stories to Philly.com," however, his or her responsibility for the story he or she had been intimately involved in constructing ended. Control over the story passed to a third type of journalist, whom I call the "web producer." This is a new position, unique to the era of Internet news. Insofar as news has moved online, web producers occupy the key place in the news production process. It is web producers (building on older, second-level newswork processes), along with aggregation-facilitating bloggers, who are doing the most to transform twenty-first-century newswork.

Web Production as News Aggregation

Philly.com, the website aggregating and repackaging the content of both the *Inquirer* and the *Daily News,* was the primary organization in which I observed the work of web production during my research in Philadelphia. It is important to note that in the summer of 2008, Philly.com was an independent institution; it had its own offices (located on the thirty-fifth floor of a nondescript office building at Market and Sixteenth streets in Philadelphia), management, work processes, and culture.[18] Surprisingly, the web production team occupied only a fraction of the space inside the Philly.com offices. In terms of space allocated and number of staff, the web production team was far outnumbered by the marketing and advertising departments. As in the newsrooms I visited, desks for lower-level employees occupied the central space of the main room, with executive offices ringing the outside walls. I imagined that the office environment would be filled with fun and games, perhaps reminiscent of the so-called new economy work spaces I had read so much about. It was, instead, a surprisingly quiet place, especially in contrast to the hustle and bustle of the newspaper newsroom. "This isn't a newsroom," I was told more than once by members of the Philly.com staff.

What exactly did newsworkers at Philly.com do, and how did I come to classify their work in the distinct category "web production"? When I began my fieldwork at Philly.com, the workday lasted from 5:30 A.M. until 11:00 P.M.; recent staff additions, however, were designed to allow the site to operate twenty-three hours a day, a process that was completed by mid-fall of 2009. A rotating team of web producers worked a total of four shifts, each lasting eight hours. Every day during every shift, one staff member was in charge of the homepage (the front page), while other members of the production team were in charge of a different section of the site, called a "channel." One producer managed the entertainment channel, for instance, while a second managed the sports channel. The day began with a 5:30 A.M. meeting between the executive website producer and the morning staff. The meeting attempted to outline how the site would unfold over the course of the day, assuming that no major news events occurred (which was rarely the case). A second, larger meeting was held at 11:00 A.M.[19] During that meeting, web producers reviewed the stories already posted online, discuss how much web traffic they had generated, and reviewed e-mails from the *Inquirer* (and, occasionally, the *Daily News*) outlining the story budget for the day, once again trying to map the day's news out as much as possible. "The *Inquirer's* online team is short-staffed today," the lead web producer said during one of the meetings I observed, "and a lot of her people are off." "They've got one dead, one critical in an Atlantic City shooting," a second producer continued, "and we think they're going to be posting that news in a couple of hours." That story could be featured in the "biggie" spot once it was filed, the lead producer replied. The staff also reviewed production decisions that had been made before the meeting. "We started the day with some coverage of the gymnastics qualifying competition," one producer began, "but I recently moved up the *Daily News* cover story. The teacher story wasn't doing that great, so we swapped it out for a feature we want to call "carnal knowledge." "I'm open to suggestions for a swap," the executive producer replied. "What about moving 'carnal knowledge' up further, for lunchtime?"

The producers also used a set of specific terms—"trio," "spotlight," and "biggie"—to refer to the process of moving content around the website. "Trio," "spotlight," and "biggie" referred to the main content containers on the recently redesigned Philly.com website. Trios were the somewhat more static, produced pieces at the bottom end of the top half of the site; often, trio stories contained links to web video and usually fell within a certain range of story types: sports, business, movies on Friday, and a "travel trio" on Sunday. "Spotlight" referred to the next level of story on the top half of the website. The "biggie," as the name implies, referred to the dominant story on the top half of the website—usually a story with a collection of related links and a large picture. "Swap" referred to the process by which one story was replaced with a different story on the site. Sometimes, an entirely new story would be added to the page, and at other times, a story already on the page would be "promoted," as in the comment, "I'm open to suggestions for a swap. What about moving 'carnal knowledge' up further, for lunchtime?" "Build out" referred to the manner in which an individual story was enhanced with graphics and, in particular, extra links, once it ascended to the biggie position.

At Philly.com specifically, the primary role of the web producer was to decide where a news story (usually written by a reporter at the *Inquirer* or the *Daily News*) belonged on the website. This was an issue of news judgment: is a story worthy of the "biggie" position; should it be downgraded a notch to "spotlight"; or should it be neither? An editor at the online desk of the *Inquirer* or *Daily News* tagged a new story "biggie breaking news," pressed the proper keys to submit the story through the paper's content management system, and informed the Philly.com offices by e-mail that a story had been submitted. Website producers then entered an internal page in the Philly.com content management system containing a numbered list of stories. Story number one would be mapped into the "biggie" spot, while stories two and three were mapped into "spotlight" positions. New stories from the newspapers tagged "biggie breaking news" automatically went into slot four. Producers controlled access to slots one, two, and three. To move something from the top breaking news "headline slot" (position four) to the biggie slot, a producer manually changed the story's position to position one, added the necessary art and related links, and updated the site. Producers at Philly.com rewrote what they saw as web-unfriendly leads and headlines, procured art, and decided on ways to beef up stories with additional links. To move into the trio, the spotlight, or the biggie website slot, a story needed art as well as an additional piece of "user-generated content" (often a comment box or a poll). A story also needed a collection of related links if it was going be a "biggie."

It is possible, then, to advance a conceptual definition of aggregators as second-level newsworkers: they are hierarchizers, inter-linkers, bundlers, and illustrators of web content. Aggregation is particularly common in journalistic networks where pieces of content are composed and submitted by producers at the ends of the news network. In many cases, these end-network producers are not formal members of the news institution doing the content aggregation; they operate instead as deinstitutionalized newsworkers. The primary role of aggregators is to coordinate a series of quasi-institutionalized content producers. The primary tasks of the aggregators are thus to build links between independently produced news stories and to rank these bundled news stories according to a rapidly changing sense of their importance, popularity, and newsworthiness.

To add flesh to this somewhat schematic description of web work, I will return to the story of the Roosevelt Boulevard car crash, this time from the point of view of a Philly.com web producer.

Building the Everyday News:
A Car Crash from the Philly.com Perspective

At about 9:00 A.M. on July 16, just as Bob Moran was being called back into the newsroom after reporting on the early-morning car crash on Roosevelt Boulevard, Philly.com concluded it had an important story on its hands. Even the first draft of the crash story was drawing web traffic, and that was before all of the salacious details about former lovers and dying infants had been fully reported. To continue pushing the story forward, however, they needed more: they need something visual. Did Moran take any video footage at the scene? a Philly.com producer asked Julie Busby, the *Inquirer*'s online editor. "There isn't any video," Busby replied. "There isn't really anything there to film anymore." The wreck had been cleared away, and there were no eyewitnesses to speak on camera. "If we were a TV station, we would have had a crew out there all night," Busby told web producers at Philly.com. "But we're not."

The problem for Philly.com was this: the story was doing well in drawing traffic, but to promote it farther up the website (e.g., to the "biggie" slot) it needed a video component, or at least a large picture. Enter once again Moran's day-old iPhone. By taking a picture at the crash scene that could be transmitted instantly, Moran enabled Philly.com's web producers to promote the story further on the website. "That's why we sent somebody like Bob," Busby noted triumphantly, "somebody who would not even need to be told to bring something visual back from the scene." By 9:40, the Roosevelt Boulevard car crash story was the main story on Philly.com.

Despite the fact that he had worked hard to please the web producers at Philly.com, Moran later told me that he saw Philly.com and the *Inquirer* online desk as "very separate enterprises. You can just tell from the content they put out and emphasize. . . . You'll have a lot of kind of tabloidy stuff on Philly.com, and a lot of girls in bikinis videos, which, you know, gets more views than any of my news videos ever will."[20] Initial evidence of this focus on entertainment and speed would appear by noon on the day of the crash. As mentioned earlier, the police beat reporter Barbara Boyer had taken over the story in the late morning, and by 12:13, an entirely new version of the story had been posted to Philly.com's breaking news channel. Nevertheless, the report was no longer in the top spot on Philly.com. A story about the opening of the movie *Mama Mia* was. Philly.com had already cycled to the next part of its news day.

I have already noted the paradoxical nature of the layering of older print and newer online news cycles during coverage of this "typical, everyday" news story. According to traditional journalistic values, the second, more detailed version of the crash report was a superior story. It was able not only to draw on the information already assembled by the other reporters but also to correct their misinformation; it had better sources and the luxury of a longer writing time. But Philly.com largely ignored the second version of the crash story. The two versions of this story contained a similar set of news objects—a crash scene, a few police sources—assembled slightly differently, with an additional set of objects in each one. The first story contained a crash-scene photograph taken by iPhone; the second contained additional sources and professional-quality photographs. Nevertheless, both stories were refracted differently through the organizational prism of Philly.com. In this case, the earlier version of the story became a "biggie"; the later version never advanced out of the headlines box. Changes in the speed of the news cycle once again played a major role in these shifts.

By the next day, major new developments in the coverage of the Roosevelt Boulevard car crash had occurred. When I arrived at 10:30 A.M. on July 17 for the Philly.com news meeting, a discussion was already under way among the staff about how to handle the latest news from Roosevelt Boulevard. The nuances of the dialogue are difficult to summarize, and so I simply reproduce the conversation here:

> **Lead Producer:** This morning's biggie was going to be a different driving mishap story, this one about a DUI accident where some baseball fan ran people over after a game. He's got a MySpace page, and the MySpace story was doing really well [in terms of website traffic numbers]. But a *Philadelphia Inquirer* journalist is following the baby from yesterday's crash [on Roosevelt Boulevard], and the baby just died. [*Pause*] So do you think that's the top story now?
>
> **Producer One:** Yes, and we should put the DUI in the spotlight.
>
> **Lead Producer:** It's already in the spotlight, so we're doing OK. [*Goes through the latest Roosevelt Boulevard developments.*] I just want to be sure people agree that this is our top story.
>
> **Producer One:** Do we have art?
>
> **Lead Producer:** We have the mug shot, and we have art of the crash. So we can [digitally layer] the mugshot onto the crash photo. . . . The thing is, we have to have art for a story to go into that top slot.

This, then, brings me to the story of a *second* photo: the picture of a crumpled car that captured the scene of the Roosevelt Boulevard accident moments after the crash had occurred. No one had known the picture existed on July 16, but on July 17, it was published in the *Daily News.* In the case of the first photo—the one by Bob Moran that appeared on Philly.com on July 16—the key element in the news network was an iPhone, a technological device that made it possible for Philly.com to move the story into its lead spot. The key element in the news network on the story's second day was a freelance photographer, as the *Daily News* reporter covering the story told me:

> I originally talked to one of our staff photographers, who been to the scene. He told me there was nothing doing there. The crime scene wreck was gone. So I crossed that off as a place to go. The problem was, the crash occurred overnight, and we don't staff photographers overnight. But we sometimes rely on these "scannerheads"—these weird guys who sit in front of the police scanner for hours at a time, and when they hear about something, they run out to get pictures of it. He was the guy who got it. He must have known we would buy it from him.[21]

The work chronicled in this chapter can be summarized, then, in the journey of two photographs:

July 16 Photograph
Bob Moran → iPhone → photo → e-mail → *Inquirer* online editor → e-mail → web producer → content management system → web page

July 17 Photograph
Police scanner → freelance "scannerhead" → camera → *Daily News* newsroom → *Daily News* print production room → *Daily News* print edition → e-mail → web producer → graphic artist → content management system → webpage

What does an iPhone have in common with a scannerhead? In many ways, very little. One is a mute technological device that bridges space and time and can be manipulated by an entrepreneurial *Inquirer* reporter. The second is a human being acting by his own agency to bring a previously unknown picture to light in the news media. In terms of their functional role in the news network, however, the iPhone of July 16 and the scannerhead on July 17 are very similar. They are both agents that exist outside the traditional, institutionally structured news network that nonetheless allows this network to function. The iPhone is a network renegade, a surprise, and an unknown factor. The scannerhead is the same. Both were essential for the story about the Roosevelt Boulevard car crash to be completed successfully.

In sum, Philly.com web producers engage in the following kinds of work. Using a particular standard of news judgment, they order ("swap out") various completed news stories within digital space and according to a rank of merit ("digital placement and hierarchization"). They add art to many of these stories, sometimes drawing on photos or graphics already produced by the newspaper staff, but more often pulling together their own graphic designs. They monitor the website for spam. They engage in a process of joint logistical coordination with the *Inquirer* and, occasionally, with the *Daily News*. They add and monitor content generated by users—usually in comment sections or polls. Finally, they "build out" individual stories by adding links to related content, either within the text of the stories themselves or, more often, in a separate box specifically designed to hold them. In every single one of these cases, then, we can see the mutation of news facts as they travel their seemingly "frictionless" digital path between the newspapers and the main website. Sometimes, this mutation manifests itself through a shift in prioritization or emphasis (e.g., a front-page newspaper article might never become a biggie). Related links both add background and change the context in which a story is read. Occasionally, as with the "scannerhead" photo of the Roosevelt Boulevard car crash, a photo is folded into a larger piece of artwork. In the most extreme cases, numerous versions of a single article can appear on Philly.com, and the addition of internal links can unpack the individual news facts contained within a single piece of journalism.

Aggregation outside the Traditional Newsroom

The process by which Philly.com and the two newspapers coordinated their journalists is just one example of how news organizations are increasingly working with other content producers that are not employed directly by their news organizations. Not only are major newspapers aggregating content. Each of the three websites I discuss below—Philly IMC, Philly Future, and Young Philly Politics (http://www.youngphillypolitics.com)—has adopted a model in which a substantial potion of its content is submitted by deinstitutionalized producers (i.e., content producers not officially affiliated with or paid by those running the website). Of course, journalism has always employed freelancers, so a model in which at least some news content comes from the edges of the news network is not entirely new. What is new is that the balance between formal employees and unaffiliated laborers (i.e., employees who cannot be controlled by being paid a salary) has shifted. These three websites receive almost all of their content from informal employees. This changes the primary responsibility of those maintaining the site: their major task is to moderate and filter the content generated from the ends of the network—not to delete it, for the most part, but, instead, to move it physically from a second-tier location to a location of greater prominence. Perhaps this is the clearest definition of what "news aggregation" actually is. In all of the examples below, the work of aggregators entails moving content from a sidebar column to a center column on a three-column web page (see Figure 3.3). In other words, their jobs are conceptually akin to the work of a Philly.com web producer.

FIGURE 3.3 A series of typical websites emphasizing three-column architecture.

News aggregation of this sort has old roots; the basic template for an Indymedia website, one of the first digital news aggregators anywhere, was established in 1999:

> The original [Seattle WTO] web site created the prototype for the typical Indymedia web page that would proliferate after Seattle. It involved three columns: one on the right, the "Newswire", for new posts which is completely open to anyone who wanted to send information or media imagery, and a centre column for "features" which was edited by a team who scanned the news wire and selected the most relevant items for the highlighted and selected central space. A third column, on the left provides a search engine and organizational information and now includes links to the growing lists of centers which continue to come on line.[22]

Today, almost fourteen years later, the primary job of a website editor at the Philly IMC is to keep tabs on the newswire, select feature-worthy posts, add art to them, and "build them out."

Karl Martino of Philly Future described his daily work routine in similar terms: "I had thought of my job as that of an editor, someone providing a focus to what was interesting and undiscovered across our regional online world. So everyday I would first scan the Philly Future Wire, our aggregator, for posts that met that criteria. Afterward I'd check our local media and larger news aggregators like Google News and Yahoo! News, then a scan of the larger blog aggregators like Technorati. I'd usually have the material for one or more posts. Ideally, I'd identify a group of blogs talking about the same subject matter and attempt to bridge that conversation."[23] Martino's job, in short, entailed pulling interesting posts from his Philly blog aggregator, as well as from other aggregators, and bridging their conversations in a larger, "featured" story.

The moderator of the community website Young Philly Politics described his job the same way, even though he wrote many of the site's feature stories himself. "It's a community blog in the sense that anyone can log on and write their own entry," he told me. "It shows up on the side. Then there's myself and a couple of other people [who] decide what gets posted on the front page, so there's some sort of editorial control. . . . [T]hen there's basic administration stuff, like seeing how many spam bots registered for usernames and trying to delete them, dealing with crazy people or whatever."[24]

Obviously, much about the daily work routine of web managers for Philly.com, the Philly IMC, Young Philly Politics, and Philly Future differs from organization to organization. Nevertheless, there is at least one important area of overlap. In journalistic networks where pieces of content are composed and submitted by producers at the ends of the network (i.e., by newspapers that are distinct from the website that aggregates them, by activist volunteers, by RSS aggregated bloggers, or by community diarists), a key aspect of journalistic work has become aggregating, hierarchizing, building out, linking together, and even selecting art. In each of these cases, information mutates as it passes through the network. Web producers are engaged in a constant, shifting process of "deciding what's news" for the hundreds of thousands of daily visitors to the various Philadelphia online news sites.

Blogging as a Site of Occupational Contestation: Between Reporting and Aggregation

In late 2004 and early 2005, blogging practices began to be absorbed into the more traditional institutions and organizations of journalism. What had once been a relatively individualized, fringe practice of personal expression carried out by amateur commentators and former journalists began to appear in such websites as Blinq (at the *Inquirer*) and Would We Lie? and Attytood at the *Daily News*. Many journalists at these more traditional news institutions spoke of "blogging" as a practice that demanded a particular writing style. "Blogging is about attitude and opinion," one *Daily News* columnist argued.[25] "Blogs depend on the cultivation of personality and voice," Amy Z. Quinn, a popular Philadelphia blogger with the website Citizen Mom told me. When blogging was framed this way—as a style—I observed a fairly high degree of personal discomfort with the practice among many traditional journalists. "A lot of journalists believe that blogging, the snark, the 'tude, the irreverence, is the antithesis of everything journalism is about," Jason Weitzel, a blogger with Beerleaguer told me disdainfully.[26]

Blogging, however, was not simply a style, even though journalists often spoke about it in those terms. As I analyzed the daily practice of blogging, it became clear that the key divisions in the blog community were not those who had an "attitude" and those who did not. Rather, the divisions were between bloggers who saw themselves as reporters and bloggers who saw themselves and engaging in aggregation. Blogging as a technical practice that used certain types of online software is being repurposed to serve "traditional" reporting needs. This repurposing is best summed up in the comments of a sports blogger at the *Daily News*: "I read the wire, I don't have time to read the blogs of the sports fans."[27] At the same time, while most of the traditional journalists I interviewed were repurposing the blog format to serve their reporting routines, a few of them have taken on professional identities and a set of work practices closer to those of the majority of unpaid bloggers. The contrast, in short, between "reporter-bloggers" and "aggregator-bloggers" can help further define the complex work roles of journalists and bloggers in the digital age.

Blogging is notoriously difficult to define. Wikipedia (ironically, a fairly authoritative reference in this instance) defines a blog as "a Web site, usually maintained by an individual with regular entries of commentary, descriptions of events, or other material such as graphics or video."[28] In concrete terms, this description could translate into virtually any sort of online work practice, including most of the practices described so far in this chapter. At the newspapers I researched, many bloggers worked primarily as reporters and used their blogs to supplement their reporting. Many bloggers at the *Inquirer* and *Daily News* told me that they used their blogs mostly as portals for breaking news.[29] When pressed about the difference between their blogs and their reporting work, many of them agreed with Dan Gross, a gossip columnist with the *Daily News*: "[There is] very little difference between my blog and my column, to be honest. If I posted to my blog more often, if I linked more to other people, if I weighed in more on what *other* people were saying, my blog would be more like a typical blog."[30] Many reporters used their blogs to supplement their reporting: to break news quickly and to cultivate sources, among other uses. "I don't see myself as wearing multiple hats," Gross told me, "being a blogger first, . . . then a columnist, then a print journalist. I absolutely see everything I do as one assignment."[31] This "one assignment," for Gross, was to break news and publicize it as quickly as possible. "We're at the presser [reportorial slang for a press conference], reading the wire, at the [team] practices, working sources and so on," a *Daily News* editor added. "So why shouldn't we use the blogs to supplement what it is we're already doing?"[32]

A description of the daily work routine of one hybrid blogger reporter—Chris Brennan, the "Clout" blogger for the *Daily News*—can help flesh out the journalistic practices of this subset of professional bloggers. On one average workday, after he arrived at the City Hall pressroom, Brennan read the *Daily News* website and logged into the newspaper's content management system, Clickability. He then read the comments left on his post from the previous day. "I'm interested in who is leaving comments," he told me. Brennan then assembled his first post of the day: a "morning post" that discussed interesting items in the day's paper and what might happen at City Hall. He described the morning post as "basically a set of single sentences with links." Several Internet browser windows were open at one time on Brennan's desktop while he read through the *Daily News* website, scanning stories and copying links. For the morning post, "I almost entirely link to the *Daily News*," Brennan told me. "Are you going up to the chambers?" a KYW news radio reporter shouted from across the room at about 9:45 A.M. "I am," Brennan shouted back. "The office has a very old-fashioned feel to it," my field notes read, despite the twenty-first-century news practices: "yellowed newspaper pages; ward-heeler-esque political signs ("Promises Made and Promises Kept. The Mayor Helped Us, We Don't Forget. Irish Vote Mayor John F. Street").[33]

The rest of Brennan's morning was consumed with traditional varieties of City Hall reportage: he attended the meeting of the Democratic caucus, sitting sat in chambers during council hearings, attended special events, and tracked down documents and sources to flesh out the day's developments. The existence of Clout, however, has created an additional mental calculation for Brennan. "It's a balancing act," he told me, "you have to decide when you've got something that should go up on the blog, when you should hold it until the paper the next day, 'cause maybe it's a scoop, and whether something is 'bloggy' or 'newspapery.'"

What did Brennan mean by "bloggy" or "newspapery"? One example of a "bloggy" item included a report that every member of the City Council was getting a car to carry out council business. "That's a classic blog item," he told me. "It's just a little nugget that people might find interesting that might not make it into a story. . . . [I]f it works out, since it is the last day of council session, I can compare it to getting a new car on graduation day." Brennan concluded, "Blogging has been a burden and a boon. It gives space to news that might not otherwise find a home, but it's more work." Blogging created a new news hole— another place to put stories that might not find space in the print paper, and it assisted with the "care and feeding of sources. People in the building [City Hall] read the blog and talk about it, and their talking about it is the first step in their picking up the phone and calling you." On the downside, blogging is more work—and uncompensated work, at that. "Even worse," Brennan said sourly, "editors don't read the blog or appreciate it."[34]

Although we see the repurposing of new journalistic forms to serve traditional reporting needs, even the most traditional reporter-bloggers alluded to several *stylistic* changes they thought were necessary to have a "real" or "successful" blog. "The thing about blogs is that they're supposed to be more informal, conversational, chatty," one reporter told me.[35] This attitude was widespread among nearly all of the newspaper reporters I spoke to, including David O'Reilly, the *Inquirer*'s religion reporter, who told me in a rueful and genuinely embarrassed way about the time he was expected to "live blog" the visit by Pope Benedict XVI to Washington, D.C., in 2008. "I never really found that blogging voice while I was doing it, and I ended up typing things like, 'The pope has arrived!' in my blog posts. The use of that exclamation point was really stupid," he said. "It didn't feel professional, and it didn't feel like me. The entire experience was pretty terrible . . . and what was worse, the story I eventually wrote for the newspaper had almost nothing to do with the Pope's visit at all."[36] O'Reilly also mentioned his surprise when he realized that his blog posts would not be edited before they appeared: "I had to call my editor back and ask him to go in to fix all the typos."

Once again, we see the invocation of "blogging as style" by traditional reporters who are uncomfortable with the practice. But we should distinguish between blogging as a supplement to traditional reporting (the gathering of news facts and the assemblage of them into news stories) and blogging as *aggregational linking*. Some of the bloggers I observed (and the majority of those I spoke to outside traditional media institutions) were not reporters. In fact, when asked to describe their daily work routine, many of them laughed and found the question difficult to answer. When pressed, most of the these "non-reporting" bloggers settled on a fairly simple job description. "We read a lot and we write a little less than we read," Weitzel, the Beerleaguer blogger, told me with a laugh.[37]

What does it mean to "read a lot" in the context of blogging? "I have a set of work process now that I take myself more seriously as a writer," Amy Quinn of

Citizen Mom told me. Occasionally, when Quinn took on a freelance reviewing or reporting assignment, she attended music events or shows at night. "But most of the job is reading, with a few hours of writing every single day," she said. Quinn had a set list of mostly online reading material: the blogs Jezebel.com, PerezHilton.com, Politico.com, McClatchyDC.com, Philebrity, Phawker, Will Bunch's Attytood, Dan Rubin (a blogger for the *Philadelphia Inquirer*), [the] *Atlantic* [*Monthly*], and the *New Yorker*.[38] Bunch, who also is a reporter and columnist with the *Daily News,* noted that his blogroll doubles as his blog reading list. "I have a dozen, maybe, A-list blogs that I'm reading on a pretty constant basis," he said. "The only local blog I try to read regularly [is Philadelphia Will Do]. That blogger basically has a newspaper sensibility, and he tries to . . . comprehensively cover the great blogging subjects of the day, which makes it a good one stop shop. The other blog I used to read everyday—and I have to confess I've kind of gotten out of the habit of reading it, because I think it's gotten too hipster and less news— . . . is Philebrity."[39]

What is it, exactly, that bloggers write? Weitzel of Beerleaguer puts his work routine into relief by comparing himself to more traditional sports reporters. "There are big differences between what reporters do and what we do," he noted. "They're talking to the guys in the locker room, writing on deadline. We, on the other hand, are always working with secondary sources, and we rarely interview players." Whereas reporters are on deadline for the whole game, he continued, "I make my own deadlines. They also have to follow the team on the road, they're away from their families." Despite the backhanded deprecation of his work effort, however, Weitzel's daily blog routine is fairly rigorous. "I arrive at my job and browse my daily headlines through Google Reader and Philly.com," he told me. "Then, by late morning, I put up a post analyzing and recapping the Phillies game from the day before. Later in the afternoon, I post something smaller, maybe a post discussing the latest trade rumor." Finally, around game time, "the blog becomes more like a chat among my readers," who discuss the game in the comments section of the latest post. "People come to the blog not only to read my thoughts[;] they come looking for what my commenters have so say."[40]

Non-reportorial bloggers read other blogs and write blog posts themselves, entries often related directly or indirectly to the online content they have consumed. How can such a routine possibly be labeled a new form of newswork? Several factors lend blogging enough of its own, unique character to classify it as an emerging journalistic form. The first is the highly routinized consumption of online media sources. The second relates to the relationship between bloggers and their audience. And the third has to do with the relationship between bloggers and other bloggers. The relationship between a blogger and his or her audience is summarized by Weitzel's statement that his readers come to read not only his thoughts but also his readers' comments. The relationship among the blogs can be tied to the manner in which the perusal of other blogs is inscribed through the linking process. A dialogue of ideas has always been a part of the writing process; in the case of blogging, however, this community aggregation is rendered visible through links and readers' comments and is valorized as an essential cultural component of the blogging process.

The earliest blog in Philadelphia produced by an employee of a news organization, Barks Bytes, fell firmly in the conversational blogging category. Written by Ed Barkowitz of the *Daily News,* Bark's Bytes was created long before the term "blog" had moved into the popular vernacular. "We didn't have a name for Bark's Bytes," Barkowitz told me. "We didn't call it a blog; I don't remember what we really called it. We always referred to it as 'conversation' starter,' as something to engage readers in a new way."[41] The structure of the blog was fairly simple: Barkowitz, who was working as a clerk for the *Daily News* sports department at the time, posted short comments and observations about the Philadelphia Eagles, encouraging his readers to weigh in with their own thoughts. This encouragement was usually explicit: "I think the Rams missing Marshall Faulk is as crucial as the Eagles having to play with a third-string quarterback. . . . Do you think the Rams would miss Faulk more than the Eagles would miss Koy Detmer?"[42] Audience responses on Bark's Bytes were usually on-topic and informed. "I think the Eagles will win this one 34 to 24. I have faith in Andy Reed's play calling for this game. I also have faith in A. J. [Feeley, an Eagles quarterback]," wrote one reader.[43]

Barkowitz described the invention of Bark's Bytes this way:

> Football in this town rules, and the *Philadelphia Daily News* takes its moniker—"The People's Paper"—really seriously. What do I mean? Well, sometimes somebody sitting at a bar will call us up and ask us to settle a sports bet. So we wanted something online to capture that interaction with readers. When I started up the blog, I just wanted to say, "Here are some ideas, here are some observations, what do you think?" So it truly was an aggregation.

Although he continues to blog occasionally about both Flyers and Phillies games, Barkowitz admitted, "I don't really dialogue with the local sports blogging community at all. I don't read a lot of blogs. Instead, I read the sports wire."[44]

One form of blogging as conversation encourages dialogue between readers and bloggers, as well as dialogue among readers themselves. The role of the blogger, in this case, is to write provocative entries, provide a forum for discussion to occur, moderate the dialogue, and occasionally engage directly with readers. A second form of blogging as conversation, however, can occur with no interaction between commenters and bloggers at all. In this second case, bloggers read the written work of other bloggers in their community and engage in a running form of inter-blog dialog. On other words, conversation occurs here, but does usually not take place in the comments section but is between websites. "Blogs fail if they are a monologue, not a dialogue or aggregation," Bunch argued. "You shouldn't just use them to clear out the journalistic notebook. One of the biggest problems for newspaper blogs is if bloggers are not a part of their community."[45]

In a the key moment in the growth of Attytood and his own emergence as a blogger, Bunch pointed to September 2003, when one of his posts was linked to by the then popular left-wing website Buzzflash. "E-mails to me went through the roof. That was the kind of national attention I was looking for," he recalled.[46] Over a period of time, this material form of community aggregation—inscribed in links to and from blogs—positioned Bunch as an "authentic" blogger engaged in a long-distance aggregation with other bloggers. Weitzel summed up the importance of community for bloggers by noting that Beerleaguer attracts readers from "DC, Chicago, the Bay Area, Boston, New York City. . . . It's a lot like the 'extra innings' package on TV—the place where people from out of town and expatriates go to be part of an expat community and find out about their hometown team. During the playoffs last year, somebody even sent us a photo from Iraq."[47]

A simple practice—blogging—thus takes on vastly different forms depending on the economic, cultural, and professional networks in which it is embedded. In one case—perhaps the dominant case inside traditional newspapers—blogging has been repurposed as an advanced, open form of "beat reporting." In this instance, the role of the blogger is to break news faster, write stories that might not make it into the daily newspaper, and cultivate sources, all carried out through work mechanisms that are fairly similar to those used in traditional reporting. An extra layer is added to the practice of news judgment in this instance, as the hybrid reporter-blogger must decide whether a particular set of assembled facts is a "newspaper story" or a "blog story." In the second case, bloggers' roles can be described as representing a form of extended aggregation, both with a community of readers and with a more dispersed community of likeminded bloggers. The mechanisms through which bloggers carry out this role include the extensive consumption of online materials, dialogue with commenters, regularized writing, and linking to others. In the case of conversational bloggers, the entire hierarchy of news judgment has been upended; rather than asking themselves, "Is this news?" these bloggers most often ask, "Is this content interesting to me and of interest to the community of which I consider myself a part?"

What explains this bifurcation of different types of blogging? One important variable, I would argue, lies in the work a blogger is being paid to perform. Local beat bloggers, my time in Philadelphia increasingly demonstrated, are most often paid reporters who use blogging as a tool to supplement their daily work. Bloggers doing aggregation, by contrast, are more often unpaid amateurs, freelancers looking to build online name recognition or, in the very rare case of Will Bunch, former full-time reporters paid partially (though not entirely) to blog. Through the time of my fieldwork in Philadelphia, and even in the years afterward, reporting remained the dominant form of journalistic work—at least rhetorically— even as the line between reporting and aggregation increasingly blurred in practice. More recent evidence that this dichotomy is finally collapsing is explored more thoroughly in the book's concluding chapter.

Conclusion

In this chapter, I have analyzed newswork in Philadelphia as primarily composed of two dominant forms: aggregation and reporting. I then discussed "blogging" as a hybrid form of reporting and aggregation, arguing that the ways its practices have been debated and redefined by many traditional news organizations highlight some of the rhetorical tensions surrounding twenty-first-century newswork. I also used the emergence and reporting of several actual news stories to highlight the uncertain status of reporting in the digital era. Distinctions between reporters and aggregators often manifested themselves as a debate between bloggers and journalists, with an attending argument about what constituted valid reporting practices and how those practices served—or did not serve—to bind the public together.

In the next chapter, I continue this discussion of newswork practices, tying newswork and news ecosystem together and documenting and analyzing the circulation of a particular set of news facts relating to the eviction and arrest of a group of homeowners in Philadelphia during a single week in June 2008, a time period in which the story of the arrests emerged, exploded, and then quickly faded away. By putting the various parts and practices of the Philadelphia news ecosystem into motion, we can gain an in-depth understanding of how this system functions from day to day.

4

How News Circulates Online

The Short, Happy News Life of the
Francisville Four (June 2008)

This chapter broadens Chapter 3's ethnographic analysis of newswork, focusing on how a single news story—the wrongful arrest of four area homeowners on trumped-up charges—diffused across the entire Philadelphia news ecosystem. Chapter 3 looked at newswork practices from the vantage point of the traditional newsrooms; the events discussed in this chapter also occurred inside the editorial nerve centers where newsroom managers, bloggers, and reporters exercised their news judgment. However, the chapter also examines how the story in question leapfrogged across different media and how different news outlets contributed original reporting, analysis, and commentary to the journalistic mix. In that sense, it fuses Chapters 2 and 3, examining how news moves and how journalists behave across the entire breadth of the local news ecosystem.

How does the story of the so-called Francisville Four highlight the larger journalistic processes and tensions central to this book? First, it demonstrates how notions of "reporting the news" have become hybridized in the web era. Second, it argues that while, from a distance, the organizational boundary markers between different kinds of newswork are becoming ever more porous, the fact that a *local news network* was emerging in Philadelphia was more visible to the scholarly analyst than to local journalists or news editors. In other words, while the researcher could trace the manner in which a news network briefly coalesced around the story of the Francisville Four, this process was not immediately obvious to working journalists. Nor was facilitating the development of that network, or tapping into it in order to produce news, the primary concern of journalists—reporting the news was, and reporting the news as seen in a particularly traditional way. In short, the story of the Francisville Four demonstrates not only a particular reality of networked journalism, but also the manner in which that "reality" is largely irrelevant in the face of a specific institutional and professional culture.

The Francisville Four: Emergence of the
Story in the Online Political Press

On Friday, June 13, 2008, at 5:19 P.M., activists with the Philadelphia-based radio activist group Prometheus Radio Project sent out an e-mail announcing that four of the city's residents, initially identified only as "critics of the police," had been arrested in a police raid earlier in the day. Most important, according to the release, the arrests appeared to have no reason beyond harassment by law enforcement. "Philadelphia Police descended upon . . . homeowners who have been questioning police tactics in Mayor [Michael] Nutter's new 'stop and frisk,' program," the e-mail read. "[Four] residents were arrested in their home at 17th street and Ridge Avenue, and the police are in the process of sealing the building. The homeowners are being held at the police station, no charges have yet been filed." One of the people arrested was Daniel Moffat, the owner of the home. The e-mail concluded by linking the arrests to larger city issues of police misconduct. "Few imagined that simple criticism of a city policy could result in the seizure of one's home and subject residents to arrest."[1]

Although Prometheus Radio's political work is primarily national in character and centers on the rather esoteric issues of low-power radio and online spectrum access, its key members are also longtime members of the local radical community, with many living in several large collective houses in West Philadelphia.[2] Word of the arrests thus spread quickly across what is known locally as the "West Philly activist scene." About an hour later, having already heard about the raid from friends, the reporter Hans Bennett (who often contributed work to "citizen media" projects) received the e-mail from Prometheus and forwarded it to the editorial group of the Philadelphia Independent Media Center (IMC). Using the open-publishing feature of the Philly IMC website, Bennett turned the story into a website "news brief" on his own initiative. His e-mail proposed that the Philly IMC turn the brief into a full feature—meaning that it should be placed at the top spot on the website. Because a previous feature—about wireless Internet access in the city—had already been proposed but not posted, and because the Philly IMC can handle only one large feature at a time in the top slot, Bennett's proposal attempted to find a way to balance the timing of the different proposed features. "Hi folks, I just got this from Prometheus Radio, and [it] looks real bad," he wrote. "I already heard about this now from friends who know the residents, and it sounds like a really legit story, esp[ecially] coming from Prometheus. What do folks think about putting it up either right now (before [the] upcoming feature [about municipal wireless]), or we could put [the municipal wireless feature] up now and put this other one up 24 hours later?"[3]

The editor of the feature on wireless Internet quickly blessed the delay of his own story, and by 6:54 P.M. on July 13 (about ninety minutes after the original Prometheus e-mail had been distributed), a feature story about the arrests had been posted to the Philly IMC website. Headlined "Police Critics Arrested, Home

Seized in Police Raid," the story was primarily a re-posting of the original Prometheus press release.[4]

While the feature-creation process was being quickly and easily negotiated at the Philly IMC, a more fraught conversation was taking place at a second activist-journalist hub, Young Philly Politics (YPP; http://youngphillypolitics.com). Bennett posted the Prometheus press release to the "blog" section of the YPP site at 6:21 P.M.[5] Unlike with Indymedia, however, a second YPP user, writing under the pseudonym "MrLuigi," quickly critiqued the post in the comments section. Particularly problematic for MrLuigi was the press release's assertion that Mayor Nutter had declined to attend community meetings at which recent examples of police misconduct had been discussed. Nutter was a marked improvement over previous Philadelphia mayors in this regard, MrLuigi asserted. "I'm very interested to hear more concrete details about this recent arrest, but to be absolutely clear the blank assertion that this mayor and this police commissioner are less then a noticeable step forward from the past in terms of community relations seems pretty dubious to me."[6] Bennett responded, again in the comments section, by acknowledging that the state of community-police relations under Nutter might mark an improvement over that under past mayors, but he also shifted the conversation to the topic of the story's inherent *newsworthiness*. "I, too, am waiting for more information. . . . But, I really want to help get the word out, so that the chances are better of these folks getting fair treatment and having the facts get out. *I've personally known the folks at Prometheus Radio for many years, and called both the folks listed at the bottom to confirm the email, so this does seem like a very serious story."*[7] In the exchange, Baker defended his journalistic credentials by emphasizing (1) the public importance of the story; (2) the goals it might serve (increased "fair treatment" for those arrested); (3) the reliability of his sources ("I've personally known the folks at Prometheus Radio for many years"); and, finally, (4) what he saw as his journalistic spadework ("[I] called both the folks listed at the bottom to confirm the email").

It was on the subject of journalistic credibility that the site's lead moderator and web producer took issue with the story about twelve hours after the original posting. Under the headline "YPP Standards," the producer wrote that "a vague email forward does not cut it here, especially if you are accusing people of fairly serious stuff. If you have more than that, post it. If not, please wait till you get something a little more concrete, like any sort of actual source."[8] This comment prompted an important exchange regarding the status of Bennett's story and the general journalistic role of Young Philly Politics. After Bennett largely repeated his original justifications for posting the story, stating that he "stood behind it,"[9] the moderator noted, "Sure, you can stand behind it. But, this isn't a democracy, and I am telling you that it doesn't meet standards here. When I say a source: how about a witness, how about a name, how about a first person account, how about a police report, how about anything at all? . . . I am not trashing Prometheus radio or Philly IMC, and what they decide to forward, report on or feature. But different places have different standards, and if you are going to post here, that isn't a debatable point."[10]

After Bennett expressed his disappointment with YPP and repeated his assertions that the Prometheus press release, combined with the public identification of press contacts, constituted reliable sources for him, a second site producer weighed in on the question:

> Also, re: "website policy" or whatever, I'd like to say one thing, generally: *a site like this exists in a weird space between journalism and, like, standing around the corner gossiping and talking politics.* I think there's a great tool here to expand awareness of important stuff. People really do listen. It's also a tool to expand mutual understanding: I don't know everything, and I learn things by talking to people here all the time. *So I'd like to think that the policies should not be so much about [us] drawing lines or playing some pseudo-dictatorial role, but rather as encouraging everyone to just recognize the power and responsibility of having a platform like this,* which even though it's virtual, creates a written record and has the power to affect the real world, for better and worse.[11]

Although discussions about the reliability of Bennett's information would continue on YPP, the conversation would be largely preempted by new developments in both the case and the coverage of it over the course of the weekend.

Several general items are worthy of note at this point, fewer than forty-eight hours into the story. First, contrary to much of the existing literature on online journalism, a nonprofessional, entirely volunteer media organization did in fact "break" the story of the arrests. However, even among more amateur media outlets, serious doubts were expressed about whether the story as it stood on the Philly IMC contained enough "reporting" to be featured in contexts that transcended the local activist community. While the original volunteer reporter expressed confidence in the work he had done—reading the press release, contacting its authors to confirm the story—other journalists were looking for more: "a witness, a name, a first person account, a police report, anything at all."[12]

Many of these discussions also revolved around questions of organizational identity, self-perception, and perceptions of "the audience." Editors at YPP were acutely aware of the homologies between themselves and the "Indymedia crowd" and thus erected institutional markers to create a strong counter-identity.[13] This need for boundary work helps to explain the unusually hostile remarks about the YPP "standards" the site's moderator expressed in his e-mail exchange with Bennett.

Finally, we should note that in all of these cases, the amateur reporters echoed traditional journalistic concerns and thought processes in their assessment of the news. Bennett defended his story by invoking notions of source reliability, public relevance, and journalistic routines ("[I] called both the folks listed at the bottom to confirm the email.") The YPP editor responded by asking for additional reporting. Finally, a second YPP editor alluded to the "public responsibility" inherent in maintaining a community website.

By the end of the weekend of June 14, however, the story of the arrests remained the tree in the proverbial forest: it had fallen, but (almost) no one had heard it, so was it really news? Simultaneously, however, additional journalistic work was occurring at more mainstream news organizations that would soon turn the Francisville Four into a major local story.

From Alternative Weekly to Tabloid to Broadsheet

On the afternoon of June 13, the editorial offices of the *Philadelphia City Paper* (one of the city's two alternative weeklies, along with *Philadelphia Weekly*) took a telephone call from "a friend of a friend" of one of the people arrested at the house on Seventeenth Street and Ridge Avenue.[14] Isaiah Thompson, the reporter dispatched to the scene, told me that he was new to the Philadelphia area, and the caller was not one of his regular sources. "I think somebody in the house knew somebody at the paper," he said. "In any case, I pretty much ran down there."[15] Thompson's article, which appeared on the *City Paper*'s daily blog, The Clog,[16] on June 14, contained the first extensive information about the arrests, as well as a number of unusually candid quotes from members of the Philadelphia Police Department. A photo of the scene of the "investigation" taken by Thompson,[17] as well as an interview with the building's co-owner Robert Gilbert "on the scene," marked Thompson's presence as a direct observer at some point on June 13. The second and third paragraphs of the story established the chain of events leading to the arrests: "[Daniel] Moffat [the arrestee] watched from the squad car as the officers entered the building and detained three other residents who were inside. Then a funny thing happened: Homeland Security showed up. And more detectives. And then the Crime Scene unit. And then more detectives. And the Fire Marshall. And Licensing and Inspection. And then more detectives. All day long and into Friday evening, the building was crawling with officials from one agency or another."[18]

The article also contained the first interview with Moffat, who repeated the original contention of the press release that the police were targeting members of his house because of their neighborhood activism. Finally, the article provided the first justification of the Police Department's actions: Captain Dennis Wilson of the Ninth District, who, along with two other on-scene officers, spoke to the *City Paper* "gravely from the building's doorway," claimed that the building contained "literature about killing cops" and "propaganda against the government." He then made a statement that would be cited numerous times in the additional reporting on the story: "They're a hate group. . . . We're trying to drum up charges against them, but, unfortunately, we'll probably have to let them go."[19]

The story was largely complete by Saturday, and Thompson and his editor engaged in a familiar debate about whether to save the story for the print edition or, Thompson remembered, "did we want to just put it online?"[20] The debate did not last long: the story was posed on The Clog at 4:23 P.M. on Saturday, June 14. When the *City Paper* hit the streets on Wednesday, a small box on the cover touted the "online-only coverage" of the story.[21]

By the start of the workday on Monday, friends of those arrested had put a media plan in place to further publicize what local activists were now calling the "illegal arrests." The first sign of the media blitz came in the form of a new, much more detailed press release that, in the words of a *Philadelphia Daily News* editor, quickly "went viral."[22] A copy of the release appeared on YPP at 8:30 A.M., complete with a prefatory note acknowledging that its authors had "seen lots of debate about whether or not the information that my colleagues and friends released Friday about the police action at 17th and Ridge was enough for folks," and adding, "There's been much conversation and support bubbling up from the city for the folks who were evicted Friday. Over the weekend they developed this press release, and decided to organize a press conference [at 1:00 P.M. Tuesday] to answer questions."[23] A city editor at the *Daily News* received "at least five" e-mails containing the press release, from reporters and sources, and another veteran reporter "got one e-mail, maybe more."[24] The press release did not originate from YPP; rather "friends of the people arrested sent out the press release to everyone and their mother."[25]

"The story was just intriguing enough to catch my interest," said Gar Joseph, city editor of the *Daily News,* who also noted that, in his experience, the majority of such activist press releases amount to nothing at all and that he is generally skeptical of them.[26] The level of online conversation generated by the story on YPP also played a role in reinforcing the potential importance of the story, adding to a sense in the newsroom that the topic was "hot." "When people are excited, we notice it," said Joseph.[27] "It was the press releases that caught our attention," said Dave Davies, the reporter assigned to report the story for the Tuesday edition of the *Daily News.* "We saw the *City Paper* article once we'd already begun the reporting."[28] As *Daily News* editors debated the next day's newspaper coverage at the afternoon editorial meeting, staff members described a mix of excitement and skepticism surrounding the arrests. "The consensus in the room was that it was a good story," said Joseph, "but there was skepticism about the motives of the people behind it."[29]

The metro columnist and blogger Dan Rubin, who was working one floor up in the *Philadelphia Inquirer*'s newsroom, recalled seeing the Philly IMC story over the weekend and bookmarking it. "Then on Monday, I got a note from Brian Howard of the *City Paper,* touting his reporter's version of it," Rubin said. Shortly thereafter, he received the widely distributed e-mail announcing the news conference on Tuesday. "I didn't have a Wednesday column lined up," Rubin said, "so I jumped on it."[30] Rubin remembers that the IMC story was not enough, in itself, to prompt him to write about the arrests, "because their article wasn't really anything more than a press release, and I don't like linking to press releases."[31] At the end of the day, though, Rubin "wasn't sure if [the arrest] was a column or a story because there was so much unknowable, and to columnize, I'd have wanted a better sense of what to make of it all. So I prepared to do a totally different column for Wednesday, which I did." However, he added, "I had all this material, and we hadn't done anything for the paper yet, so [on Tuesday morning] . . . I start[ed] writing. For the blog. Because I could."[32]

Philadelphia's major news organizations first reported the Francisville arrest story on Tuesday, June 17. The *Daily News* article, "The Cops Came, Searched and Left a Mess for Puzzled Homeowner," which was promoted on the cover and featured on page seven, was the first appearance of the story in printed form.[33] Rubin's blog post "Who Wrote 'Kill The Pigs' at 17th and Ridge?" was posted at 8:52 A.M. Both stories would eventually move to the top slot of Philly.com. The online version of the *Daily News* story contained no links, although it prominently quoted the *City Paper* article;[34] the post on Rubin's blog, Blinq, linked to both the *City Paper* and Davies's story in the *Daily News*.[35] Both pieces were extensively reported and contained a wealth of new information: the Police Department claimed that its original visit to the property was prompted by the defacing of a neighborhood security camera, that someone had written "kill the pigs" on the wall of the raided home, that the residents of the building refused to identify the owner of the house, and that there was a "bunker" on the roof of the building. Moffat, who served as the lead interviewee in both stories, denied that anyone in the home had written "kill the pigs" on a wall ("If anyone did that, it was the police themselves," he was quoted as saying). He also noted that the police had not said they were investigating a defaced security camera when they arrived and that the so-called bunker was really a greenhouse. He produced a property receipt showing that his laptop computer was "in the possession of the State Police Bureau of Criminal Investigation, Intelligence Division," and admitted that because he "panicked" when the police arrived, he denied he was an owner of the building.[36]

Despite their many similarities, however, the two stories also contained a wealth of subtle differences, owing to both the nature of the medium in which they appeared and the character of the institutions that produced them. The *Daily News* article was an entirely "straight" news piece; although it contained a wealth of potentially damning information about police misconduct, it explicitly allowed both "sides" in the arrest dispute to address the claims of the other. The bulk of Rubin's Blinq post did the same thing, yet it was framed in a subtly different fashion. Whereas the *Daily News* led with "Four young residents of a North Philadelphia house who circulated petitions questioning police-surveillance cameras were rousted from their home Friday and detained 12 hours without charges while police searched their house," Rubin took a slightly more skeptical attitude toward the activists. "Now that he's had time to think—and 10 hours in police detention gives you time for introspection—Dan Moffat concedes things might have gone better if he'd cooperated," Rubin began. His conclusion was even stronger: "All I know is that if a bunch of cops came to my door and woke me up—at 3 A.M. even—my instinct would be to cooperate to the point of blurting out anything I'd ever done."[37] Nevertheless, the bulk of the actual reported material is quite similar to the material gathered by the *Daily News*—and, to repeat, it contained a great deal of damning information about police conduct. Part of the difference, as already noted, stemmed from differences in the story form. While it is a truism that reported journalism should be "objective," I noted an equally prevalent notion during my time in Philadelphia: that "blog material," even if it was mostly straight reporting, should contain, if not an explicit opinion, at the very least a strong authorial voice.[38]

An additional explanation for the differences in the two articles—and indeed, for differences in the arc of the story coverage in general—stems from differences in professional self-awareness and brand identity at the two newspapers. "This isn't an *Inquirer* story," one *Daily News* editor told me early in the week. "It's more of a gritty, *Daily News*–type piece."[39] Indeed, no story about the arrests appeared in the print version of the *Inquirer* until Wednesday, using the press conference on Tuesday as a news hook but largely driven by the fact that the *Daily News* had already reported the story.[40] Even more telling were the differences in follow-up planned by the two papers. While the *Daily News* mounted a "mini-crusade" around the issue of the police raid, the *Inquirer* quickly moved to expand the meaning of the arrests in a far more general and skeptical direction. "I got the [Licensing and Inspection] report and this house had a million violations against it," said Kia Gregory, the *Inquirer* reporter who covered the press conference on Tuesday. Possibly alluding to the *Daily News,* though not by name, Gregory continued: "I think we make characters out of the news sometimes." More than a month after the arrests, Gregory said she thought the deeper issues brought to light by the story included the redevelopment of the North Philadelphia neighborhood in which the arrests took place and the relationship between the arrestees and longtime community members. "This whole thing about people coming into the neighborhood and are their tensions between them and the community—that's the story I and my editor care about," Gregory said. Alluding to a post on a local blog, she recounted another incident in which "anarchists" and members of a different neighborhood clashed over gentrification. "Some of the underlying stuff [that is important to this story] is how do these two groups work together?"[41]

Despite these differences in tone—though not in the actual substance of reported material—the fact remained that the arrest of the Francisville Four had become "news." It had gained certification by both of the major newspapers in Philadelphia and had produced a well-attended press conference. The story would now expand into the local and national blogosphere. Indeed, it is at *this moment* in the development in the story that much of the academic literature on the "journalism-blogger" relationship begins.

The Local and Global Blogosphere

Hours after the *Daily News* story appeared on Tuesday, the local Philadelphia blogosphere began devoting considerable attention to the travails of Moffat and

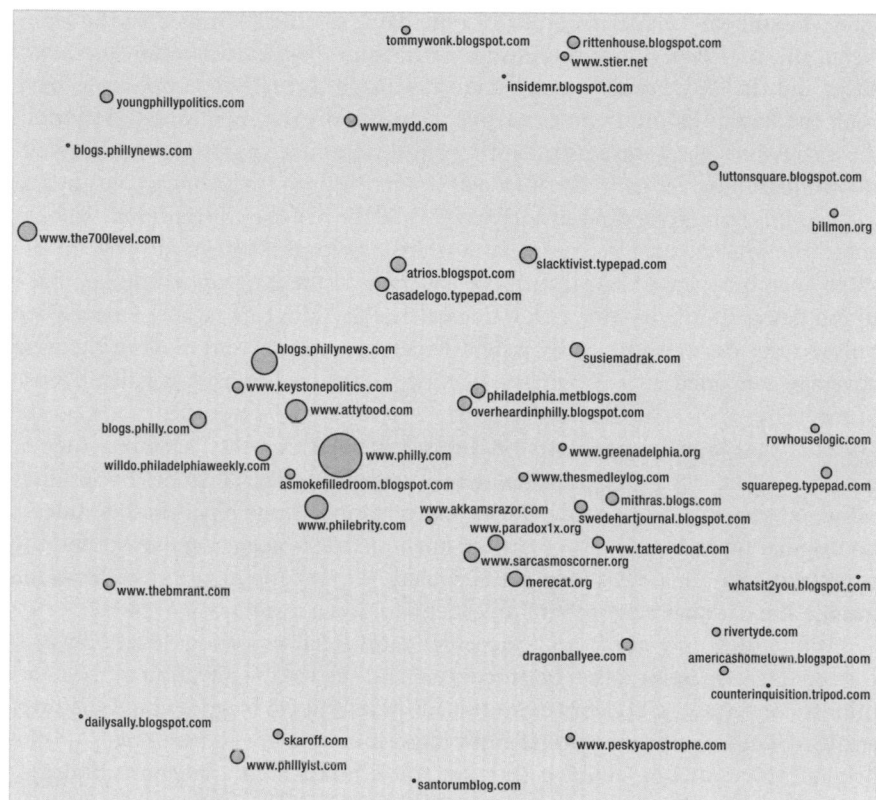

FIGURE 4.1 The Philadelphia blogosphere, circa 2008. This diagram is the visualization of a network analysis, based on co-link frequency, that represents the relationship of various media entities in digital space. For further information about the methodological implications of this sort of analysis, see the Appendix. *(Source: Adapted from Morningside Analytics.)*

his Francisville housemates. In particular, four local blogs—Philebrity, Philadelphia Will Do, Attytood, and Phawker—ensured that the story would have a life that went beyond the confines of the regular *Daily News* and *Inquirer* readership. In addition, the work of "local bridge bloggers" (bloggers who occasionally bridge the gap between local news and a national audience) helped briefly move the story into national prominence (see Figure 4.1).

Several websites jumped on the story before Tuesday, linking to the early *City Paper* and Philly IMC reports. Nevertheless, it is clear that the major Philadelphia blogs were spurred to action by some combination of the original *Daily News* story and the Rubin post, along with the prominence given to both of those stories on Philly.com. In its 12:24 P.M. story, "It Would Be Hilarious If It Weren't True,"[42] Philebrity linked to the *City Paper,* the *Daily News,* and Blinq; in "Cops

Raid Dreamboat Terrorist's House," Philadelphia Will Do linked to the *Daily News,* the *City Paper,* and the Philly IMC;[43] and Phawker linked to the *Daily News* and the *City Paper.*[44] In all, the story in the *Daily News* appears to have been the key: in addition to the three websites already mentioned, Attytood, the discussion board on Stormfront (a white-supremacist group), and the well-known local blog Fables of the Reconstruction (http://mithras.blogs.com) linked to it. At this point, one can see fairly clear validation of the conventional wisdom about the journalism-blogging relationship: key local bloggers jumped on the story once it appeared in print; most coverage in the blogosphere linked back to the newspaper story (to such a degree that the bloggers largely ignored the online-only story produced by a newspaper columnist); and most of the blog coverage contained little "original reporting" in the traditional journalistic sense of the term.

That said, a more qualitative appraisal showed that this "classic" story of news diffusion was more complex than it initially appeared to be. Local blogs reframed the story and broadened the conversation. Some bloggers did, indeed, do original reporting. The thoughts of one journalist-blogger demonstrated the complexity of online news judgments. Finally, the way the story moved from the local to the national blogosphere provides additional insights.

While they may not have done much additional reporting, local blogs reframed the story in ways that both reflected and shaped the direction of the community conversation. Philebrity and Philadelphia Will Do blogged about the story early on Tuesday afternoon, and both blogs immediately added "snark" to the original story, writing about it in ways that typified their trademark brand of sarcastic humor. In addition to recapping the arrests, Daniel McQuade of Philadelphia Will Do noted that Moffat had "dreamy" eyes—eyes that were, in fact, "too dreamy for Philadelphia."[45]

At the same time, however, local bloggers seemed genuinely outraged by the police raid. "Frankly, we don't know where to even begin with this," wrote Philebrity. "But let's start here: This is one of those Culture Wars arrests that cops are always going to lose by virtue of both sheer stupidity (illegal search and seizure, giving the press ridiculous quotes) and cultural ignorance (the inability to discern a hipster from, say, Ramona Africa, cue Domelights thread, blah blah blah)."[46] Philebrity took the additional step—important from a journalistic point of view—of adding background and context to the story and framing it, through a series of links back to previous blog coverage, as part of a pattern of recent police misconduct in Philadelphia. Will Bunch of Attytood also added context to the story (minus much of the sarcasm), linking back to posts he had written on civil liberties and the record of Philadelphia's new Police Chief Charles Ramsey during his tenure in Washington, DC.[47] "I was interested [in the story] because a) civil liberties is one of the main issues that I blog about and b) I'd specifically written last year about the lousy record of the DC cops on civil liberties under Charles Ramsey," Bunch told me. "So I waited for our story to come out, and added some commentary about Ramsey and how such an apparent abuse of power is harmful to fighting crime."[48] In contrast to the newspaper's highly reported stories, then, the three most prominent local bloggers made it a point to deeply contextualize their posts, usually linking back to previous coverage of the topic. All three key local blogs would revisit the story several times over the next few days.

A second factor complicating the usual pattern of diffusion lay in the fact that the local blog Phawker, alone among the media outlets, did indeed do some important original reporting the day after the *Daily News* story broke. "While everyone else was at City Hall for the press conference concerning the police raid of a Francisville building last Friday," wrote the blogger Jeff Deeney, "I was on Ridge Avenue hoping to find my old friend Ms. Edna Williams, of the Mary Jane Enrichment Center."[49] Deeney's connection with Williams went back to his days as a writer for the *City Paper*: "I wrote about Edna in a *City Paper* article about grassroots homeless services not long ago. . . . She's a strong voice among local community activists, and she's respected by social service providers as a tireless advocate for the downtrodden."[50] Deeney turned to Williams to try to answer one of the more pressing journalistic questions at this point in the development of the story—namely, what was the character of those who had been arrested? Were they little more than "hipster" gentrifiers, or were they actually members of their North Philadelphia neighborhood? "If anyone would have a good read on the situation, it would be Edna at the Mary Jane," Deeney wrote. "When I asked her about the building up the street, she became gravely serious and told me to get the word out that Daniel Moffat and the friends that lived with him were good people."

Deeney drew on his reportorial background—a high comfort level with basic reporting; a stable of relevant contacts; the ability not only to identify "the story" but also to collect, represent, and collate basic news facts—to advance the news of the arrests. Deeney might be called a "blogger," but perhaps it might be better to call him a "freelancer," and he is certainly "a journalist." His journalistic identity, however, is deeply deinstitutionalized. He was once a reporter for an alternative weekly but was identified in his biography on Phawker as a freelance writer and a "caseworker with a nonprofit housing program that serves homeless families."[51]

There is a third complication in the traditional blogging-journalism narrative. Although Bunch's description of how he decided to blog the Francisville Four story for Attytood does not contradict the general pattern of news diffusion, it does adds nuance to the conventional wisdom. Because it offers such a window into the blogger-reporter mindset, I quote from one of his e-mails to me at length:

> I actually first heard about the arrests the day before I wrote about [them]. Brian Howard of the *City Paper* and their blog [T]he Clog sent me an email and said something about Homeland Security being on the site. Ironically, I was really tied up with non-work stuff on Monday and didn't have time to pursue it, but then one of our reporters [Davie Davies] made a point of telling

me about the story he was working on when I came in to the office Monday night. . . . For me, the key was the fact that this particular reporter thought the police actions were pretty egregious—he's a solid reporter and someone who takes an open minded approach to every story. He's what bloggers mean when we talk about "a trusted source" of information. Had the story been reported by a different news outlet, or a blogger, I'd be less likely to pick it up.[52]

The quote contains two items of importance. First, the role of the print reporter is fleshed out to an unusual degree. It was not simply that a "real journalist" wrote about the arrests but that a *particular* real journalist, Dave Davies, wrote about them—a "solid reporter," according to Bunch, who is "open minded." While it is unclear whether bloggers who were not that particular reporter's colleagues (as Bunch is; their desks are opposite each other in the *Daily News* newsroom) would have been influenced by Davies' high reputation, it is a fact that a considerable number of reporters I spoke to in Philadelphia—bloggers, radio reporters, Indymedia journalists—spoke highly of him. Second, we again see that the *City Paper* story, marketed aggressively by its editor, played a key role in reinforcing the importance of the Francisville story in the minds of many journalists within the more institutional journalistic community. While the direction of news diffusion from newspaper to blog holds in this instance, the arrow that connects them is more complicated than it might first appear to be.

Finally, in the diffusion of the Francisville story across the blogosphere, we can see evidence of what I call "bridge bloggers" at work: blogs that maintain their connections to local communities (in terms of both their physical location and the topics they write about) but usually blog about national or international issues. It is these blogs to which more prominent sites in the blogosphere are likely to link, which occasionally give bridge blogs the opportunity to take local issues to broader audiences. This was the case for the Francisville Four.

By 10:46 P.M. on Tuesday, June 17, news about the arrests in Francisville had reached the pages of Boing Boing, a prominent weblog of "cultural curiosities and interesting technologies."[53] The key moment in the path from local story to global news (at least in the blogosphere) began when Bunch e-mailed Duncan Black (a.k.a. Atrios), a Philadelphia area blogger who writes primarily, though not exclusively, about national politics. "I emailed [the post] to Atrios, who's also interested in civil liberties and picks up local issues from time to time—he did link to it," said Bunch.[54] Atrios's blog Eschaton is a bridge blog, as well as one of the most popular liberal blogs in the United States. His brief post titled "Hate Group" linked back *not* to Davies's story but to Bunch's blog post and was then picked up by the science-oriented national blog Futurismic, which reframed it as a story about the dangers of urban surveillance cameras.[55] It was the Futurismic story, now reported in terms relevant to the tech-minded Boing Boing audience, that helped the Francisville Four make the final leap into the upper-level blogosphere. "Privacy activists in North Philadelphia who circulated a petition opposing the spy-cameras that were going up in their neighborhood were busted by cops on a warrantless raid," the Boing Boing blogger Corey Doctorow noted.[56] The quote from Captain Dennis Wilson (who later gave the interview in which he called the arrested activists a "hate group" and said he hoped to "drum up charges against them"), first reported by a rookie reporter for a small alternative weekly in the sixth-largest city in the United States, had now reached the pages of "the most popular blog in the world."[57]

We have seen how the general division of labor between journalists and bloggers—that is, journalists report and bloggers comment—is both an accurate and simplistic way to describe the relationship between traditional and new media during the coverage of the arrests. The circuitous journey of this news item, however, was not complete. After a brief moment in the national spotlight, the saga of the Francisville Four would quickly become local news again. It would be the *Daily News,* the most resolutely local of Philadelphia's major news-papers, that would carry the story to its unsettled conclusion.

Live by the Tabloid; Die by the Tabloid

The much-hyped activist news conference on the Tuesday afternoon after the arrests presented something of a dilemma for the *Daily News.* "There wasn't much news there, and that makes it difficult to write anything new," said Davies.[58] Reporters and editors also expressed renewed skepticism about aspects of Mof-fat's story. "Basically, I don't think he's being entirely up front about his politics," an editor noted. But both the reporter and the editor expressed the opinion that the story was deeply troubling. "Unless I hear otherwise," the reporter said, "[I think what happened] is fucking bullshit. I think the police wanted to bring the full weight of the city down on these kids."[59] An editor joked that the situation reminded him of the 1960s, "with the presence of outside agitators and all," but he also seemed to accept the activists' version of events.[60] Davies said that one interesting angle behind the arrests was the use of the Department of Licensing and Inspection to enforce city codes selectively and politically, and he suggested writing a column that made that point. "The idea behind columns is to not let the story disappear," an editor told me, even when there is no immediate news hook.

Davies, however, was not the only *Daily News* journalist who had the idea to write a column about the arrests. Jill Porter, a columnist at the paper, was think-ing along similar lines. "There are certain stories that just jump out at me" as good column material, she said, "and I read the Dave Davies story on Tuesday and thought, 'This is a total outrage.'" The situation was a bit unusual, Porter said, insofar as Davies was also considering writing a column. "So I called Dave, and he said, 'Well, let's just see what happens.' . . . So I went ahead, thinking I was going to write a column [about something else], and then [an editor] said to me, 'What do you mean you're not going to be writing about this?' So I went ahead with the column on this, especially once I heard that [Dave] was going to be taking a slightly different angle and would be focusing more on selective enforcement at [Licensing and Inspection]."[61] According to Porter, writing a column is often a way to keep a particularly important story in the public eye and involves more than just giving opinions. "Reporting is involved," she said— and, indeed, Porter made a special trip to the City Council session on June 19 specifically to question Mayor Nutter about the Francisville arrests.[62]

By the end of the afternoon editorial meeting on Thursday, June 19, a decision had been reached that the two columns would not only run but would also lead the next day's paper. "In the absence of anybody being honest" about what had actually led to the arrests, an editor argued, it made perfect sense to keep the story alive with the hope of pressuring city leaders to get to the bottom of the affair. Discussions surrounded the question of how to work two columnists into a single cover story rather than just one ("It might be worth putting just one of their stories on the cover," an editorial designer said) and what to do about the problem that the arrestees no longer wanted their pictures taken. Although there appeared to be some uncertainty about the exact contours of Friday's paper, it appeared certain that Moffat's story would lead the cover of the *Daily News*.[63]

By Thursday evening, however, the editorial calculations had changed. In the late afternoon, it emerged that the local news anchor Alycia Lane was filing a lawsuit against her former employer, a local CBS News affiliate. Over the course of the previous several months, the *Daily News* had pushed Lane's story relentlessly; it was one of the items that led to the early success of Dan Gross's Philly Gossip blog, and it was a story—despite competition from the *Philadelphia Inquirer*—that the *Daily News* felt it "owned."[64] Indeed, by the end of June, a full one-fifth of the top-fifty year-to-date stories on Philly.com involved the attractive, arrest-prone TV anchor.[65] Even Bunch was not immune from the Lane frenzy that swept the newsroom at the *Daily News* the evening of June 19; indeed, in the absence of the usual gossip columnist, who was on vacation, Bunch ended up writing what turned out to be the cover story on Friday, June 20: "Alycia Tells Her Side—in Suit."[66]

After a brief flirtation with the front page, Moffat and the Francisville Four would be bumped by an obsessively over-reported story about the court filings of a former local news anchor. While one can argue that the choice of cover material represented a betrayal of the *Daily News*'s "public" mission, it is difficult to imagine editors making any other decision. Indeed, it seems clear that the same news practices that put Moffat into consideration as cover material in the first place—the *Daily News*'s tendency toward sensationalism; its willingness to "crusade" on the behalf of those it feels have been wronged by city government; its tendency to bypass reporting on deeper cultural issues (in contrast to the *Philadelphia Inquirer*) in favor of turning news events into "characters"; its comfort in putting two opinion columns on its front page—doomed his story when it went head to head with Alycia Lane's. The Lane story, after all, was the bread and butter of the *Daily News* in the summer of 2008. While Porter's and Davies's columns about the Francisville Four did run together in the June 20 edition, Porter noted that "where a column is placed shapes a lot of the impact it has." Although she thought it "a great idea to have two strong columns on [the Francisville Four] lead the paper," she said, she was not particularly disappointed, or even surprised, by the eventual decision to lead with Lane. "It goes with the turf."[67]

The Aftermath

In the days following the appearance of the columns in the *Daily News,* the story of Moffat and the Francisville Four disappeared from public consciousness. The Philly IMC, retaining its strong links with the activist community and largely insulated from the normal cycle of what counted as "meaningful" news, published a fairly extensive piece of "first-person" reporting from two of the arrestees on June 22.[68] That article marked Indymedia's first bit of original reporting since it had posted the Prometheus press release more than a week earlier. The *Daily News* blogger Chris Brennan followed up with a brief item in his "Philly Clout" column on June 27, noting that Moffat had been placed on a "watch list" at City Hall, despite the absence of any additional evidence against him.[69] Other than those brief items, the story seemed to have been forgotten by the end of the summer. According to Kia Gregory of the *Philadelphia Inquirer,* the disappearance of this particular piece of news had as much to do with the actions of the Police Department and the activists as it did with formal editorial decisions. The arrestees appeared more interested in using their brief moment of notoriety to push their larger political goals through the media, Gregory told me, and the threat of an American Civil Liberties Union lawsuit against the city seemed to place the Police Department in an official "no comment" posture. "[The activists] still haven't filed a complaint," Gregory said. "I contacted one of the people from the press release, just to see, hey, what's going on, and they said, well, they don't really want to talk about this per se, they want to talk about the larger issues of gentrification and police brutality, and I'm thinking, that's what this whole thing is about. To get their agenda out . . . [the activists] won't even follow up on their own story, so it makes you, think, well, how serious, how aggrieved could you feel if you won't file a complaint? . . . So, honestly, I don't know what this [was] about."[70]

It would also appear that the speed of the news cycle had as much to do with the disappearance of the story as did any specific decisions made by the actors in it. I have noted throughout this book that a primary impact of the Internet on journalistic work is its fostering of a dramatically sped up sense of the news cycle. In this example, news of the arrests reached the Internet only a few hours after they occurred; a reporter working for a *weekly* newspaper posted his story several days before his paper officially went to press; and it took only a few hours for the first *Daily News* story to reach the pages of the most popular blog in the world. And then? Nothing. The story vanished. "News is what's new," goes the old journalistic saw. In the case of the Francisville Four, what is new is no longer new—and therefore no longer *news*—for long.

Conclusion: Hybrid Practices and the Invoked Authority of News Reporting

As Chapters 1–4 have demonstrated, the "institutional containers" holding different types of newswork appear to be breaking down. At the very least, they are becoming more porous. One aspect of these blurred boundaries can be seen in Table 1.1, which shows a variety of institutional actors traversing the boundaries of blogging, paid reporting, "traditional" journalism, and radical activism. Some professional reporters began their journalism careers as activists with the Philly IMC; some bloggers were once professional reporters employed by large newspapers, and so forth. The overview of different forms of newswork described in Chapter 3 also highlights porous boundaries. "Blogging," for instance—once seen as a fringe activity carried out by journalistic amateurs—is now being actively embraced by traditional media organizations. And this chapter, finally, has demonstrated that many of the key processes of journalism—breaking news, corroborating it, analyzing it, and creating public action around it—have been distributed to a variety of players scattered across the local news ecosystem.

Alongside this growing institutional hybridity, however, the act of reporting also seemed increasingly to be cited as the "jurisdictional core" of professional newswork. The bulk of daily reporting continued to be carried out by traditional newsroom professionals. Reporting was the most rhetorically valorized form of newswork inside Philadelphia newsrooms. The bloggers employed by Philadelphia news organizations most often reappropriated the blogging form to facilitate reporting. Finally, more "traditional" bloggers, such as Jason Weitzel of Beerleaguer, rhetorically diminished their own occupational standing by sheepishly noting that they "don't do reporting." There is a paradox here, the full implications of which become clear in later chapters. Under jurisdictional pressure from a variety of new journalistic and quasi-journalistic work practices, there was a growing newsroom-based invocation of *reporting* as the heart of Philadelphia newswork. This very act of reporting, however, also appeared to be under technological and economic stress and suffering from a diminished occupational authority: reporting was becoming more reactive, less specialized, more prone to speed-induced errors, more dependent on the "culture of the click" and the desires of the active audience, and, consequently, less autonomous. So at the same time that traditional reporting was emerging as the valorized capstone of journalistic work, its very operations were becoming less insulated, more hybridized, and more difficult to sustain.

Chapters 1 and 2 focused on how local reporters' conceptions of the public were changing as journalistic production moved into seeming boundless digital space. Chapter 3 and this chapter have described the simultaneous hybridization and valorization of reporting within the journalistic imaginary. At this point, it seems safe to argue that the core of modern journalism in the years leading up to and immediately following the onset of the web era was the notion that journalists *reported the news in order to call a particular form of public into being.* Previous chapters presented evidence to buttress this claim and chronicled how it is changing in the age of digitization.

Chapters 5 and 6 turn to examining one strategy journalists, academic thinkers, foundations, and newsroom managers adopted to deal with the problematization of reporting and the public: the idea that the future of the news is *networked.* In my discussion of the Francisville Four, I noted that the existence of the Philadelphia news network might have seemed obvious to an external analyst, but it was not for reporters and editors, all of whom pursued their reporting duties in fairly traditional ways. Chapters 5 and 6 explore attempts to both strengthen Philadelphia's journalistic network and make the ecosystemic mindset more central to the lives of working journalists.

III

Building
News Networks

5

What We Have Here Is a Failure to Collaborate (2005–2009)

"[It's like] Three Different-Size Legs on One Stool"

At approximately 10:00 A.M. on an ordinary Monday at the offices of the *Philadelphia Daily News* on 400 North Broad Street, a well-sourced columnist took a surprising phone call: Anne d'Harnoncourt, longtime director of the Philadelphia Museum of Art and a leading member of the city's cultural elite, had passed away suddenly the previous night. She was only sixty-four and seemed to be in excellent health; her death came as a shock to members of the tabloid's staff. Also something of a shock was the possibility that, if it could report the tip quickly enough, the *Daily News* might scoop its upstairs competitor, the *Philadelphia Inquirer,* which had not yet heard about the death. Since the *Daily News* lacked a large online staff, the death of d'Harnoncourt "normally would have been an *Inquirer* story all the way," the reporter Barbara Laker told me. "But we got this information first, and the powers that be have told us they want more rapidly updated breaking news coverage from the *Daily News.*"[1] The *Daily News* editor David Preston added, "We're trying to beat the *Philadelphia Inquirer* every few minutes." He asked one of the few reporters already in the office to throw together a single paragraph on the story to put on the *Daily News* website as a breaking news item. That paragraph, limited to reporting the most basic facts (who d'Harnoncourt was and that she had died) was posted by 10:14 A.M. and constituted the first published report of the death. By 11:00 A.M., Preston and the reporter were working on a longer story that they hoped to post on the *Daily News* website as soon as possible.

Between 10:30 and 11:30 A.M., the *Daily News* and the *Inquirer* (which had launched into the story a few minutes later, drawing on its greater institutional resources and well-staffed breaking news desk) were each reporting and editing their own versions of the d'Harnoncourt story. A longer but still skeletal news item (fifteen to twenty column inches) by the original *Daily News* reporter and a research intern was e-mailed to the online desk at the *Daily News* and posted to the paper's website at 11:30 A.M. Nearly simultaneously, a three-paragraph *Inquirer* story about d'Harnoncourt both led the paper's website and sat in the "biggie" position on Philly.com. This version of the story contained less information about d'Harnoncourt's life but included the purported cause of her death (a stroke). After posting its 11:30 update, the *Daily News* started working on a third version. The original team was joined by another reporter, who began calling notable public figures in Philadelphia for reaction. A thirty-inch story was posted online by 2:00 P.M. that added details and local reaction and updated the cause of death. All the while, reporters and editors at the *Daily News* regularly checked Philly.com to see how the *Inquirer*'s reporting was progressing, making frequent comments about their upstairs rival.

One of the remarkable things about the development of this fairly mundane story was how the seriously and substantively the journalistic competition between the *Inquirer* and the *Daily News* played out over the course of the news morning. This was surprising, given that the papers had a common owner, worked from the same building (though on different floors), and were aggregated by the same company website, Philly.com. Examples of this professional competition ranged from the mundane to the serious. For instance, there was minor glee in the *Daily News* offices when interns at that paper managed to get their hands on a shared archive of news clippings about d'Harnoncourt before the *Inquirer* did. "[Reporters at the *Inquirer*] will be wondering where the clippings went," one editor said, chuckling. There was also competition over the basic facts of the story. The two papers disagreed about the cause of d'Harnoncourt's death, and the *Daily News* strategically decided to hold off publishing a fourth version of the story online to save a second scoop for the printed newspaper—that d'Harnoncourt was undergoing breast cancer treatment shortly before she died.

The journalistic rivalry between the two Philadelphia newspapers ultimately played out across around the digital webspace of Philly.com—specifically, in a competition over which newspaper's story was placed in the top website position. The fact that the shorter *Inquirer* report led Philly.com for most of the morning was a source of consternation for the *Daily News* reporters working on the story. At some point in the late afternoon, a city editor sent an irritated e-mail to a producer at Philly.com complaining about the continuing subordinate placement of the *Daily News* story, and for most of the rest of the day, the stories at the top of Philly.com ping-ponged back and forth between the two papers. "Ideally, Philly.com would just be aggregating the content from the two newspapers [without having to make editorial decisions about which newspaper's reporting got top priority]," David Preston told me, "but when both papers are going headlong into the same item, it presents something of a challenge." The speed and transparency of competition—although not the existence of competition in the first place—between the *Daily News* and the *Inquirer* appears to have increased in the online era. Each newspaper can see, overtly and in real time, what its competitor is doing—a situation Pablo Boczkowski has referred to as imitation in an age of information abundance.[2] There are battles over which paper gets onto the "biggie" slot on the front page of Philly.com, as well as competition over who can produce the most "moving parts" (blog posts, background content, and so on) that supplement basic reporting.

For reporters and editors at the *Daily News* and *Inquirer,* the relationship between the two papers is competitive. From the point of view of executives and web producers at Philly.com, however, the driving impulse is to *coordinate* the papers' competitive journalistic impulses as part of their own aggregative newswork. In describing the development of the d'Harnoncourt story from the point of view of the Philly.com newsroom, Wendy Warren, a vice-president at Philly.com, recalled:

> When I walked in the door of the [Philly.com newsroom,] the *Daily News* had just filed a flash that [d'Harnoncourt] had died, . . . and the *Inquirer* quickly followed suit. That happens a lot, you know, on a big breaking story: we will typically have one newspaper doing one thing, and then the other newspaper doing the exact same thing, especially at the beginning. . . . So you had this constant flow of newspapers updating their stories and Philly.com attempting to juggle them.[3]

Indeed, a close reader of Philly.com would have noticed that its top two stories reported different causes of d'Harnoncourt's death for most of the day.[4]

These coordination problems ironically stemmed from what everyone at the Philadelphia newspapers identified as a position of journalistic strength: the existence of three separate news "brands" under one ownership umbrella, each with a tendency to market itself to a different kind of news consumer. Many of the complex management factors alluded to above arose from the aggregation of the content produced by these brands on an organizationally independent website. "Someone once described it as a three different-size legs on one stool," an executive at Philly.com told me. "Is it a difficult thing to manage? Yeah, very difficult. Three brands give you so much freedom. But it really does make it incredibly difficult." While the rationalized structures of most news organizations in Philadelphia enabled the production of valuable journalism, in short, they also erected high barriers around a variety of networked, collaborative possibilities. The halting efforts made to coordinate content production within the same news organization, described above, are reminiscent of what Joshua Braun has called the difficult process of "heterogeneous engineering" that is required to get "smaller companies, all with their own legacy publishing platforms and organizational subcultures[,] . . . to work together harmoniously within a large media corporation."[5] Even as the Philadelphia newspapers began to merge many of the reporting desks of their formerly competing papers in 2012, the competition between the two brands was unlikely to fade away quickly. Even more important, the struggles of two media companies to coexist within a larger framework sheds light on the larger complexities of networking together news institutions in the digital age, even after the specific institutional relationships I discuss here have changed.

This chapter, drawing on several years of fieldwork and numerous site visits to Philadelphia after 2009, explores the possibilities of (and barriers to) building a more networked local news system. The chapter begins with an overview of the different ways that scholars, policy analysts, and media pundits have articulated the notion of networked news and ties these conceptions into larger questions about the nature of reporting and the idea of the public in a digital age. I then move into a discussion of three Philadelphia case studies, each of which was chosen to illustrate a particular potentiality of the networked news environment. The first looks at the Philadelphia-area "norgs initiative," a coalition of individuals and news institutions dedicated helping build a new news organization that would operate in a more web-centric, networked fashion. The second looks at the Next Mayor, one of the first special projects undertaken by the *Daily News* that attempted to foster collaboration with a broader range of communicative actors (blogs, new media organizations) to cover the city's mayoral race in 2007. The third and final case study looks at digital linking practices in the Philadelphia media ecosystem and elaborates the various cultural, organizational, economic, and technological factors that facilitated or blocked the construction of these "inscribed networks." The take away from these three case studies is that the process of "networking the news" in Philadelphia remains, even in 2013, in its nascent stages. Ironically, Philadelphia media organizations found it easier to collaborate on complex, one-time projects than they did on the relatively mundane process of reporting the daily news. Collaboration and interorganizational linking were primarily confined to special projects.

Rebuilding the News

The previous chapters examined both digital-era changes in the work of journalists—how they understood and undertook *reporting*—as well as changes in journalists' vision of the public, insofar as that seemingly unproblematic body was now increasingly encountered online. Faced with these challenges to concepts of reporting, as well as to the public toward whom that reporting was directed, many thinkers both inside and outside the traditional news industry have argued in favor of building a more networked news ecosystem in which both the definition of the public and the meaning of reporting is further problematized. For many of these analysts, the first step on the road to building a more networked news ecosystem lies in increased journalistic collaboration between organizations. Jeff Jarvis, a professor of journalism at the City University of New York, and Joshua Stearns, a policy analyst and organizer, have done much to advance our understanding of the varieties of collaborative journalistic work—Jarvis by positing the existence of an organizational ideal type (the "networked journalism organization") and Stearns by mapping the real-life examples of this ideal type.

For Jarvis, the ease of collaborative work in the digital media environment, the explosion of online content (much of it increasingly specialized and targeted in nature), and the diminishing resources of traditional news organizations have made the emergence of networked journalism inevitable in the news business. Jarvis writes:

> "Networked journalism" takes into account the collaborative nature of journalism now: professionals and amateurs working together to get the real story, linking to each other across brands and old boundaries to share facts, questions, answers, ideas, perspectives. It recognizes the complex relationships that will make news. And it focuses on the process more than the product.[6]

Charlie Beckett, a professor of media at the London School of Economics and the director of the Polis journalism think tank, has expanded on Jarvis's definition in *Supermedia* and a series of related articles. For Beckett, "Networked journalism gives rise to more decentralized decision making and nonhierarchical structures as well as to greater heterogeneity and diversity. This confronts the traditional practices of journalism, which tend to be much more centralized, homogeneous and less pluralistic."[7]

Beyond these definitions, however, the nature of the causal arrow and the dynamics of the underlying forces driving the emergence of networked news collaboration are unclear. Is "networked journalism" the inevitable outcome of large-scale processes of technological, organizational, and economic change? Is it a prediction about something that might happen, given the convergence of a set of contingent factors? Or is it more of a call to arms, an exhortation that a particular type of organization should be built? Like all provocative blog posts, Jarvis's speculation about networked journalism is a little bit of all three, which makes it an excellent spur for creative thought but a poor substitute for more rigorous scholarly analysis.

Josh Stearns has done much to shift the discussion about networked journalism away from a collaborative "call to arms" and toward a more grounded analysis of actually existing collaborative projects.[8] Stearns divides his examples of collaboration into five categories: (1) commercial news sharing; (2) private-public partnerships; (3) public and non-commercial media organizations; (4) university news partnerships; and (5) legacy/hyperlocal collaborations. While Stearns's categories focus primarily on the nature of the collaborating organizations, we can also rearrange his typology to more strongly emphasize the purposes and outcomes of the collaborative work. Drawing on Stearns's list of more than thirty-five collaborative projects, as well as my extensive fieldwork observations, I would argue that three categories emerge when we focus on the nature of the work being done and the eventual journalistic output. All of the examples that follow are Stearns's:

1. Sharing resources, or combining the back-end resources needed for the regular production, analysis, and distribution of journalism. Examples range from the sharing of resources (e.g., "Fox and NBC: These stations are sharing one camera crew and consolidating equipment under one assignment desk in cities across the country") to a more content-based type of sharing ("The Ohio News Organization: The eight largest papers in Ohio have partnered to share content, including sports coverage, state government and local events."[9]

2. Cross-organizational content partnerships, or different organizations' agreeing to work together to produce journalism, with a focus on the collaborative nature of the resulting content rather than the sharing of existing back-end resources. This may be the most common example current collaborative work ("ProPublica works with a range of commercial and noncommercial news outlets. Their stories have appeared in the *L[os] A[ngeles] Times, New York Times, Washington Post* and everywhere in between" and ("The *New York Times* and [New York University's] Arthur L. Carter Journalism Institute are collaborating on a hyper local news site based on NYtimes.com and covering the East Village in Manhattan").[10]

3. Materially inscribed collaboration, or the slightly more obscure notion of a partnership that exists and is recognized in material space—that is, one that signals its partnership by "linking out" to its partner organizations. After all, organizations can collaborate on content production without ever acknowledging each other through hyperlinks, and it was the notion of linking across brands that formed one of the core precepts of Jarvis's original notion of networked journalism. Likewise, organizations can engage in collaborative work without explicit agreement.[11] Collaboration can exist simply in acknowledging that other news organizations have done important work that your organization might not have done and linking to it ("News organizations in Washington State are using a Publish2 Newsgroup to collaborate on creating a *link newswire* of top regional news").[12]

Along with these three potential forms of networked journalism, Stearns tacitly acknowledges a second axis of comparison when he notes that there is a difference between long-term collaborations and one-time partnerships. Not all partnerships between new organizations are long term. Many are temporary. By further breaking these three categories down along the second axis, we can construct a six-quadrant typology of different forms of newsroom collaboration (see Figure 5.1).

Admittedly, these categories function more as ideal types than perfect descriptions of actual collaborations. Many projects include the simultaneous sharing of back-end resources; a focus on the finished, collaboratively produced content; and links. But not all do. Indeed, I think the categories get at some very real distinctions: there are differences among a type of collaboration that is primarily a "link newswire" of hyperlinks to outside websites, an intensive organizational partnership producing several pieces of distributed long-form reporting, and the back-end sharing of existing newsroom resources. During my ethno-

	Resource Sharing	Collaborative Content	Inscribed Networks
Temporary Partnership			
Long-Term Partnership			

FIGURE 5.1 Typology of networked news partnerships.

graphic research in Philadelphia, I discovered that news organizations in the city were far less likely to collaborative over the long term than they were to collaborate on short-term reporting projects and that the act of materially acknowledging another media organization in digital space—simply linking to it—was far less common than partnering with another organization over either the short term or the long term. Formal partnerships involve meetings; shared—or, at least, jointly articulated—goals; collaborative teamwork; and the negotiation of eventual outputs. Linking, making clear that an external partner simply exists, involves, seemingly, a few keystrokes and a bit of technical code. If considered in terms of economic and technical logics, the fact that linking was less common than more formal partnerships makes little sense.

To elaborate on and complicate these ideal types of collaborative newswork, and to investigate further the odd discrepancy between formal collaboration and linking, I now turn to the case studies of collaborative news projects: the oddly named norgs initiative (designed to facilitate a collaborative atmosphere in Philadelphia), the Next Mayor project, and, finally, hyperlinking practices at traditional and nontraditional Philadelphia news organizations.

Building a New Local Partnership, or Just What Was "Norg" Anyway?

It was yet another blog post about the future of journalism, much like the millions of blog posts about the media that had come before it and have come since. This post, however, was different—not really in terms of what it said, but in terms of what it did. "The New Philadelphia Experiment: Saving the *Daily News,*" posted on October 25, 2005, by the *Daily News* journalist Will Bunch crystallized one of the most ambitious recent attempts to reimagine the future of local news production. The manner in which Bunch's blog post was used as an organizing object by a set of well-networked local media makers and technologists, the immense amount of work required to draw what became known as the norg network together, and the inherently uncertain future of this temporary assemblage (along with the impressive number of digital artifacts it has scattered like crumbs across the Internet) make it a fascinating example of what I link to think of as the "ontological flatness" of news networks. The norg network was assembled out of people: their words crystallized as online blog postings, their organizing work, their physical spaces, their academic support, the documentation of meetings and of online listservs, and (occasionally) by actual changes in newswork practices. Key to these processes of assemblage is what Fred Turner has called "network entrepreneurs" (actors "positioned between multiple discursive and institutional networks [that fill] 'structural holes'") and "network forums" ("places where members of [various] communities came together, exchanged ideas and legitimacy").[13]

The newswork routines that went into the daily crafting Bunch's Attytood blog are described in Chapter 4; Bunch had been thinking and blogging about the changing nature of the journalism profession at least since the now forgotten "Jeff Gannon" controversy of early 2005 (a scandal in which a Republican public relations manager posing as a journalist gained access to the White House pressroom). "Blogging about Gannon was one of the things that set Attytood apart from Campaign Extra" (Bunch's previous blog, which covered the presidential election in 2004), an editor at the *Daily News* told me. "There was politics in Campaign Extra, [but] the Gannon event was what began Will's self-reflections about what journalism was, how it was changing, and how to fix it."[14] In late October 2005, rising anxiety about the financial condition of the *Inquirer* and *Daily News* (focused on the impending layoff of 15 percent and 19 percent, respectively, of the papers' newsroom staff) prompted Bunch to write his most explicit reflections on the future of local news. The early paragraphs of his blog post "The New Philadelphia Experiment" began by sketching an imaginary future in which "news organizations" (Bunch named them "norgs") had replaced "newspapers" as the key providers of local news; in Bunch's Philadelphia of the future, Phillynorg.com (the "People Norg") was the first stop for most Philadelphians during their morning web-surfing routine; Bunch idealistically described Phillynorg as a web-native, personality-heavy, blog-friendly, news-providing, money-earning institution.[15] For Bunch, this sketched future "may have been fictional but it was no fantasy," as he sought to turn the economic tsunami bearing down on the *Daily News* into an occasion to think boldly about the future of local journalism:

> With a staff that is now too small to cover every news story, we can learn how to cover just the stories that truly matter to people, and cover the heck out of them. Because a newspaper with 20 personalities that the reader knows and seeks out every morning is better off than a newspaper with 200 faceless reporters covering zoning meetings. Hence, the "norg." "Norg" because we need to lose our old identity with one dying medium, newspapers, and stress our most valuable commodity, the one that we truly own, and that is news—without the paper. Thus, we must now be news organizations, or "norgs."[16]

The overall tone of Bunch's post implied that divisions that had long beset the emerging media community—between bloggers and journalists, between print and digital media, between corporate and "alternative" journalism—needed to be overcome in favor of a new spirit of collaboration, work coordination, and mutual respect.

The major impact of Bunch's post, however, came not through his theorizing about the "new Philadelphia experiment" but, rather, in his call for a public dialogue about what local journalism in Philadelphia should look like in the new online era and how news providers in it might work together more productively. "It's a cheap gimmick, and 'norg' is a word that might never live past these blog entries," he wrote. "But it's a cheap gimmick aimed at starting a valuable conversation that should have begun years ago. . . . [I]n the end, what I think isn't paramount. What do you think should be done to save America's news organizations?"[17]

The on-site responses to Bunch's post were fairly innocuous. It was what happened next, however, that shaped the direction of what quickly became a local reform movement. As Jeff Jarvis, an early participant in the dialogue, recalled, the conversation "started with Will Bunch writing on the *Daily News* blog Attytood. [The] Philly blog king [and founder of Philly Future] Karl Martino picked this up and sent e-mail to folks he knows—bloggers, journalists, educators—suggesting that we get together to help explore this with Bunch."[18] In his description of how the larger conversation inspired by the norg post began, Martino described the organizing process in more detail:

> I've been online for a long while, working on Philly Future for many years, and had many contacts in online media and technology I thought I could bring together in discussion and possibly a meeting—with members of the local newspaper community—to build bridges and possibly discuss solutions to the problems the news industry was facing. I contacted Will Bunch of the *Daily News* (after he wrote his piece, which kicked things off) and Daniel Rubin of the *Inquirer,* Fred Mann and Kevin Donahue of Philly.com and Susie Madrak of "Suburban Guerrilla" along with other regional bloggers, technologists. Chris Satullo of the *Inquirer* was instrumental in contacting members of the Penn community to get the University involved. Jeff Jarvis was a huge part in raising awareness and in participating. Wendy Warren, Susie Madrak, and Will Bunch collectively led the effort to pull this together.[19]

This is a process of network assemblage using an online artifact (Bunch's blog post) as an object around which to organize, creating what Susan Leigh Star and James Griesemer call a "boundary object": "objects which are both plastic enough to adapt to local needs and constraints of the several parties employing them, yet robust enough to maintain a common identity across sites."[20] Each of the key organizers of the first Norgs Unconference held at Annenberg on March 25 might be seen as a hybrid actor sitting between two or more networks: Martino as a former Philly.com employee with deep contacts in the local blogosphere and the tech community, Bunch as both a blogger and traditional journalist, Madrak as a blogger and former journalist, and Warren as a *Daily News* editor with a background in the "public journalism" movement. Each of these organizers, in other words, sat not only at a central point in his or her own network but also on key nodes of network overlap, well positioned to translate the language and concerns of one network community (e.g., that of traditional journalists) into the language and concerns of another (e.g., that of bloggers).

Along with the structural positioning of the key members of the early "future of local journalism" conversations, the desire to *materially represent* these conversations in the form of on- and offline artifacts also helped contribute to the early success of the norgs initiative. In examining the evolution of the idea, we can point to multiple key moments of what scholars of science and technology have termed "inscription": "all the types of transformations through which an entity becomes materialized into a sign, an archive, a document, a piece of paper, a trace."[21] Examples of inscription in the 2006 norgs initiative abound: Bunch's original blog post and the comments and conversation it engendered; the move from a closed e-mail chain to a semi-public listserv through which to discuss the possibility of a norg; small, in-person meetings; the organizing of a norgs conference; and the extensive documentation of that conference that was later posted online. Similarly, each of these meetings and digital inscriptions—particularly the norgs conference and its associated mailing list—can be viewed as an example of a particular "network forum."

In early November 2005, Martino outlined the attempts that had been made to date to build a conversation around Bunch's call for reform. "We are having [a conversation] via email, with a group of bloggers, journalists, and educators to discuss what can be done [to reinvent local news]," he wrote on Philly Future. "Talk has grown into bringing a very small working meeting here, where over a few cheese steaks . . . we can discuss, face to face, best practices, tools, and solutions. We're calling it, and not so jokingly, the 'Real Journalism in Philly Change or Die Study Group.'"[22] This in-person meeting encouraged further back-channel e-mail brainstorming, which itself prompted the move to a larger, public e-mail list. In fact, a key moment in the transition from a small, one-off study group to an actual working community came with the decision to move the conversation from a "cc list" to a Yahoo Group. By shifting to Yahoo, Martino and others created a permanent repository for the discussion that could be accessed at any time and that rationalized the structure through which new members could be invited to join. Although participants expressed an early concern that the new, more formal structure would limit the intensity of the conversation, members soon re-engaged as a number of dramatic local developments occurred in quick succession. Just as plans were being finalized for a larger, in-person journalism reform meeting hosted by the University of Pennsylvania's Annenberg School for Communication—what participants were awkwardly calling a "norgs Unconference [to] save local journalism in Philadelphia"—word arrived that Knight-Ridder, the company that owned the *Inquirer* and *Daily News,* along with thirty other U.S. newspapers, was being sold to the McClatchy Company, which planned to resell less profitable parts of the Knight-Ridder chain, including the Philadelphia media properties, immediately. By the date of the Norgs Unconference speculation that the *Daily News* would be significantly downsized or closed had reached a fever pitch. I attended the "unconference," which was held on March 25, 2006, and observed complex mélange of fear and optimism gripping participants as it got under way.[23]

According to its organizers, the Norgs Unconference aimed to extend, enhance, and solidify discussions about the future of journalism in Philadelphia that had been occurring mostly online, discussions inspired by Bunch's original blog post and that drew energy from the changes shaking the Philadelphia newspaper market. More than forty people "from blogging, independent publishing, and newspaper industry backgrounds" participated. The fact that the Norgs Unconference happened at all was something of an achievement; keep in mind that there was no larger umbrella sponsorship of the meeting—no permanent structure like the Online News Association or the Newspaper Association of America under whose auspices the meeting occurred. The meeting included everyone from "the upper management of traditional news organizations to the trenches of independent media, from seasoned journalists to young news consumers, from personal bloggers to online community hosts, from software engineers to media entrepreneurs," groups with their own sets of internal hierarchies, cultural boundary markers, and deep sociocultural needs to distinguish themselves from other groups—that is, "Folks that normally don't see eye to eye—let alone see common cause."[24] Many of the participating institutions historically had been hostile to one another. Included in the conversation, for instance, were members of the Philly IMC, a group founded in explicit opposition to the very newspapers now driving the conference, one of whose early members told me that they would never even *link* to a "corporate" media outlet.[25] By 2006, however, members of the Philly IMC were both participating in and (true to form) videotaping the entire day. Writing in his blog later in the day, a second attendee tried to capture the excitement of the event: "Industry types mixed surprisingly well with non-industry types. Ideologies were varied, bloggers, students and people simply passionate about the future of news delivery. It was pretty exciting."[26]

Despite the fact that many of the post-conference conversations with interested academics and journalists revolved around these notions of occupational identity, professional cooperation, and competition, the conference *itself* largely steered clear of rehashing the more philosophical debates around the relationship between journalistic professionals and amateurs. Instead, the tenor of the talks was practical, following the original mandate to "reinvent local news" in Philadelphia. A "lightning round" of brainstorming about "what we want a norg to be followed morning introductions" and included answers like the following:[27]

Should empower its users to be citizens.

Has a voice. Have a personality.

Enables the community to inform each other. . . .

Willing to see the union as a partner.

Interactive. Gives voice to the readers.

Realizes that journalism is not always a story. It might be a database.

Multiplatform, including a free print edition. Multimedia, offering different platforms for different audiences.

Not a one-way street. Not print into multimedia—both ways. . . .

Allows reporters to express what they think and feel.

A watchdog of the eternal spin machine. Please, of state government. . . .

Supports the acts of journalism.

PERSONAL. Facilitates actual human interaction. . . .

Devoted to Media literacy—not how to use the media, how to BE the media. . . .

May offer layers of journalism: old-school, trained journalism; community journalism.

Uses a new metric for measuring success. Clicks are not the only way.[28]

Brainstorming about the nature of the news organization for the twenty-first century led into an agenda-setting conversation that was notable, once again, for its practical focus. Three breakout groups tackled three major agenda items: what the content and culture of a "norg" should be, what business model it should adopt, and what its ethical responsibility was. Later feedback on the "business models" discussion noted laughingly that the group vacillated "between socialism (functioning as a community co-op) and capitalism (discussing new ways to monetize content) and back again," and noted the difficulties funding investigative journalism online.[29] The culture and content discussion, somewhat surprisingly, focused on questions of legal liability and management functionality, while the ethical responsibility working group dealt most explicitly with the "big ideas" surrounding changes in the local news ecosystem. "What are we trying to *grow*," one set of notes asked rhetorically?

> How can we redefine what local news can be and ought to be? Find what ties us together—psychographic, not geographic. Importance of storytelling. Finding new ways to use technology to tell the story. Beyond even our new toolbox (podcast, blog, etc., these are old technologies in web time). [Should we] consider partisan journalism? How would that work? [We want something with] tone and attitude. . . . How much do we let non-readers, including corporate interests, dictate our business? And what is the role of citizen-journalists? Can they help answer the "geography paradox"?[30]

Another distributed digital object that pointed to a lowering of barriers and walls was the collective statement[31] hammered out after the meeting and signed by members of the *Inquirer, Daily News,* and the Philly IMC (all acting in an individual rather than organizational capacity), as well as by numerous bloggers.

The twenty-one-point document was "an attempt to summarize concepts and ideas that attendees of the March 2006 Norgs Unconference agreed on" and emphasized the necessary disaggregation of news and the newsprint, the inherently social and collaborative nature of the web, the importance of collaboration that went beyond the newsroom, and the fact that some companies (such as Amazon.com and eBay) had been able to turn the "sociability" of the web into a functional business plan. "Collections of stories, and our interactions with them, define communities," the statement concluded. One historically important category of stories had been crafted, for the past century or so, through "acts of journalism and "a norg is an organization that provides infrastructure to support [these] acts of journalism."

The news network crystallized by the conference seemed to provide many of its participants with the hope that more solid and permanent networks might result from the dialogue. What, indeed, did all of the talk amount to in the end? I have already alluded to the fact that I think the very existence of the conference— along with its e-mail list—was no small accomplishment, but actual participants in the conversation clearly wanted more. Notes from the final session summarized:

> We will create a Wiki and a blog and a message group to define the still-changing architecture of a norg and—with our users—begin filling out the details, completing the model. We will start developing an Evangelist's Calendar of ways to promote the norgs idea at conferences, etc. (and set up another meeting, inviting new people). But we aren't waiting for a norg to be built. We will publish all the ideas that came up today, begin shaping them in communication with our users, and begin using what ideas we can in our current jobs. We'll be working on three tracks: Building the model; putting the ideas to work during the drama at Philadelphia Newspapers Inc. (because it is so dominant in Philadelphia); and working to have the ideas applied in all local media.[32]

"But what has your group done that's *concrete*?" asked a journalist from the University of Massachusetts during an information sharing videoconference several months after the Annenberg meeting. "We're doing lots of things that are concrete," Wendy Warren, replied, noting that Philly.com's deliberations over a new content management system, as well as its recent embrace of user-driven, interactive web tools, were deeply influenced by dialogue on the norgs list. "But you have to keep in mind that we are doing two things at the same time," she noted. "We are dreaming of a future that does not exist and we are practicing in a reality that we've got. . . . The thing that's wild about this project is that we started the year thinking, 'Maybe we have to reinvent local news in Philadelphia,' but what we're doing is more a *philosophy* than it is a *thing*. And the philosophy and the discussion is helping me, anyway; I don't know about anyone else. . . . [I]t's actually helping the media participants expand their minds, and at the same time it's helping . . . independent media broaden their minds."[33] Another organizer, speaking several months after the event, agreed that the spirit of "cooperation was really one of the most amazing things about the conference" and emphasized his hope for the continued lowering of occupational barriers and for an extension of news networks:

> Every day you hear this "journalists versus bloggers" discussion occurring when that discussion shouldn't even be happening. . . . [I]t's a silly and distracting argument between two groups of people that aren't as dissimilar as people like to think and want to do their best to serve their communities. We had a number of prominent bloggers who were at the Unconference, including folks from Indymedia, Duncan Black of Eschaton, and Susie Madrak, who actually helped organize the Unconference, and it was a terrific discussion and a terrific meeting of ideas. [There were] different takes on what journalism is and how to support it.[34]

One specific outcome of the norg meeting, then, might be described as a cultural reorientation on the part of the participants, a greater tendency to see media makers less as "bloggers" or "journalists" than as potential contributors to "acts of journalism" whose merits should be judged on those grounds rather than according to more traditional categorical divides.

Many participants also hoped this intangible spirit of collaboration might result in a second outcome: a growing dialogue, both in person and on the Yahoo Groups listserv. One crude measure of overall dialogue—the number of posts to the norgs list—shows that, indeed, the excitement of the conference did translate to a larger number of list posts. The number of posts prior to the conference averaged 42.3 per month; except in March (the actual month of the meeting), the number of post-conference posts averaged 117.3 per month. While this is a deeply crude measurement, there can be little doubt that the energy of the conference served to spur discussion, the sharing of ideas, and collaboration in the months that followed.

A third outcome of the conference was simply its documentation; in more technical language, the sheer number of digital objects it scattered across the Internet. Unlike the normal whiteboards used to document meetings and brainstorming sessions, the March meeting produced a mass of online material. I have already mentioned that the Philly IMC videotaped the meeting and that a "Statement of Principles" was agreed to at the conference's conclusion. A complete list of digital objects produced from the meeting includes the following:

- A norgs Wiki at http://norgs.pbwiki.com/FrontPage
- The "The Norgs Unconference Statement of Principles," available at http://norgs.pbwiki.com/The+Norgs+Unconference+Statement+Of+Principles
- The meeting notes at http://123.writeboard.com/50f77441c4d21a4a8
- An MP3 recording of a breakout session originally posted at http://www.jgregorypalmer.com/media/norgsbreakout.mp3
- An organized summary of the meeting notes at http://blogs.phillynews.com/dailynews/norg/2006/08/what_we_did_saturday.html

- An edited conference video originally posted at http://phillyimc.org/en/2006/03/20081.shtml
- A photo set, available at http://www.flickr.com/photos/dragonballyee/sets/72057594090659485
- Posts by Karl Martino, Jeff Jarvis, Philly Blogs, Will Bunch, Amy Webb, Dan Rubin, Howard Hall, Albert Yee, and me, among others, on a variety of blogs[35]
- A video of a later meeting between Philly Norg representatives and the Media Giraffe Project originally posted at http://psg2.princeton.edu/media giraffe/MGP2006_062906_conference.mov

In response to the question "What has your group done that's *concrete*?" one could reply that the conference had produced a "concrete" feeling of collaboration, a "concrete" increase in dialogue about Philadelphia media, and a "concrete" number of digital objects documenting the conference—objects that, much like Bunch's original blog post, could serve as organizing tools and links between different journalism reform networks. I suspect, however, that what the questioner actually meant when he challenged the norg group was something like the following: "How have you *actually* succeeded in 'reinventing' journalism in Philadelphia? What new permanent or semi-permanent news-gathering organizations have come into being, and how have news practices inside existing organizations changed?" In short, "What is the value of a network forum during those moments when intense collaboration and conversation have yet to call a true network into being?"

In many ways, the networked norg reform group accomplished a great deal, but in other ways, it was a quickly forgotten idea. The norg group did not succeed in rebuilding Philadelphia journalism. In a post to the norgs list a few months before Philadelphia Media Holdings filed for bankruptcy protection, Will Bunch reflected on the failure of his initiative in 2005 to bring about the kind of change for which he and many other attendees at the first Annenberg conference had hoped. Conversation on the list had slowed to a crawl, and many of the projects that had been discussed in the excitement that followed the initial conference had never materialized. Rather than acting as a network forum, the initial participants appeared to have fractured off into their own projects, and all the while the economic prospects of many local newspapers continued to decline. "As the person who kicked off the whole discussion three years ago this fall," Bunch wrote,

> I have a pretty good sense of why [the norgs initiative] failed. I think by 2008 there's an irreconcilable conflict between the reality most of us know in our heart—which is that there are far too many barriers, mainly cultural and psychological but also certainly economic, for a traditional news organization like the Philadelphia Media Holdings empire or any other legacy newsroom (especially print) to make the kind of changes that will be needed to compete— and what we hoped to see happen back then. The only way to build a news

organization that would make any sense in this day and age is to blow everything up and start over from scratch. But who wants to contemplate that?[36]

In her reply to Bunch, Warren noted that the failure of local Philadelphia
journalists to seize control of their own fate did not mean that news organizations were not changing or that new models, collaborations, and network forums
were not being proposed. But the emerging networks might not be local, she
said, and might not even be based within the community of journalism. "This
conversation is happening," she said, "but it's not been a community discussion,
and it's not involving local journalists, either. Instead, it's being held by technology companies, potential investors and by potential funders, including foundations. If we don't jump in, we will risk losing our voice at a time that is critical
for our community. There's wisdom built up in the minds of professional journalists, and energy in the hearts of non-professional journalists; we should inject
both into this ongoing conversation."[37]

Provided with enough distance—temporal or geographic—examples of successful network forums and network entrepreneurs might be easy to find. It may
be that the network entrepreneur I was looking for when I began this research is
to be found elsewhere, perhaps at one of the technology companies or foundations to which Warren referred. It may also be that this successful network entrepreneur will emerge from the foundation world, a possibility I explore further in
the Conclusion. To date, however, the journalistic world envisioned by the participants in the Norgs Unconference has not become a reality. In retrospect, the
successful Louis Pasteur, or even Stewart Brand, appear as networked geniuses
who bend the materials of the world to their will, creating new institutions, dis-
courses, and ways of working and knowing.[38] There is little doubt that a future
historian or sociologist will eventually chronicle for us the triumphant history of
the actor or institution that successfully rewove the news. Network failures out-
number successes, however, and a focus on the deeply local, contextual, and
time-bound can help draw our attention to the obstacles lying in the path of the
network mode.

To further probe these questions, I turn to other recent attempts to assemble
news networks in the city of Philadelphia. The norgs initiative sought to carve
out a collaborative space in which it would be easier for organizations to coordinate their newswork. Projects like the Next Mayor, discussed below, represented
concrete attempts to perform these acts of organizational coordination.

The Next Mayor Project

For the *Daily News,* the mayoral race of 2007 started early—in the winter of
2005. It was then that the tabloid, in partnership with the public radio station
WHYY and the Committee of Seventy good-government group and with funding from the William Penn Foundation, launched the Next Mayor, "an innova-

tive, two-year, multi-media partnership . . . [focusing] on the issues—not just the personalities—leading to the 2007 mayor's race."[39] The Next Mayor was an part of the "Rethinking Philadelphia" series, "probably the most successful example of 'public journalism' in the country,"[40] and began with the unveiling of the Next Mayor website, which aimed to "offer in-depth coverage, history and perspective on the regional issues that will fuel the mayoral campaign."[41] While the norgs group was a formal attempt to build a network forum through which to bridge the gaps that separated various local networks of journalists, bloggers, and programmers, the Next Mayor was an example of a functional networked news project that was assembled and deployed to cover a particularly meaningful public event.

There is a remarkable homology between the "public journalism" movement, which reached its apex in the mid-1990s,[42] and the earliest and most innovative online journalism projects, such as the Next Mayor. Further research would certainly be required to map out the institutional, personal, and ideological connections between these two reform initiatives. For now, I simply want to note that the Next Mayor originally began as a project firmly in the public journalism mold. Zack Stallberg, the editor of the *Daily News* at the time, had extensive experience with public journalism projects. An article in the *American Journalism Review* in November 2000 quoted Michael Days, then deputy managing editor, saying that the *Daily News* was "doing a lot more advocacy journalism or public journalism or whatever you call it."[43] With its emphasis on "the issues, not the personalities"; an informed citizenry; its use of research and polling data; and its convening of periodic, in-person citizen forums, the early design of the Next Mayor set the project firmly within the mold of public journalism. As time wore on, however, the ambition and shape of the project would gradually evolve; it would, in a sense, "go native" on the web. This evolution of the Next Mayor offers us a window into what many media makers in Philadelphia called the closest thing to an actual norg that the city has ever had. At the same time, the limitations of the Next Mayor project can highlight some of the limitations of the norg concept in general.

Wendy Warren, then at the *Daily News,* was one of the project managers for the Next Mayor. "The Next Mayor started very early," she recalled, noting that her own involvement grew out of her earlier work on "Rethinking Philadelphia," which was a "classic civic journalism" initiative:

> Zack was not the biggest fan of the Internet, but I was really curious and wanted to play and experiment with online journalism. We wanted to create a fan site for the mayor's race. We wanted it to be one of those places where you would find every scrap of anything that had anything to do with the mayor's race. We wanted to really aggregate just everything we could, and just come at it from this point of "the race doesn't have to be cynical and bad." The race can be great. We can ask people for their position on issues, we can force the candidates to tell us their position on issues.

Beyond the journalistic work needed to make the site successful, Warren remembers "marketing the heck out of the Next Mayor website. . . . We spent our own personal time stomping around the city, gong to street fairs, going to College Day on the Ben Franklin Parkway, we handed out buttons that marketed the project."[44] The website grew to include a calendar, profiles of candidates, "reported guides (including video segments) to the top issues in the race, comparisons of candidates' positions on a variety of topics, and a blog."[45]

In discussing the Next Mayor, Warren repeatedly referred to the "networked" nature of the project: "I always envisioned the Next Mayor as more like a movie studio than a manufacturing plant—more like a nimble network of different people doing different things rather than a permanent institution." We did our best to build a wide network out of the various actors in the City."[46] One of the most innovative partnerships during the two years of the project's existence was a voter-registration collaboration with the popular blog Philebrity: "The Next Mayor is delighted to announce that we are joining forces with Philebrity to make it even easier for you to change the city," announced a post on the Next Mayor blog. "Soon, we will launch a joint voter-registration effort. We'll be throughout the city, signing up people who deserve a voice in this election."[47]

Warren was keen to emphasize that the Philebrity partnership was only one of many efforts at community network building undertaken during the life of the Next Mayor project. There were also partnerships with the business community: "More than three dozen groups . . . will contribute their knowledge, passion, and expertise for the issues they represent to the rest of the electorate," a press release for the Next Mayor Community Network announced.[48] Warren remembers approaching community groups. "We wanted their content, of course, but we also told them: if you join us in this endeavor, you'll have an easy path to us," she said. "But in return, we might help you to participate in or host a forum, and we might ask you to tell your members about us."

The Next Mayor project began in the winter of 2005, nearly simultaneously with the norg initiative. What was the relationship, if any, between the norgs Unconference and the development of the Next Mayor project? Warren took pains to emphasize that, in her eyes, the two events were largely separate. "My goal has always been to be inclusive, journalistically, and so the Next Mayor and the norgs meeting were united by that spirit of inclusiveness, but I wouldn't say that one was a big influence on the other," she said. "I will say that the norg meeting was useful for getting the word out about the Next Mayor, though."[49] Warren's denials aside, there is, at least some *visual* evidence that the norgs meeting prompted a change in the vision of the Next Mayor; the project released an updated version of TheNextMayor.com a few weeks after the Annenberg conference that looked much more like networked news site than a "public journalism voters' guide." Some discussion on the Yahoo Group listserv, in addition, seemed to indicate that the Next Mayor project was in the spirit of the Philadelphia norgs initiative, even if there was no direct collaboration. "I think [the Next

Mayor] *is* saving local journalism," a participant from the Philly IMC said. "At least, it is the type of cross [between] journalism, informational resource, advocacy, community building, good citizenship, etc., that local media should aspire to. I don't know what the profit model is for this type of project (teaming up [with] a non-profit probably doesn't hurt), but the end result is definitely an exciting model."[50]

Once again, however, Warren resisted attempts to draw a line between the site's redesign in the spring of 2006 and the norgs discussion. "I think the reason the site changed when it did is because we went from a project that was trying to 'start a discussion' about something that hadn't really happened yet to a project that was reporting actual news," she said. "One of the problems with public journalism—and there's a lot I like about public journalism—is that it's trying to get people to talk about something they haven't really thought about before, and after a certain point, the Next Mayor wasn't doing that anymore."[51] It is probably safe to conclude, then, that while the Next Mayor was norg-like in character, this character ran largely parallel to the Annenberg summit.

In many ways, the Next Mayor attempted to knock down the traditional silos separating political actors (community advocates, politicians, the media), different media outlets (WHYY and the *Daily News*), different media types (the web, print, radio, and TV), and different groups of journalists (bloggers and more professional reporters). This, at least, was its stated goal. But how were these new relationships *inscribed* in the fabric of the web? In other words, how often and in what fashion did the Next Mayor link to other websites? The answer to that question points us toward a deeper understanding of the manner in which the Philadelphia media community did and did not assemble itself into a collaborative network.

As shown in the analysis of blogging and web production in Chapter 4, linking is increasingly becoming a form of newswork, and archived linking practices demonstrate one aspect of that newswork in process. What the Next Mayor participants did, in terms of their linking practices, casts a slightly different light on what they said about what they did. In particular, linking highlights one of the ways in which traditional news institutions come to terms with the plethora of voices on the World Wide Web. News organizations did not necessarily see everyone, to quote the idealistic words of the Norgs Unconference, as potential participants in "acts of journalism." Rather, evidence from the Next Mayor project shows that many news organizations saw much of the online community as "bloggy" and dealt with that bloggy component by creating their own blog-like websites rather than interacting with them on their primary news sites.

The second iteration of the Next Mayor website resembled an actual news site more than the original voters' guide–like version (see Figure 5.2). One of the changes made to the second iteration of the site was the addition of a "blogroll" that included links to weblogs such as Young Philly Politics, Philadelphia Will Do, and Philebrity. By the time the third version of the site launched, however,

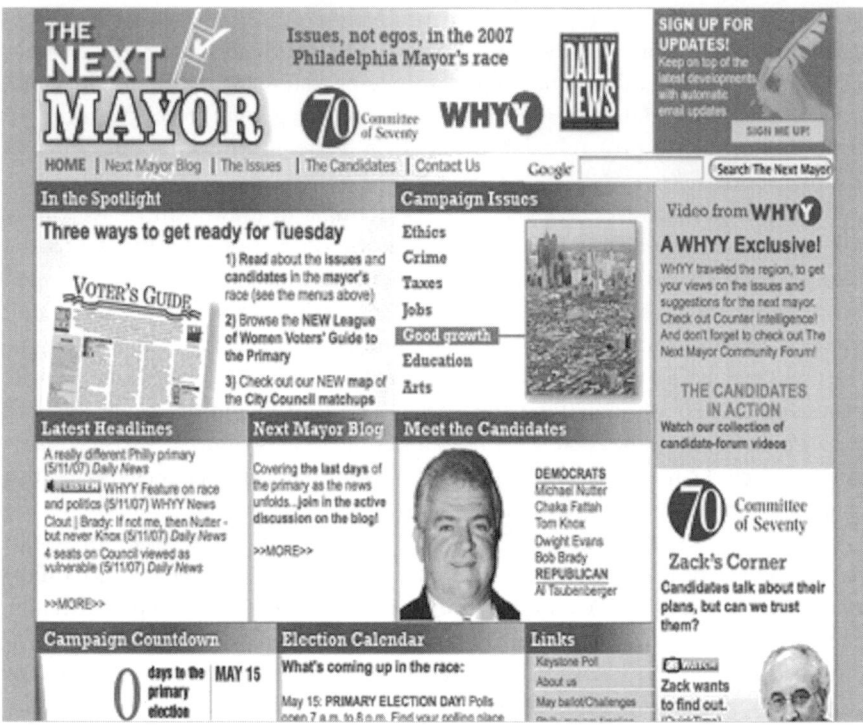

FIGURE 5.2 The Next Mayor website, version 3. At this stage, the site was reemphasizing news and de-emphasizing community interaction. *(Source: http://archive.org.)*

the blogroll had been replaced by a link page (itself one page deep) that mostly included links to other printed newspapers and to community groups. The blogroll, in other words, had disappeared.

Did this disappearing blogroll signal a change in priorities on the part of those organizing the Next Mayor project? Were they suddenly uninterested in the work done by deinstitutionalized journalists such as bloggers? The evidence is contradictory. When previewing their coverage of primary day, the Next Mayor's producers explicitly drew attention to the fact that journalists would be "contributing posts to TheNextMayor.com, while reporting on what other political blogs are saying about the elections"; they made this claim despite the fact that their links to other blogs had recently vanished.[52] Warren was also emphatic in claiming that the Next Mayor was primarily interested in aggregating "anything about the Mayor's race we could get our hands on,"[53] and that this would include outside blog content. Because the archives for the Next Mayor no longer exist online, it is impossible to conduct any form of content analysis that might definitively answer questions about the degree to which the website linked out and whether its linking practices changed over time. Another possibility, however, also seems likely: the work of the Next Mayor that most resembled the dialogical, web-native, cross-linking practices of the blogosphere were primarily sequestered on the Next Mayor's own *blog*. The primary Next Mayor website, in other words, served as a hybrid public journalism–online project, aggregating information, presenting issues, discussing candidates, and holding dialogues with community groups. The Next Mayor blog, on the other hand, behaved like, and engaged with, the local "blogosphere." While many of the ideals of the norgs initiative were thus realized by the Next Mayor—the disaggregation of news and newsprint, the inherently social and collaborative nature of the web, and the importance of collaboration that went beyond the newsroom—the project ultimately divided its labor, with the most collaborative interactions with the Philadelphia blogging community occurring on a *second* Next Mayor website.

Why was such a bifurcation of work inscribed within a project as innovative as the Next Mayor website? One way to ratify that you really are part of a news network, after all, is to materially embed yourself within that network by linking to a second, affiliated node. If the simple act of "linking out" to other websites is rare—and, in the following section, I argue that it is—and remains rare even in the face of overwhelming managerial rhetoric about the "networked nature" of the news ecosphere, then perhaps other factors are at work. The next section thus turns to an analysis of these factors: the dynamics that affect the material inscription of organizations within networks. In other words, the next section examines reasons that so many news organizations in Philadelphia had such a hard time linking out.

"Binding the Public Together": Hyperlinks in Local News

Chapter 3 described the growth of the Philadelphia blogosphere and the creation of blogs such as Citizen Mom, Philebrity, and Mere Cat against the backdrop of larger changes transforming digital media between 1997 and 2009. Each of the blogs described in Chapter 3, I noted, was both individualized and open; often the idiosyncratic product of a person or small community of interest, these blogs were simultaneously open to the entire online universe through their ability to link out. As numerous web commentators have argued,[54] the act of linking to other websites is one of the core practices of the online world; links are "not only ubiquitous[;] they are the basic forces that relate creative works together for fun, fame, or fortune."[55] In this sense, links can be seen as an inscribed acknowledgment of a networked relationship.[56] They are inscriptions and are thus embedded in the digital fabric of the Internet itself.

More than just embedded inscriptions, however, links are also an acknowledgment that a relationship exists between two online entities. This relationship can be one of citation ("This is where I obtained my facts"), affinity ("These are the people/websites/groups with whom/which I agree; they are my community"), reciprocity ("You linked to me, so I will link to you), or even disagreement

("These are the people/websites/groups with whom/which I disagree; they are my enemies"). In each of these instances, the act of linking is simultaneously the act of creating a network, and any news organization that links to other news organizations, facts, or websites is in that moment engaged in an act of network inscription.

The explosion of blogs, user-generated content, new online activist groups, and nontraditional journalism institutions presented the earliest batch of web-native, local Philadelphia media organizations—groups such as Philly.com, Philly Future, and the Philly IMC—with a potentially endless opportunity to inscribe their own networks. They offered an opportunity for organizations to supplement their journalistic work by linking to the work of others, to acknowledge perspectives different from their own. They offered, in short, the ability to network the news in a deeply material sense. At the same time, however, each of these organizations approached the seemingly simple act of linking differently. Indeed, two organizations that seemed radically different from each other in nearly every possible way—the Philly IMC and Philly.com—deeply distrusted linking and had difficulty doing it for many years. Philly Future, by contrast, quickly saw linking to others as the key to its identity. The differences in organizational linking practices, and in their self-understanding of what these practices meant, provides a clue that networking the news is not a simple act but, rather, is fraught with cultural, economic, and organizational considerations. In the pages that follow, we can also see the advantages to this book's ecosystemic approach to studying the news. It is hard to think of two more journalistic enterprises that are less similar than Philly.com and the Philly IMC, but the organizational obstacles *both* institutions have faced when it comes to the seemingly simple task of linking beyond their borders provides valuable evidence about the self-understanding of newswork in the twenty-first century. It is a comparison that is possible only if we take the decentralized nature of digital journalism seriously.

The act of linking offers news producers a chance to digitally ratify their relationship with other journalistic organizations. Above and beyond meetings aimed at fostering greater collaboration and special projects, linking provides insight into the manner in which news institutions understand their place in the digital media ecosystem. Philly Future, with little institutional emphasis on original newsgathering or "citizen journalism" per se, found the notion of creating of a local blog network to be entirely consistent with its conversational mission. The radical, politically motivated Philly IMC struggled with how to balance commitment to media democracy with its political identity and its open publishing system. Philly.com, despite moves in 2008 to build a "user-centered" website and attempts to more effectively "network the news" in 2010–2011, still largely refused to engage in external linking practices and preferred to link to the multitude of journalistic and quasi-journalistic institutions housed under the corporate umbrella of Philadelphia Media Holdings. The different ways that each of these early, and very different, news organizations thought about linking provides insight into larger questions about the relationship of digital culture, the public, and notions of original reporting.

For Philly.com and the major newspapers in Philadelphia, the limited success of projects such as the Next Mayor did not lead to related success in creating more long-term, inscribed network forms of collaboration. The major news organizations in Philadelphia chose not to open their websites to a more permanent, linked form of journalistic collaboration. In short, they simply did not link outside their own media properties. While there are exceptions to this general rule, these continued even in late 2011 to be exceptions. Philly.com still does not link out.

The greatest divergence from this general refusal to link out could be seen in 2008 in an initiative on the sports page of Philly.com titled "From the Bleachers," described as a "fan blogroll." In From the Bleachers, "Philly.com takes a look at what Philadelphia-area sports fans are saying on their blogs. Want your blog listed?" the website asked. "Let us know!" A Philly.com producer described the general thinking behind From the Bleachers: "We were all under an order to do [user-generated content] as part of the new site design, and this was a way I thought I could do it." From the Bleachers went beyond simple user comments in its commitment to user-generated content, the producer told me proudly, while also noting that providing "user interactivity" in this fashion amounted to less work than constantly moderating comments. "Basically, all I had to do was add an RSS feed container to the website," the producers said, "but what really made it work was when I could automate it to have the most recent headlines at the top, so it would be like a scrolling series of headlines, from all the sports bloggers in the area. As long as it's clear that I'm not in charge of the content going up there—that it's not our content—it's fairly simple." Interestingly, local sports bloggers seemed unaware of From the Bleachers or thought that it generated comparably little traffic to their websites. From the Bleachers appeared to have been more of a cultural statement by producers at Philly.com that they considered the area's sports bloggers to be a valid part of the conversation rather than a major contribution to the web-traffic ecosystem of the local media sphere. Sometime after 2008, From the Bleachers was discontinued and replaced by a partnership with another website, called Bleacher Report. Described as "the web's leading publisher of original and entertaining sports editorial content," Bleacher Report used data and narrative science (turning statistics into written text) to create digital sports content.

When quizzed in 2008 about Philly.com's general refusal to link to outside websites, Wendy Warren pointed to the power of old institutional practices and beliefs, along with what she labeled a conservative professional culture:

> I think that Philly.com is a pioneer in a lot of stuff, but we've still got to move a great distance from an old mode. [It was a model] where we owned our content, and we control our content, and we don't link, and we don't share. It's honestly just a job of convincing people [about] the power of being a

nimble network, and it's not the easiest thing to do. . . . I don't think we're alone in that. Reaching that "Jarvis moment" where you say "do what you do best and link to the rest"—that's a real conversion for a lot of professional journalists."[57]

For Karl Martino of Philly Future, by contrast, the solution to the problem of how to digitally inscribe visions of a networked news ecosystem was different. Martino began rethinking the mission of Philly Future in the post-blogosphere world as early as 2004, alluding to problems of work duplication and original content brought about by the explosion of digital content in 2003. The problem for Philly Future was that "folks already had great blogs in their own right," Martino said in an interview published in 2004. "I found attracting people who have their own blogs to post at Philly Future to be difficult. Why should they, after all? I would leave my own best work for my personal site, and so did they. Asking people to double-post didn't make sense."[58] If everyone in Philadelphia had his or her own blog, Martino wondered, why would anyone ever bother posting to his community website? But if people did not post, how could Philly Future ever accomplish its goal of "serving as a Philadelphia area, community building clearing house"? Philly Future, born out of wave of digital empowerment and institutional fragmentation of the late 1990s, was now confronting a new wave of fragmentation in which even relatively deinstitutionalized projects like his were being rendered superfluous by new, easy-to-use content-creation technology.

For Martino, the answer to questions about the role of Philly Future in an era of blogging would be found partly in new technology: RSS (for Really Simple Syndication), "a lightweight [extendable markup language] format designed for *sharing headlines and other Web content.* Think of it as *a distributable "What's New" for your site.* . . . RSS has evolved into a popular means of *sharing content* between sites."[59] Through RSS, in other words, any content published on a website or blog with RSS feed functionality can be distributed automatically to any RSS reader or website capable of aggregating it.

Every time a blogger publishes an entry, the headline of that entry can be distributed automatically ("pushed out") across the web. For most of its earlier history, the Internet had relied on random browsing, search-engine *technology,* and the previously discussed practice of linking to filter and display content. Thus, RSS can be seen as a fourth way to manage web content—one that has placed more power in the hands of producers (who now have an increased ability to distribute content) as well as of consumers (who can now individually tailor the information they wish to consume, as well as where and when they want to receive it).

While the increased adoption of RSS might be viewed as rendering the linking practices of blogs less important, RSS can also be seen as supplementing the existing tendencies of bloggers toward content aggregation. Martino certainly saw the potential of the technology in these terms. "I originally started Philly Future to provide a weblog clearinghouse covering Philly," he wrote when he announced the relaunch of the website in 2004. "I was hoping to attract a team of webloggers to post regular updates at Philly Future. It never happened. The best [media makers and bloggers] want a place to express their *own unfettered* view. . . . [But now] thru RSS, Philly Future can fulfill its original purpose and much more."[60]

The process of web production had democratized to a remarkable degree, but websites that truly valued aggregation could find new roles. "I wanted to experiment with online community," Martino elaborated in an interview, "but this time in a distributed, open way. RSS and Atom blog syndication provided a framework that enabled me to build something that, instead of trying to be some kind of walled garden, attempting to pull people in to contribute, could instead highlight the growing online community dispersed across our region."[61] With the advent of RSS, Martino realized, the tedious process of scanning headlines could be largely automated, and the need for direct posting to Philly Future had become unnecessary. Martino, along with other members of the Philly Future volunteer team, could shift their energy toward the curation of web content and the continued fostering of what Martino called "the public conversation" of the Philadelphia community:

> Instead of attempting to get people to write for Philly Future, Philly Future would highlight the writers already out there, encourage more to join (get their own blogs), and encourage them to read one another. Initially, I had a front page consisting of only their headlines flowing thru. But that's not enough. Anyone can collect blogs and read them thru an aggregator. I moved to highlight certain bloggers I thought were exceptional and to point out stories they've posted that I thought should be shared. . . . Philly Future highlights a local blogger each week by providing a space for their headlines where I hope you see them right away.[62]

Through RSS, in short, Philly Future could regularly ratify its inscribed local community network.

During the fall of 2004, the Philly IMC also began to grapple with the shifting parameters of participatory media creation. Unlike at Philly Future, however, the creation of an inscribed network through RSS aggregation at Indymedia was fraught with controversy. By and large, the Philly IMC had struggled with varying levels of stagnation since the protests of 2000.[63] "We did a handful of really good things in the early days," one early Indymedia organizer said, but a second confessed that the organization "felt hollow" for much of the post–Republican National Convention period.[64] By early 2005, with an influx of volunteers, the Philly IMC seemed ready to try come to grips with the new online media world in which it now found itself embedded, a process documented across a number of IMC meetings held in the summer, fall, and winter of 2005. Under the subject headline "Blogging and Philly IMC," for example, the agenda notes for a meeting in the winter of 2005 asked attendees to "take a look at Philly Future" to get a sense of how the online media landscape was changing. "Does Philly Future, and blogs in general, perform the principles of Indymedia better than Indymedia does?" the notes rhetorically asked. "Doesn't blogging live out the anarchist vision of the Indymedia vision better than Indymedia? Does blogging give life to 'Be the Media!' ethos Indymedia has tried to cultivate? How is Philly IMC similar and how is it different than Philly Future?"[65]

Discussions about how to redesign the new Philly IMC site were inherently implicated in questions about what the organization was and *whom its news was actually for.* The questions of how and whether to integrate RSS feeds into the new site exposed deep tensions surrounding the Philly IMC's place in the new web ecosystem. "The struggle of Indymedia," a volunteer recalled, "is that it initiated open publishing, and all of a sudden open publishing was nothing special. Blogging now is considered a legitimate expression. Even in 2005, it was still not as widely accepted as it is now. . . . But in 2000, that [type of participation] didn't exist, and so Indymedia was more unique."[66] Some volunteers remembered discussions in 2005 about integrating RSS "feed capacity" into the Philly IMC website as having been fairly muted, but meeting notes on the topic document several areas of major disagreement:

> There are two viewpoints right now on the website, and we discussed heavily the two sides and informed each other about concerns and the reasoning behind ideas. [People who feel] discomfort with the new website structure argued that there is a more fluid interacting with blogs and other news sources that are not IMC related. If we start taking news from other places— we could just become a news feed; we don't want to be something that just looks like everything else. [Second], what is our relationship with blogs? Have to keep the open news wire open and make it more prominent—let people know that they can publish and make it easy for anyone and everyone to get involved with the open news wire.[67]

The differences between Philly Future and the Philly IMC are instructive. Philly Future envisioned itself as a nonpartisan website designed to encourage community dialogue and mutual understanding, thus making the adoption of a universally inclusive RSS aggregation mechanism easy. The Philly IMC, by contrast, had always been an explicitly political organization. At the same time, its radicalism was always partially camouflaged by its commitment to reporting and to open publishing. In theory, the open-publishing perspective advocated by early IMC techs would treat all content equally; the embrace of a universal system of open publishing thus would naturally lend itself to the inclusion of all RSS content from local websites in Philadelphia. But as documented in most of the early research on the Philly IMC, open publishing never actually "meant that 'anything went' in practice: there [were] always criteria for 'hiding' postings [published on Indymedia]. . . . Contrary to its own policy on hiding articles, the reasons for hiding posts were specified in some cases but not in others."[68] This is not surprising. It is hard to imagine any organization as deeply political as the Philly IMC ever sacrificing its politics for a pure open-publishing model. What the concept of open publishing did provide, though, was a ready-made metaphor through which the Philly IMC could fudge the contradictions between its claims of all-encompassing openness (its exhortation to "be the media") and its deeper identity as a radical political platform. In 2000, this was a tenable contradiction. By 2004, the explosion of participatory media content and the fragmentation of the local media sphere meant that the Philly IMC had to take sides. The need to take sides manifested itself in debate over deliberate linking to outside content through RSS.

By explicitly confronting long-deferred questions about web architecture, whether to include RSS feeds as part of the website redesign, and so on, the Philly IMC was finally grappling with the tension inherent in its open-publishing model. Part of this tension stemmed from the fact that the Philly IMC, unlike Philly Future, was founded as an explicitly journalistic organization; much of it also stemmed from the fact that, as one former Philly IMC volunteer told me, "We would never link to the corporate media, and we would never link to right-wing media. We just wouldn't do it."[69]

The notes from the Indymedia meetings in which these questions were debated conclude on a plaintive note: who, participants asked, was the Philly IMC actually a resource *for*? "Who is our audience?" they asked somewhat desperately. "Just activists? Communities? Neighborhoods? Groups? All of Philadelphia? We have to decide who we are targeting before we can really make decisions on various issues."[70] Or, as an early Philly IMC organizer summarized, "The thing Indymedia wanted was this diverse multiplicity of voices, a multiplicity that would go beyond the corporate media monotone, . . . and once the multiplicity of voices existed, then the IMC had different reasons for existing, [it] had to shift and change. Or it had to stop."[71]

The act of linking—of "networking the news" in a material sense—thus meant different things to different organizations. Some nontraditional reporting organizations were surprisingly hostile to linking practices while others embraced them. At Philly.com, linking was almost universally a fraught process. Why? Stepping back, one can see economic, organizational, and cultural explanations.

In economic terms, it was clear that many of the for-profit news organizations I studied did not work together because they feared that doing so would hurt their bottom lines. To them, a necessary level of newsroom income seemed to be dependent on occupying the central node in a local information ecosystem. In short, online ad rates would decline if online traffic declined, and online traffic would decline if news production routines and journalistic content were shared with too many other people. It should be noted that there is actually a great deal of debate over whether the economics of networked news ecosystems actually encourage sharing and collaboration. The debate here is not over what the economics of online news production actually demonstrate but what behavior news organizations *think* are in their economic interest.

Organizationally, four cross-cutting dynamics internal to the rationalized nature of the news production process tended to push news organizations away from networked collaboration. First, most of the large news organizations I observed in Philadelphia were hierarchical and set up to produce a news product in a silo-like manner. As Herbert Gans described them nearly forty years ago, news production routines most resembled "assembly lines managed by decision makers with quasi-military roles. . . . [A]s one executive producer put it: 'The daily routine is like screwing nuts on a bolt.'"[72] In organizations like this, internal rewards lie in the regularized production of branded news articles, not in collaboration with others. Second, the perceived economics of digital production have encouraged media organizations to adopt a what Dean Starkman has described as a "hamster wheel" approach to the production of news that consists of "volume without thought. It is news panic, a lack of discipline, an inability to say no. It is copy produced to meet arbitrary productivity metrics."[73] This approach of "more content, faster and faster"—an approach I certainly observed in Philadelphia—tends to reinforce the inability to deviate from the obsession with internal news production I have already noted.

Third, I observed a mismatch between the rationalized production routines of news professionals and the routines (or non-routines) of journalistic amateurs. To the degree that collaborative news production depended on working with journalists outside the professional sphere, the lack of standards among amateurs—whether they were standards for sources, standards of objectivity, or, most important, standards for routinized production—made it unlikely that amateur production could be easily integrated into professional newsroom routines. In other words, never knowing exactly when a blogger would post, whether that blog post would come in by deadline, and whether the content would be relevant for today's article made it seem irrational to work with others. Fourth, the news organizations in Philadelphia most likely to want to build collaborative news networks between 2005 and 2008 (such as the news-curation blog Philly Future) were run by news amateurs working out of love and for free. The organizations that embraced collaboration were also the most *organizationally precarious* and thus unlikely to be able to make change in any systemic, long-term way.

Finally, beyond organizational factors, I think that deep-seated aspects of journalistic culture played a role in the lack of cross-field collaboration. They may, in fact, have played the most important role. Quite simply, reporters and newsroom managers in Philadelphia expressed fear and uncertainty about the veracity, commitment, reliability, and "journalistic-ness" of potential outside partners. If an organization was seen as being too partisan, too sloppy, or too snarky, it was inherently suspect and taken less seriously. A related attitude common in most traditional newsrooms can be stated simply: "The journalists are *us.*" Large news organizations, after decades of monopolistic positioning inside local news ecosystems and the accompanying professional pride that came from real local power and journalistic standards, tended to see themselves as a one-stop shop for news of local public import. Traditional journalists in Philadelphia often failed to see a meaningful, publicly legitimate communicative world beyond their own organizational walls. The *Inquirer*'s old building, a classic example of modernist architectural design, faces the famed Philadelphia City Hall in a way that speaks volumes: "*We* are the ones who watch *you*." Encoded in design choices are attitudes about the world. In Philadelphia, the attitude was clear: *we journalists* are the central node of communicative public.

Conclusion

Over the course my conversations with various traditional and nontraditional journalists, I kept hearing notions of *reporting* and *the public* invoked as an explanation for why particular decisions about networking the news were or were not made. Organizations that touted reporting as central to the newswork process often seemed hostile to linking out. Remember the sharp contrast between the blogging carried out by reporters at Philly.com and the blogging of more conversational, deinstitutionalized reporters discussed in Chapter 4. The Philly.com bloggers, with a few exceptions, have repurposed the blogging format to help with their reporting practices; more traditional bloggers see the their work as a type of interlinked community conversation. The Philly IMC, too, has traditionally focused on the basic reporting of news, especially protest news, rather than on the facilitation of conversation. Due to these institutional biases, it might be possible to argue that the notion of conversation as a "legitimate" form of newswork continues to be devalued, resulting in a simultaneous devaluation of conversational linking by both Philly.com and the Philly IMC. Both Philly.com and the Philly IMC value traditional news and fact gathering more than blog dialogue and thus tend not to link to dialogical media outlets.

One barrier to forming inscribed news networks may thus be a dominant understanding of journalism as *reporting*. While it is clear that the Philly IMC has always been torn between multiple definitions of what it was trying to accomplish—it has always been part tactical propaganda and part "citizen journalism"—evidence abounds that it has always seen itself in a representational journalistic role. Submission forms on the Philly IMC website ask users "under what name (byline)" they would like to see their submissions posted. "Byline" is a somewhat technical term that deliberately invokes traditional journalistic practices and jargon. In contrast, according to Martino, Philly Future never saw itself as a journalistic project; while it linked to citizen journalism institutions and organizations, it always saw itself as a facilitator of community conversation.[74] Thus, it never seemed to have a problem with devoting nearly all of its organizational energy to linking and aggregation.

Part of the reason that the seemingly simple act of linking out was so difficult for so many news institutions may thus have to do with the very nature of newswork. Another reason may lie in the "problems of the public" first addressed in Chapters 1 and 2. In those chapters, I noted that the Philly IMC, Philly.com, and Philly Future all struggled with questions of community—with questions about whom their projects were for. Despite contradictions between their rhetoric and their practices, moreover, I argued that both Philly.com and the Philly IMC glossed over tensions between online fragmentation and claims to comprehensiveness—Indymedia with gestures toward universal open publishing, and Philly.com through its inheritance of an industrial-era belief in the capacity of the newspaper to capture a mass audience on the web. How do problems of the public and questions of community relate to linking practices? When an institution links out, it acknowledges that other institutions exist. Acknowledging that other media institutions exist—and exist as equals in an endless digital space—renders problematic the public-making claims of traditional journalistic institutions. More than simple economic fears and cultural dislike of rowdy bloggers might account for the dearth of inscribed news networks. Part of the reluctance to network the news may stem from journalism's vision of the public—a public that, many news organizations believe, can continue to be enclosed within a particular series of digital walls.

By the winter of 2009, following the bankruptcy of Philadelphia Media Holdings, the local situation had begun to change. The William Penn Foundation had moved toward launching a networked journalism hub. The public radio station WHYY had introduced Newsworks, which it described "an innovative Web portal that covers the news from around the Delaware Valley . . . in ways that are distinctively participatory, insightful, community-based and solutions-oriented."[75] In both cases, networked collaboration was driven by a traditional institution (a newspaper company, a radio station, a foundation) that had decided that collaboration with outsiders had value.[76] The future of digital networked news may lie in the survival and emergence of traditional brick-and-mortar institutions that think collaboration is important.

Paradoxically, however, the job of sustaining traditional institutions devoted to journalistic work has emerged as one of the key challenges in the twenty-first century, particularly in local communities. Changing technology, the implosion of newspapers' economic models, and the shifting cultures of newswork have all played a role in this decline, which are examined in detail in Chapter 6. Along with bankruptcies and what I call the "fragility of underfunded news enterprises," however, new opportunities for networked news have also emerged. Many of the emerging models have been created not by reporters, activists, or newsroom executives, but by foundations, technology companies, and computer programmers who work inside news organizations. Chapter 6 turns to an overview of 2009 and 2010, years that contained many dark days that hid the tenuous possibility of new beginnings.

6

Dark Days and Green Shoots
(2009–2011)

As the first decade of the twenty-first century drew to a close, the Philadelphia media ecosystem seemed to be perched a knife's edge between rebirth and collapse. While earlier parts of this book alluded to the various pressures affecting the professional status and occupational stability of journalists and journalistic organizations, this chapter explicitly discusses exogenous factors reshaping journalistic work: the encroachment of web metrics into formerly autonomous journalistic practices, the increasing precarity of newswork (as the number of digital content producers increases and the ability of news organizations to extract revenue from advertising declines), and the fragility of modern informational institutions. The chapter, however, does not end in despair. The second half chronicles the bankruptcy's aftermath, from 2009 to 2011, when a new group of innovators struggled to network the Philadelphia media ecosystem on their own terms and a reborn Philadelphia Media Network attempted to retrofit its legacy newspapers for the web era. Even these reborn practices and institutions, however, face the strains on newswork that this chapter chronicles; they cannot escape the factors that humbled earlier institutions in the Philadelphia news ecosystem, as my discussion of post-bankruptcy stress and instability at Philly.com shows. While the future of local journalism remains to be written, it is likely that the structural factors discussed below will continue to shape efforts to network the news in Philadelphia and elsewhere.

Strains on Newswork: Audiences, Web Metrics, and the Reshaping of Journalistic Autonomy

The authority of journalism has been based, in part, on professional autonomy to decide what makes the news.[1] This professional autonomy is under increasing strain, however, as audiences exercise their own digital freedom not only to create their own informational content but also to gain access to a wide range of unbundled informational options. One aspect of this increase in the influence of the audience is deeply technical: newsrooms are making use of seemingly transparent web metrics that confront professional journalists with the judgment of the audience on a daily or even hourly basis.[2] News organizations are rethinking what audiences are and the role audiences should play in deciding what is news. The behavior of these audiences is captured, quantified, and allowed to shape what news is determined to be important. For journalists I observed during my research—journalists used to basing their professionalism on their own autonomous, insulated news judgments—this was a profoundly stressful change.

The most obvious change in journalistic attitudes could be seen in the daily rhetoric that newsroom workers and managers directed toward their online audiences. During my time at Philly.com and the two Philadelphia newspapers, I noticed an increasing emphasis on the creativity and autonomy of journalistic audiences. I also noticed, however, a tension between the image of the audience as articulated by editors, website consultants, and executives (who waxed overwhelmingly positive about audience creativity, generativity, and empowerment) and the attitudes of reporters, which were far more conflicted. When discussing a redesign of the Philly.com website, for instance, consultants with the firm Avenue A Razorfish summed up the new attitude toward Internet consumers prevalent in much of the marketing end of the news industry. "Philly.com should do what only the web can really do," one consultant told me. "Brands across the board have shifted. You can't push from the mountaintop anymore. . . . Unless you let your users have some kind intimacy with the brand, and maybe even some control, you're going to fail. They have to play with it. It has to be 'of the people, by the people, for the people.'"[3] The web audience, in short, was seen as a *generative* one. It was active and had needs and desires. Journalists could no longer assume that their readers were entirely passive.

A newsroom manager also took pains to emphasize to me that Philly.com needed to be a *useful* website in addition to simply an *informative* one. "I think news people care about a whole pile of headlines, but I think that what we were trying to get in our website was more like, 'What would help people plan their lives in Philadelphia and live their lives in Philadelphia?' So that, yeah, you want to know what the mayor has done, but you also want an idea of what's going on in town tonight, what's going on this weekend, what you can do with your life. Audiences are active now. They create things on their own . . . and 'news' is good for building the sustaining interest, but for building utility, to be useful for people, you have to throw all the other stuff in."[4] Throughout my time in Philadelphia, I heard a steady drumbeat of commentary regarding the empowerment of audiences, the creativity of audiences, the fact that audiences' preferences needed to be taken into account, and the fact that audiences were "partners" with journalists in the creation and consumption of journalism.

Nevertheless, news reporters (as opposed to news executives and website consultants) displayed a welter of contradictory attitudes toward the empowerment of audience members. "Philadelphia is really full of a bunch of boorish jerks," one journalist said out loud after reviewing a series of particularly nasty comments on one article. Interns at Philly.com, aided by an aggressive spam-filtering system (so aggressive that it censored comments discussing Iraqi "Shi-ites," for instance) worked to keep articles clean but were often unsure about the line between passion and abuse. Other journalists were curious about their read-ers. "I'm interested in who is leaving comments," the City Hall reporter Chris Brennan told me one morning.[5] Other journalists mostly ignored the com-menters, dismissing them as unrepresentative of the bulk of their readership. "You have to understand: these are people that have nothing better to do than surf the Internet at 11:00 A.M.," one journalist confided to me in a conspiratorial whisper. "They're losers."[6] Many other journalists (and even some of those who tried simultaneously to dismiss readers' feedback) were upset by rude or vulgar posts, feeling that such comments from reader reflected poorly on them as jour-nalists or on the articles to which the comments were attached. The line between article and readers' feedback, in other words, was not always clear to reporters. In many ways, they seemed to regard the comments as affecting the professional-ism and neutrality of the articles *they had written,* even though the difference between comment and article seems clear enough to outside observers.

If discussions of how journalists should relate to their newly empowered audience were only centered on visions of the active audience and audience feed-back, we might simply chalk the perspectives up to difference in the attitudes of newsroom managers and "on the ground" reporters and move on. However, qualitative audience impact, in the form of comments and other such user gener-ated content, was not the primary manner in which the audience seemed to be affecting news routines. Rather, technological developments allowing for instan-taneous audience metrics and newsroom management strategies that empha-sized the widespread diffusion of these metrics marked the primary axial shift in the journalist-audience relationship. And when it came to questions of the role of audience metrics and traffic figures, much of the ambiguity expressed by jour-nalists with regard to their audiences disappeared. They, like newsroom manag-ers, were obsessed with "traffic."

In other words, while discussions of users' comments at Philly.com partially concerned the quality of the dialogue, they primarily revolved around the *num-ber* of comments and the manner in which commenting was affecting website traffic overall. A PowerPoint slide that was distributed to all employees docu-menting the impact of making comments a "default" for all articles is fairly typi-cal. In effect, much of the discussion about comments concerned their ability to generate website hits.

Based on the PowerPoint slide, which was widely displayed during public presentations about the Philly.com website, editors and managers concluded that comments were a useful way to generate traffic. One of the most interesting things about working at Philly.com, Wendy Warren told me, was that "you get constant feedback on your work . . . and I don't mean emails, I mean constant exposure to traffic."[7] At Philly.com and its affiliated Philadelphia newspapers, editors used a system called Omniture to track visitor data and, quite often, made major editorial decisions on the basis of website traffic numbers. The simple existence of a tracking technology does not mean journalists or editors will use it, however. My observations showed that the strategic use of web metrics was part of a deliberate strategy for online management in Philadelphia newsrooms.

Details of website traffic numbers were widely available for journalists in Philadelphia who wanted access to them. During my time at the *Philadelphia Inquirer,* I was approached by one online newsworker clutching pages of Omniture website data in his hand. The reporter handed me a page of "click counts," sorted by authors' names. "We're probably headed toward a new model where reporters get paid by clicks," the reporter said darkly, only half in jest. "People who are concerned with their careers know these things, but most people still aren't concerned with stats, but I am." The reporter then told me about a powerfully written, extensively researched *Inquirer* story about a local army company that "just bombed on the website, it just did terrible. You want to throw fear in to the hearts of journalism professionals? That's a way."[8]

A producer at Philly.com echoed this sentiment:

> Even when I first came here, we had a much cruder system [to measure traffic], but we had skilled programmers . . . and we would get e-mails in the middle of the day that would be about which stories were doing well, and we would take them to the [newspapers'] news meetings. I think they were a little shocked a lot of the time, because even then we knew that a lot more people clicked on the gossip story than on your story, which you spent all this time investigating—that was maybe not something readers cared about as much. Papers don't have that same way of following what it is people care about.
>
> But in the old days, we thought different things were more important than they are.[9]

"The bottom line is, we are not old-style journalism," a Philly.com executive said, proceeding to tell a story about a *Inquirer* report on a special eye virus that brought sight back to the blind. "It was an amazing story—or, rather, it was an amazing whole package of stories. But it bombed. It got no traffic. And it was then that I realized we're in a new world."[10] As further evidence that a focus on metrics was part of a deliberate newsroom management strategy, the top Philly.com stories as of the end of May were collected and distributed to staffers as an Excel spreadsheet.

Website traffic numbers, no matter what the content of actual clicked articles, were invoked often at the *Inquirer* and almost obsessively at Philly.com. "We hit 35.8 million in November," said Wendy Warren in a presentation about the new website to the news staff: "37.9 million in December, 38.8 million in Jan, 42.1 million in April, 39.1 million in May, and 33.9 million in June."[11] However, she continued, "This is not good news on traffic. We're in a summer slump—and we aggressively need to find way to end it. We will protect our growth in page views! Everybody here should be thinking, 'What can I get to Philly.com now?' in terms of content. And, 'What can I add to the story that's good for the web?' There should be an urgency around the idea of sending stuff to Philly.com." There was a similar rhetoric about page views during staff meetings at Philly.com. "We're trending low for the day," said an editor at a typical summer meeting in 2008. "But uniques [a website metric meaning "unique visitors"] were up for the day." And so on. This would then be followed by a discussion among the group as to why numbers were down—perhaps it has to do with summer vacations, a producer might suggest. "Either way, it can't last," another producer concluded.[12]

Even outside official meetings, traffic patterns played a major role in the selection of stories for Philly.com. "I just pulled this story off the spotlight. It was underperforming. It only had 137 page views" were common phrases shouted across the Philly.com office. "Usually I give a story at least an hour to prove itself," one web producer told me. "Five hundred page views is pretty good, and a thousand is great. It's easier to compare story traffic in the morning when everything goes up at the same time. Then you can basically compare different articles with each other. The afternoon, when things are more erratic, it's tougher to compare."[13]

It is not an exaggeration to say that website traffic often appeared to be the *primary ingredient* in Philly.com news judgment. Phil MacGregor argues, "[Although] data are directly revising the way 'news values' are implemented in the respondent sample, overall, social and organizational context rather than technology alone shape the way these online professionals react to their new tool."[14] My ethnographic research, however, demonstrates that Philly.com lacked a strong organizational culture that could mitigate against the dominance of a website management strategy based on clicks. I probed this topic in three ways during my conversations with Philly.com web producers and newspaper journalists. "Is there an organizational culture that can mitigate the primacy of web statistics when it comes to choosing stories?" I first asked bluntly. Rephrasing my question somewhat during later interviews, I put forward the following hypothetical scenario: "Say that a member of the technology staff came up with a way to automate the Philly.com website so that well-trafficked stories were automatically placed in the biggie, spotlight, and trio slots. What would be left for a web producer to do?" Finally, I simply asked, "What's the perfect Philly.com story?" A story "that is going to get tons of hits, and is going to elicit a lot of comments," I was told.[15] "Is there a news culture at Philly.com yet?" said Yoni Greenbaum, a web editor at Philly.com, in response to one of my questions. "Let's put it this way: if there was, the personnel has changed so much I think there probably isn't anymore. Literally in the last couple of months, there's four of us on the entire team who are not new, and the bosses are new."[16] "Occasionally we'll buck the trend toward click thinking, if there's a strong local news story or breaking news—we tend to do it more with breaking news—or if there's good stuff in the paper," a web producer said. "But, in general, moving away from click driven thinking is the exception."[17]

"We're trying to be a real strong local news site that appeals to our audience and gets traffic," Greenbaum concluded in an earlier interview:

> You just sort of get used to knowing what kind of news gets clicked. A story about the Middle East, a national story—no. We're trying to pick out strong local stories or strong state stories that we know will appeal to our readership. We're a news site, but we don't feel tied to the definition of news, as in breaking news. As far as the spotlight versus the biggie goes, it's intuitive, but we put just about anything we think will get clicked up there at this point. You just have a gut feeling about it. Like for an article about Michelle Obama: your gut instinct is that it's not going to get picked up, but if it's getting clicked, we'll bump it up.[18]

In sum, the sudden availability of news metrics were making journalists and editors more sensitive to the implications of what their audience was reading and why. In Philadelphia, a deliberate emphasis by management on the widespread diffusion of metric data, along with a fairly desperate need for greater traffic numbers that could increase revenue for online ads, were leading web producers at Philly.com to base more and more of their news judgments on raw quantitative data. Along with this reliance on metrics there was a rhetorical valorization of the audience. I would argue, then, that underlying rhetoric of the active audience might be seen as laying the groundwork for a vision of the professional reporter that is less autonomous in his or her news decisions and increasingly reliant on audience metrics as a supplement to news judgment.

Strains on Newswork: The Precarity of Journalism

The encroachment of technology on newsroom judgment was not the only exogenous factor causing worker strain among members of the Philadelphia media ecosystem. The work situation at many of the newspapers I observed might be characterized as one of precarity—a condition of work whose dominant characteristics include unpredictability, insecurity, and emotional and psychological uncertainty.[19] A condition of precariousness is now dominant within the U.S. journalism industry as a whole—a precariousness that, along with the discussed reliance on audience judgment and news metrics, is dramatically reshaping journalists' conceptions of their own professional autonomy.

Uncertainty and instability have always been attendant consequences of work in the news industry.[20] What is new is the impact of temporary work, freelance employment, technological change, and economic developments on newswork. My fieldwork, with its broader analysis of both institutional and deinstitutionalized aspects of journalistic work, also points to a second consequence of technological and economic shifts: the fragility of journalistic networks that accompanies conditions of precarious work. In this section, I present evidence of the growing precariousness of journalistic work, then expand the analysis to include a discussion of "networked fragility."

The current feelings of many journalists are best summed up in a comment by an award-winning *Philadelphia Daily News* photographer who was trying to recast himself as a flexible new media worker and videographer: "My old medium is dying, and my new one doesn't pay."[21] Throughout my time at the *Daily News*, the *Inquirer*, and Philly.com, I was constantly approached by journalists who made comments such as, "So, you've come to observe a dying industry"; "You're here for the final days"; or "You're interested in the last rites, are you?"[22] Indeed, there was an overwhelming, crushing feeling of anxiety throughout the Philadelphia newspapers at 400 North Broad Street; while my purpose there was to discuss how journalistic authority was changing in the face of citizen media and growing deprofessionalization, most reporters seemed uninterested in such topics or interested in them only momentarily and in the abstract. Most often, my question "How has journalism changed since you started reporting?" would be answered with a comment such as, "There are fewer people doing it with me" or "The newsroom is a lot emptier than it was twelve months ago." A veteran reporter with the *Daily News* told me:

> What's the biggest development in local news gathering? The steady attrition of news gathering resources. The Internet is hammering the newspapers, and cable TV has already impacted the [television] networks' news gathering abilities. . . . I was at City Hall for three different news organizations from 1984 through 2002. . . . [T]here is a newsroom there, across from the Mayor's Office. When I started, there was a cacophony of typewriters and [a lot of] cigarette smoke. In the fall of 2005, the [*Daily News* cut one-third of its full-time reporting staff]. We never quite recovered. We went from four people at City Hall to one. Now we're back to two, but it still isn't the same.[23]

When asked a fairly esoteric question about whether "reverse publishing" (moving news copy from online into print rather than from print to the Internet) had changed her job at all, a journalist involved in the design side of the news operation responded in practical terms: "What's changed my job is that the paper has gotten smaller and smaller."[24]

While I was conducting fieldwork, Philadelphia Media Holdings—the company that until 2010 owned all three major media properties in Philadelphia—missed an interest payment to its creditors, prompting widespread industry speculation regarding the financial health of the company.[25] Later in the summer, the decision was made to merge the photo and copy desk staffs of the *Daily News* and the *Inquirer*, the first step in what was widely feared would become a large-scale consolidation of the two papers.[26] In July, the *Inquirer* eliminated two of its sections.[27] In January 2009, rumors circulated about a government "bailout" of the Philadelphia papers. In August 2008, *Philadelphia Magazine* summarized the state of the papers in bleak terms:

> As the financial troubles of Philadelphia Media Holdings (PMH) continue
> to mount, more layoffs are coming at the *Philadelphia Inquirer* and *Daily
> News*. . . . PMH is currently involved in a forbearance agreement with its
> creditors that lasts through September 10th, which appears to be undermin-
> ing the market's confidence in the company. . . . In a new twist, the papers are
> said to be eyeing the ranks of newsroom managers for layoffs rather than
> reporters. "Our members have taken enough hits over the last couple of
> years," says [Bill] Ross [administrative officer of the Newspaper Guild], "and
> new management under Mark Frisby has realized there are layers and layers
> of management that haven't been touched."[28]

All this, of course, was written before Philadelphia Media Holdings filed for bankruptcy in February 2009.

Sam Wood, the reporter at the *Inquirer*'s online news desk, as discussed in
Chapter 3, summed up the mixture of personal anxiety, uncertainty, sharp aware-
ness of economic realities, and simultaneous embrace and fear of the Internet
that I found prevalent in the more traditional Philadelphia newsrooms. "The big
fear, and you'll hear this over and over again," he said, "is that we're doing this
[adapting to the online news cycle] too late. I moved over to the online desk to
build transfer[able] skills. I'm a middle-aged guy with two three-year-old kids.
. . . [W]ho's going to hire me?"[29]

When not contemplating the tenuousness of their basic job security, reporters found numerous other ways to articulate their feelings of precariousness.
When asked about the technological consequences of employees' using portable
digital devices, the City Hall reporter Chris Brennan reframed the question in
terms of resource deprivation. "Most reporters on these papers don't even *have*
BlackBerries because the papers can't afford them," he told me. "We purchased
our own BlackBerries once we moved into the City Hall beat, and then we had to
hook ourselves up to the system." Brennan also asked his newspaper whether it
would pay to dedicate a laptop to the City Hall bureau so he could blog live but
was told that "the paper couldn't afford it."[30]

Even at the relatively healthy Philly.com, where management had made
growth "a priority,"[31] resources were strained. During a newsroom meeting, an
editor made a comment that the company "had a dramatic shortfall of programmers and designers." Wendy Warren replied that, after some recent additions in
the web production department, hiring had ceased, and even if the paper did find
itself in a position where it could one day hire again, "You have to pay programmers [a lot of money] compared to web producers."[32] That comment about the
relative inexpensiveness of web managers compared with unionized journalists
adds insight to the situation of precarious labor in Philadelphia journalism. Web
producers at Philly.com generally were younger that their counterparts at print
media, and, importantly, they had been non-unionized for many years. Indeed, it
was widely speculated that Philly.com had moved its offices downtown (with all
of the accompanying logistical aggravation such a move entailed) partly to protect its employees from unionization drives at the company[33]—although, as one

active Newspaper Guild member told me, "There wasn't much of a chance they were going to sign the cards anyway. They were in the [*Inquirer*] building for a year, and we couldn't convince them to sign the cards, because they're terrified they will lose their jobs."[34]

The career path of one video producer at Philly.com can be seen as emblematic of the emergence of a young, flexible workforce within the walls of a historically older, unionized community. A journalist who requested anonymity—I will call him Gary German—was working as a cameraman and producer at Philly.com during my research in 2008. He held a master's degree from the Columbia Graduate School of Journalism. Instead of the shirtsleeves and ties that are common at the *Inquirer,* or the polo shirts often seen at the *Daily News,* many video producers at Philly.com, including German, wore European-style glasses and "hipster" jeans. Several had "faux-hawks," a hairstyle in which a strip of hair across the top of the head is longer than the hair on the remainder of the head. While I was conducting my fieldwork, German announced his departure from Philly.com to work at what another journalist described sarcastically as "some hip media company in New York that was an Internet startup but also pays more than we do."[35] Another reporter commented that one of the problems with Philly.com was that it paid very little, "so then people leave pretty fast."[36]

Several of the Philly.com web producers were hired after they had been laid off by the *Inquirer* in the fall of 2006, an employment shift that interrupted the once typical pattern of successful journalistic career advancement.[37] A senior web producer described his career path this way: he had started out with a weekly suburban paper, then moved to a daily in Florida; he then spent four years at the *Inquirer* news desk. In decades past, this job at the *Inquirer* would have marked a career peak and could have amounted to a job for life. But "I was laid off at the end of 2006," he said, "and started at Philly.com in January 2007."[38] Another *Inquirer* reporter described job turmoil at Philadelphia Media Holdings in similar terms. Because her professional path from the *Inquirer* to Philly.com (and then back to the *Inquirer*) captures the precarious nature of journalism in the 21st century (with its attendant uncertainty, stress, sacrifice, and occasional exhilaration) so well, I quote her here at length:

> I was sort of at the higher end of the layoffs in 2006 in terms of [the fact that] the last reporter laid off had been hired in 1999, and I had been hired in 2000. . . . First we heard there were going to be 150 layoffs, and numbers were sort of wild. Several attempts were made to save my job, but ultimately I was laid off. . . . From the newsroom [they fired] about seventy [people], and thirty-some reporters. You know, it's a very fluid number, because some of those people were called back. I know all the copy editors on the list ended up getting all their jobs back if they wanted them; they realized they had cut too deep. . . .
>
>   I was laid off on Friday, and on Monday I met with [an executive]. He sort of had this proposal: "Why don't you work at Philly.com?" The thought of working in the online world had never even occurred to me. I didn't know

HTML or anything like that, but I was certainly aware that it was the future of journalism. And frankly, I wanted to stay here and work with this company. Several of my . . . reporter colleagues who were laid off went to work at Philly.com, which is a separate company.

My heart has always been in the writing and reporting end of things, so when the opportunity came up to go back to the paper, I went. . . . I thought about staying at Philly.com, but I had to do this. For as long as newspapers exist, I have to pursue this dream.

When I came back to the *Philadelphia Inquirer,* and when I came back to being in the [Newspaper] Guild, I remember talking to one of the editors and asking, . . . "Am I gonna get laid off again?" This particular editor said to me, "Well, we can't control the industry." That was when the economy was bad; now it's worse, so I don't think anyone was under the impression that things had stabilized. But when they talked about media cost-cutting moves—"We're going to close these sections . . . and we're going to merge the [desks]"— I think people thought that all this cutting was inevitable, but maybe not so soon as now.[39]

It was a common refrain, voiced throughout my research, that there were too few journalists at the Philadelphia papers to do the minimal level of reporting that once would have been expected of them. One morning, for example, when a Southeastern Pennsylvania Transportation Authority (SEPTA) trolley collided with a school bus, an editor at Philly.com asked reporters at both papers to cover the story. Although Gar Joseph, city editor at the *Daily News,* thought that the story would work best as a visual rather than a full story—a photo of the crash with a caption—no photographers were available. A photographer walking by the metro desk responded to Joseph's request for help by shouting over her shoulder, "I can't cover the SEPTA thing, I have two assignments already," as she ran off. "There's just not enough people here," Joseph noted glumly. In a second incident, a *Daily News* editor took a phone call from a woman whose son had been arrested by the police and engaged in an extensive conversation. "That shouldn't be," a second city editor sighed. "It should be a reporter having such a lengthy conversation. But there's nobody around who is experienced enough to actually take the call, There are too few employees." Incidents like this were common during the summer of 2008. Office clerks performed some of the web functions at the *Daily News*; at Philly.com, marketing staff members outnumbered content managers by a ratio of at least three to one.[40]

This shortage of staff also manifested itself in less incidental ways. My field notes for a day in mid-July read, "This place is like a tomb, except for the one online area, where things are popping. Literally, there is no one else in the entire office."[41] I also wrote this about the famous *Philadelphia Inquirer* building a few days earlier:

Things are scattered around. It would be impossible to find anything if you just walked in. There appear to be tons of signs and spaces devoted to these weird newspaper things—printing, paper things—that seem like they've been totally abandoned.[42]

Importantly, as the once grand buildings of the newspaper business slowly emptied, more paid reporters were being asked to do more work for less money. "In the new new media marketplace, you're still only getting paid for a seven-and-a-half-hour day," one *Daily News* columnist told me, explaining why he refused to blog, "and until the people upstairs decide that that's how they want me to spend my time, it doesn't make much sense to [blog]."[43] It was not the extra time spent writing, the columnist added. "That's the least of it; it's the tech time spent getting the blog up, and then you have to deal with the comments." Conflicts about the degree to which reporters could be "required" to blog by management led to significant tensions with the Newspaper Guild and almost led to a strike in 2006.[44] Because blogging was uncompensated work, one reporter-blogger told me, it had to be voluntary—meaning that while guild members could not be "forced" to do it, they could not get extra compensation for it, either.[45] Hai Do, an editor at the *Inquirer,* told a meeting of the Philadelphia Area New Media Alliance that he "spent a lot of time trying to grab people, shake them, and get them to understand . . . we have to change." In training photographers to be videographers, he noted, he first found people who were willing to add video to their resume. It then became a viral "spreading out." Hai argued that his employees "got the sense pretty fast that if they want to be successful within the organization, they will have to learn video skills in addition to the skills they already have, whether they're 'forced' to do it or not.'" Soon, Hai concluded, "everyone wants to learn video."[46]

While it might be argued that management simply uses labor precariousness to increase the output of individual journalists, more work is not necessarily rationalized work. Perhaps the clearest manifestation of this tension between free labor and organizational control came in the discussions surrounding the creation of a new Philly.com music page called Phrequency (www.phrequency.com). The idea behind the page was that it would be a Philly.com website providing coverage of the local "indie rock" scene, music that appeals primarily to the twenty- to twenty-six-year-old age demographic. At the same time, the costs of the page would need to be kept low. During one of the planning meetings, an executive laid out a series of very specific requirements for the reporter-bloggers who would "populate" the site with content. They would need to attend a certain number of music events per week and blog a certain number of times per week. If the did this correctly, they could earn bonuses on top of their base salaries. In answer to the question of who would do the actual reporting, the preferred answer was clear: interns or freelancers. "Frankly, we don't need to re-create an entire staff around music," the Philly.com executive said during a second meeting.[47] However the preferred solution, obviously designed to keep costs as low as possible, risked sacrificing the regularity and predictability of content production. According to a lawyer also present at discussions surrounding Phrequency, employment law mandated that management could not set the terms of freelance work (e.g., require a certain number of blog posts per day of freelancers). However, if the reporter-bloggers were going to be interns, then the purpose of the work had to be "truly educational" in nature. In this example, Philly.com's dreams of a team of low-cost laborers to run its music website appeared to conflict with its desire to structure the content production of its workforce rationally.

Strains on Newswork:
Fragile News Institutions and Bankruptcy

The inability to pay reporters is not the only process destabilizing news networks. From the fragility of voluntaristic news organizations to the bankruptcy of some of the oldest, seemingly most stable journalism outlets in Philadelphia, 2009–2010 was marked by the collapse of many formal and informal news organizations. I first discuss the structural factors pulling older blogs and citizen media outlets apart before turning to the more widely discussed bankruptcy of the *Inquirer, Daily News,* and Philly.com.

Foremost among the factors affecting the early wave of largely volunteer-driven online news organizations was a conflict between the free labor time necessary to sustain a functioning volunteer organization and the need to gather personal resources such as income, food, and shelter—the problem described by Yochai Benkler as "keeping body and soul together." One of the earliest volunteers at the Independent Media Center of Philadelphia told me that a motivating factor behind her initial heavy involvement in the project lay in the fact that, after being laid off at the magazine she had worked for in the spring of 2000, she received a severance package, unemployment package, and *free time.* "I was able to volunteer with the Philly IMC nearly full time between April and August 2000," she said.[48] A second Philly IMC volunteer, who later went on to journalism school and a job in traditional media, said simply, "I needed health insurance. What can I say?" Alluding to the conflict between the committed energy needed to engage with a volunteer media project and the demands of "everyday life," she added:

> [People] have their lives. You know after the week of the 2000 RNC, that's what happened. People like Mark [an Indymedia volunteer who also worked in the newspaper industry] actually had to go back and file some stories for the *Philadelphia Inquirer.* Maybe he came for a couple of IMC meetings after that, but, you know, he had his life. You know, other people had their lives, and they just sort of went where they were going to go, you know, like, "I don't really like writing journalism; I'm more of a creative writer. Why do I want to sit in these meetings?" I mean, and some of the people I remember saying, "Why would I sit in these horrible meetings with these people arguing, and I don't want to do this and I'm not getting paid?" . . . [S]o at the end of the day it just kind of fell apart.[49]

The more individualized and community-oriented blog projects discussed in this volume also appear quite delicate. They require time, personal commitment, a set schedule ("If you leave people hanging, they'll notice, and they'll go away," one blogger told me), and, as shown in earlier chapters, regular updating. Limited research on the topic of "blog death" reveals that the majority of blogs (60–80 percent) are abandoned within one month of their creation.[50] Even more striking than the number of blogs started and quickly abandoned, however, is the degree to which even the most *successful* blogs remain at risk of collapse. In short, there is often very little to keep them going except the blogger's time and passion. As the founder of the community website Young Philly Politics put it:

> What keeps [Young Philly Politics] together? I don't know. Actually, I think it's always a little tenuous, to be honest. . . . [I]f we stopped writing our readership does go down. People don't log on to write—they log on to read stuff. Not, you know, because they're bored, but its not like . . . I don't know how many people are necessarily invested in keeping it going, like they're shareholders or employees. I mean, there are a fair number of regular writers, and then there's a number of regular readers, a lot of them don't even write anything, and presumably some of them believe in what we're doing, some are just interested, some hate us . . . so I don't know. I think, if we shut down, I think eventually something would come to replace us, but [pause] you know, you see it in all these little blogs, and maybe they're smaller blogs than us, these blogs don't shut down. . . . [*Speaking slowly*] [T]hey just slowly stop.[51]

Success seems to be no guarantee of stability in the new media world. While institution building does occur online, these institutions seem to possess a character that is fundamentally different character from that of their offline predecessors. In the absence of a regular wage or the type of rationalized, bureaucratic commitment demanded by traditional, hierarchical organizations,[52] many media managers wonder how their organizations can continue. The tale told by Karl Martino about the difficulties in keeping Philly Future running illustrates this point. "As of a couple years ago, [my community blog] needed an infusion of new ideas, energy, and resources to help it become more of a resource for the region," he said. "But I became a dad, my mom became ill with lung cancer and passed, my responsibilities at work increased, and my back pain issue escalated—so I've been sidelined, and that has hurt the blog as its volunteer team has shrunk down and I haven't fought hard enough to push it along. . . . For now it remains, a set of half-implemented ideas and ideals."[53]

The changing conditions of news production, described throughout this book, also played a role in increasing the fragility of journalistic networks. Newswork used to be factory work, a reporter at the *Inquirer* told me, half-nostalgic and half-relieved. A reporter went out and reported a story, typed it up, and then sat back and watched it ascend a labor chain of increasing specialization, from editing to typesetting, photo toning, layout, and on up the ladder of industrial production until it was at last placed in the next day's newspaper.[54] News organizations have attempted to rationalize their work routines in multiple ways. Occasionally, these routines have offended implicit newsroom values or have been stated so bluntly that they have drawn the ire of professional journalists.

The following description of workflow management and story quotas highlights an important belief of many of the media managers I spoke to in Philadelphia that the newswork process must be rational to function:

> In 2007, I wrote 337 stories. Some days, like when I do rewrite, I might do up to four stories. Some days [I do] just one or none if I'm working on a Sunday story. But to compare, when I worked at the police shack in 2005, I wrote 655 stories. (Some would be really short.) And if you are an investigative reporter, you might only do a handful. . . . When I worked at the *New Haven [Connecticut] Register*'s Milford bureau, I had a two-story-a-day quota. Some days I had to do three and . . . a Sunday story. The quota was no joke. When I moved to the city desk there, I had to do maybe one a day and something for the weekend.[55]

This is a description of a highly ordered production process.[56] Even if managers do not track the number of bylines or institute quotas for articles, journalists historically have not sat around waiting for inspiration (or the news) to strike. The paper (or the thirty-minute newscast or the three-minute radio spot) must be filled, and a certain number of column inches are required. Production of the news has thus demanded a regular supply of content applied in regular doses.

Rather than decreasing this insatiable demand for news content, the Internet is requiring more work—what Dean Starkman has called the "hamster wheel" of digital news production.[57] Web producers at Philly.com groaned under the weight of a nonstop news cycle in which "non-performing" features were downgraded after a half-hour. "To be effective, I really need eighty new pieces every eight hours," Yoni Greenbaum told me, "and I don't even come close to getting that much."[58] for their part, reporters at the *Inquirer* and *Daily News* bristled at the new demands. "Why they have this frantic thing about 'getting the news up now' doesn't make a lot of sense," said one journalist at the *Daily News*. "They're throwing good stuff away because they're cycling it through so fast."[59] Philly.com staff, however, disagreed. "The problem with [the *Daily News* and the *Inquirer*] is that they're still not thinking in terms of the web," a Philly.com web producer told me. "They're thinking in terms of a sixty-four-page paper, which means that when the paper is filled, the job is done. The paper is never 'filled' anymore."[60] Every newsroom meeting I observed in which staff members of the *Daily News,* the *Inquirer,* and Philly.com were present inevitably circled back to the insatiable demands of the digital news cycle. As shown in Chapter 3, a major impact of the Internet has been to alter conceptions of news time.

We have now come face to face with one of the great paradoxes of online newswork: the Internet, with its endless need for more and more content to fill its bottomless pages at faster and faster speeds, has run up against the increasing inability of media organizations to rationalize the production of that content through traditional means—that is, through the payment of wages. We have entered a journalistic moment in which news institutions need more and more material, yet to obtain it, they find themselves ever more dependent on alliances with derationalized, often unpaid news producers. The stability and permanence of journalistic networks—whether they are community blogs, radical news websites, or more traditional media organizations—will depend on news producers' either rediscovering a means of providing formal monetary compensation for newswork; rationalizing the production of news through alternative, non-wage means; or, finally, bypassing bureaucratic and market rationality in the production of cultural goods. The first two possibilities require organizational adjustments; the third would mark a major shift in the conditions under which informational goods are produced. While legal and social theorists have pointed for at least a decade toward technological and economic trends that make these transformations in the information economy likely,[61] my analysis of newswork in Philadelphia has exhaustively demonstrated that these changes are slow and halting and often are impeded by organizational and social factors. Among the largest of these factors was the dramatic bankruptcy of the Philadelphia newspapers in early 2009.

Bankruptcy

In Chapter 1, I introduced the Philadelphia news ecosystem by chronicling the consolidation of the local newspaper industry, the development of Gene Roberts's "Alpha Plan," and the profit margin battles of the 1980s and 1990s. These fights over resources, however, were primarily waged in an era flush with cash; owning a local newspaper, it was joked, was like owning a press that could print money.[62] Between 2005 and 2009, however, four key business developments in Philadelphia piled quickly on top of each other to shape the media institutions I observed between the spring of 2008 and the winter of 2011. All of them ended up shrinking the organization. After years of steady and painful but relatively small cuts, Knight-Ridder slashed staff at both of its Philadelphia newspapers in the fall of 2005, eliminating seventy-five positions (15 percent of the newsroom staff) at the *Inquirer* and twenty-five positions (nearly 20 percent) at the *Daily News* through a combination of buyouts and, for the first time, layoffs. The cuts, some of deepest in the industry to date, were widely covered by the local and national press and left a lasting mark on psyches at the *Inquirer* and, particularly, the *Daily News*.[63] Combined with the second major development, the breakup of Knight-Ridder and the sale of the two newspapers to local owners (discussed in Chapters 2 and 5) in May 2006,[64] these changes solidified a full-scale reversal from the trends of the 1980s and 1990s. Rather than publicly traded corporate ownership, growing staff levels, and high newsroom morale, the *Inquirer* and *Daily News* found themselves locally owned and privately held, with shrinking staffs and plummeting morale. A second round of cuts occurred at the *Inquirer* (though not at the *Daily News*) seven months after Philadelphia Media Holdings, owned by the local businessman Brian Tierney, took control of the two papers and weeks after a new union contract was finalized. Oddly, the 17 percent cut (dropping the newsroom headcount to 325 people) prompted far less obvious angst than the gutting during the waning days of the Knight-Ridder regime. A review of press accounts and public statements highlighted a certain odd peace with the layoffs. "Leaders of the Greater Philadelphia Newspaper Guild, meanwhile, were urging staffers who are not on the layoff list but considering leaving the company sometime soon to consider taking a voluntary layoff as a way to reduce the number of forced job cuts," according to one account.[65] It may be that, after fifteen months of staff decimation, numbness had finally set in.[66]

The numbness, however, was not to last. Barely a month after I completed my first round of ethnographic research, on February 22, 2009, Philadelphia Media Holdings filed for Chapter 11 bankruptcy. The filing, which was aimed at reorganizing finances rather than liquidating the newspapers, primarily stemmed from the massive debt load the new owners of the *Inquirer, Daily News,* and Philly.com had taken on when they purchased the properties from the McClatchy Company.[67] The bankruptcy process, which lasted from the winter of 2009 until the spring of 2010, was something of a paradox. The legal process was fraught with drama, public relations posturing, and lawsuits and counter-suits as Tierney and the local ownership group struggled to retain control of the properties.[68] Daily life at the newspapers, by contrast, went on largely as it had for the past several years. With the papers facing reorganization rather than liquidation, a sense of change was largely absent from the editorial desks and the corridors of Philly.com. One the one hand, two journalists with the *Daily News* won a coveted Pulitzer Prize during the period in which the paper was in bankruptcy.[69] On the other hand, a worker at the *Inquirer*'s online news desk described the bankruptcy period as entirely stagnant, "a time when, left to its own devices, the newspaper seemed to morph backwards into the 1980s."[70] The lengthy period between the declaration of bankruptcy and its resolution seemed to bring the best and worst aspects of the online news era into stark relief: the continued vitality and importance of routine investigative reporting carried out by trained professionals working inside stable news institutions, combined with a continuing inability to find either the money or the willpower to innovate digitally in a way that would preserve the reportorial functions that had carried the *Daily News* to a Pulitzer Prize.

In April 2010, a day-long bankruptcy auction resulted in the newspapers' creditors seizing control of the media properties, bidding $135 million for them—less than a quarter of their purchase price in 2006.[71] "Hardly just another routine sale of yet another bankrupt company," reported Chris Nolter in *The Deal*, the auction of the newspapers "featured high drama, controversy and personalities well beyond the relatively small-dollar bids and the strictly local nature of the business."[72] By late 2010, Philadelphia's largest journalism properties were officially owned by a consortium of banks and hedge funds, just like an increasing number of city dailies and websites across the country.[73] The brief experiment in local ownership chronicled by this book had come to an inglorious end.

In many ways, comparing the inability of citizen-powered news organizations to survive when faced with the conflicting demands of real life and the collapse of large news organizations under a mountain of restructured debt may seem like comparing apples and oranges. These aspects of network fragility, however, lie at a level deeper than that of institutional size or organizational prominence. Chapter 2, which mapped the emergence of the Philadelphia media ecosystem, told a story of growth and infinite possibility; the digital realm, it seemed, offered ordinary citizens the opportunity to "be the media" and at the same time gave print newspapers the opportunity to reinvent themselves online. This chapter is a sobering corollary: in a world where emergence is easy, rapid disappearance also appears endemic. The solid institutions of the industrial age of communication appear to be dissolving under the weight of a digital tsunami unleashed by the Internet. Whether we tell the story of journalism on the World Wide Web through the chronicle of single-person blogs or hundred-person newsrooms, the years between 1997 and 2011 tell a story of radical instability. The website you visited today may be—and far too often is—gone tomorrow. When examining the now long history of journalism on the web, it is perhaps the dizzying dynamic of emergence and collapse that emerges most clearly. To date, it remains unclear how—or whether—the cycle of creation and destruction will come to an end.

Rebuilding the News, Again

On October 14, 2010, a dozen or so journalists, foundation heads, researchers, nonprofit funders, and academics gathered in a conference room at the William Penn Foundation to help fund the future of journalism. Unlike the Norgs Unconference nearly five years earlier, the foundation's gathering wanted to do more than simply hold a dialogue about how to repair journalism. The foundation had made a commitment to provide ten local Philadelphia news organizations with $5,000 to undertake collaborative reporting projects in partnership with other groups. The small awards, part of what was being called the Philadelphia Enterprise Reporting Fund, ended up funding fourteen groups instead of the planned ten. According to the press release announcing the awards:

> The Philadelphia Enterprise Reporting Awards are funded by the William Penn Foundation to help develop and amplify public affairs journalism in the Philadelphia region. The goal is to help reporting projects get off the ground and to explore collaboration opportunities among various news providers in the region. The winners, selected from 27 applicants, will launch their projects over the next six months.[74]

In 2010–2011, three major new actors emerged in the world of journalistic production that have been little discussed in this book until this point. They are, first, local and national foundations; second, not-for-profit news organizations; and third, a less formal but vitally important group of technologically minded newsworkers variously referred to as hacker journalists, hacks, hackers, and programmer-journalists.[75] While I can only sketch the import of these developments here, I would argue that the primary dynamics shaping the future of journalistic work lie at the intersection of these emergent actors and the larger structural factors of technology, fragility, and precarity discussed in the first half of this chapter. Indeed, each of these actors can be seen as arising in partial response to some of the debilitating problems discussed earlier. Programmer-journalists bring a nuanced appreciation of digital technology that goes beyond "the shock of news-metrics" attitudes often expressed by traditional journalists. Nonprofit newsrooms, for their part, can be insulated at least partially from the declining advertising revenues, high expenses, and crippling debt loads that have plagued local newspapers. Foundations, finally, occupy a strategic position in the informational ecosystem that allows them to broker creative collaborative work and to build networks of news and information producers that cooperate in new ways.[76] An analysis of these three emergent institutions, along with a very brief discussion of changes at the revamped for-profit Philadelphia newspapers, makes up the remainder of this chapter.

As the financial resources of traditional news institutions have dwindled, interest in foundation-supported and not-for-profit news media has grown. If the relationship among advertisers, newspapers, and consumers once promised enough revenue to support large-scale news gathering enterprises,[77] that dynamic now appears to be irretrievably broken. As John Thornton, chairman of the non-profit, award-winning *Texas Tribune,* wrote in 2010:

> The business of serious journalism news ain't in the top 100, probably never was, and certainly won't be again. Commercial efforts will persist because they just will. But expecting investors to continue to fund for-profit, Capital J journalism just 'cuz: doesn't that sound a lot like charity? . . . Public media, privately funded, will be a bigger part of the media landscape in ten years than it is today. This will require the inhabitants of Fantasy Land to do a good deal of consciousness raising in the general public for membership support, and among foundations and major donors to give us the runway we need to establish sustainable business models.[78]

The argument that one aspect of the future of journalism lies in "pubic media, privately funded"—neither traditional public media nor the purely commercial media enterprises of the past but, rather, public-minded and member- and foundation-funded—is controversial.[79] However, my discussion of foundation and nonprofit journalism is not primarily geared toward analyzing whether such funding will "work" in a financial sense; rather, it is geared toward exploring the many ways in which foundations have reframed the debate over journalism's future. As Seth Lewis has written, "By recasting the rhetorical and actual boundaries of journalism jurisdiction, [the Knight Foundation] has opened space for professional innovation—principally, the introduction of participation as an ethical norm, through which the profession may adapt more effectively to a networked media environment."[80] I would argue that my research helps localize and generalize Lewis's point: by making targeted interventions in the journalistic sphere, foundations in Philadelphia are redrawing the boundaries of the debate over the future of journalism itself.

This is not to say, of course, that the decision to make these interventions was unproblematic or free of controversy. Indeed, the manner in which foundations such as the Pew Charitable Trust and the William Penn Foundation came to engage with the journalistic sphere between 2006 and 2011, in many cases, mirrors the uncertain and halting efforts of Philadelphia institutions more generally. The Pew Charitable Trusts, founded in 1948 and with more than $5 billion in assets, is a nonprofit nongovernmental organization (NGO) based in Philadelphia but with a national mandate. In 2011 Pew, maintained the Project for Excellence in Journalism and the Pew Research Center for the People and the Press, but its largest recent intervention in the world of journalism was the Pew Center for Civic Journalism. The Pew Center, which was established in 1994 and closed its doors in 2003, was dedicated to funding experiments in "civic" or "public" journalism.[81] The William Penn Foundation, founded in 1945 and with $2 billion in assets, has a more localized mission to "improv[e] the quality of life in the Greater Philadelphia region through efforts that foster rich cultural expression, strengthen children's futures, and deepen connections to nature and community." The William Penn Foundation came to its interest in journalism through a somewhat circuitous route; it was disappointed in how its program areas were being covered by the press and in response helped to fund several journalism experiments, including the discussed Next Mayor project. WHYY, finally, is Philadelphia's National Public Radio (NPR) station; it is well known nationally for productions such as *Fresh Air* but occasionally criticized for underinvesting in local news coverage.[82]

In 2006, the same convergence of forces that inspired the Norgs Unconference—most prominently, fears over the impending sale of the *Inquirer, Daily News,* and Philly.com by Knight-Ridder—led the Pew Charitable Trusts to explore creating its own "norgs-like" entity informally known as the Phly, which would rely heavily on user-generated content and citizen journalism.[83] When the newspapers were sold to local owners, some of the fear in Philadelphia dissipated, and the plan was shelved. In 2008, the notion of a Pew journalism initiative returned, this time under the informal moniker of Y-Factor. The initiative would be large scale: a staff of nearly sixty reporters, editorial desks, six or seven verticals (branded website sections such as "sports," "fashion," or "cars"), an embrace of "citizen journalism," and an initial cost of $4 million–$5 million. Fresh off the success and buzz of the Next Mayor project, WHYY was seen as a

FIGURE 6.1   The WHYY Newsworks website, 2010. *(Source: http://www.newsworks.org.)*

natural Pew partner.[84] Once again, however, Pew's plans did not come to frui-
tion. The year 2008 saw the start of the global economic meltdown, the meltdown of newsrooms everywhere, and the meltdown in foundation portfolios
across the country. A combination of shrinking resources, sticker shock over the
cost of actually running a newsroom, and a loss of support from Pew executives
once again conspired to shelve the initiative.

The two major networked journalism initiatives that emerged in Philadelphia in 2010–2011—WHYY's Newsworks and the William Penn Foundation's
Networked Collaborative Journalism Project—were thus smaller, more targeted,
and more sustainable versions of the aborted Y-Factor. Each initiative, however,
drew on particular organizational resources unique to William Penn and WHYY
(see Figure 6.1).

On November 15, 2010, WHYY shuttered its existing news website and
launched Newsworks, a web-only news page that, according to the tag line,
would be "For you. With you. By you." As Chris Satullo, the station's executive
director of news noted, Newsworks was in part an attempt to "pick up some of

the pieces" following the collapse of the larger Y-Factor. Newsworks was more than simply a fall-back option, however; even in the years between discussions about the aborted Y-Factor and the fall of 2010, the conventional wisdom about online journalism had evolved. Perhaps as a nod to Satullo's background in civic journalism, Newsworks paid particular attention to thoughtful, respectful community dialogue and used the latest in online moderation technology. Satullo also took pains to emphasize that the site was as much a news network as it was a place for original journalism. The website listed more than fifteen partners in community journalism, including the Philadelphia Public School Notebook, PhilaPlace.org, PlanPhilly.com, and the Temple Multimedia Urban Reporting Lab. Even more, regular analysis of the site confirmed that at least several of the stories on the site's front page linked directly to other news websites.[85]

In organizational terms, Newsworks was launched with two main goals. Following the termination of WHYY's nightly Delaware newscast, the decision was made to retrain the radio and television journalists as multiplatform digital reporters. A second goal was to increase WHYY's levels of hyperlocal journalism by focusing deep, community-driven coverage on particular Philadelphia neighborhoods in the northwest of the city. But as Satullo noted, "The original idea was all about hyperlocal news and community conversation. But it quickly became clear we still needed to do the [original, more ambitious project called Y Factor] on a reduced scale. Just doing hyperlocal news won't work because you don't have enough of a user base to sustain a robust operation. So we needed to cover the city, but we needed to do it in a way that made use of the people in it, networked with the informational resources that we already had."[86]

The William Penn Foundation also took steps toward founding and funding a nonprofit news organization in the fall of 2010. As in the Newsworks project, William Penn sought to leverage its existing partners to build a *news network* rather than create a stand-alone journalistic organization from scratch. Perhaps mindful of the problems encountered by the overly ambitious Y-Factor, the foundation launched its project slowly and deliberately over several years.

A central aspect of the Networked News initiative was a survey of the Philadelphia media ecosystem conducted by the Institute for Interactive Journalism (J-Lab), founded in 2002 at the University of Maryland's College of Journalism, a think tank headed by the former *Inquirer* editor and Pulitzer Prize-winner Jan Schaffer. The report, which concluded that the future of Philadelphia journalism lay in networked collaboration, argued that Philadelphia had suffered an erosion in public affairs coverage between 2006 and 2009—an argument that was bound to disappoint Schaffer's former colleagues at the *Daily News* and the *Inquirer*.[87] Also controversial were the organizations Schaffer included in her overview of the local ecosystem and those that she left out. Although the report surveyed "both newspapers and . . . the city's 260 blogs, and hyperlocal or niche websites," other longtime observers of Philadelphia journalism, such as Joshua Breitbart of the Washington, DC, think tank New America Foundation argued that the exclusion of other media groups "implied . . . the media ecosystem is younger, whiter, and wealthier than the actual population of the city."[88] Particularly noteworthy was the exclusion of the Media Mobilizing Project, a successor to the Philly IMC. On the one hand, it is possible to see the boundaries of the J-Lab report as indicative of a continued conservatism in deciding who gets called a "journalist" in 2011. But it is also arguable that, in expanding the boundaries of the news ecosystem, William Penn and J-Lab definitively ratified the once controversial premise that publicly meaningful newswork occurred outside the walls of local newspapers. The controversy over the J-Lab report highlighted the difficulties in mapping a local news ecosystem in the endlessly shifting digital era, but it also showed just how far the conversation about journalism had moved since the late 1990s.

Following the J-Lab report, the William Penn Foundation issued a series of fourteen small awards to local news organizations in October 2010. While allowing these organizations to experiment with limited collaborative news projects, the foundation also began to lay the groundwork for a larger, more permanent networked news partnership that winter. Based at Temple University, the Networked News initiative envisioned a larger collaborative ecosystem that would make up for the growing holes in local coverage exacerbated by the decline of the Philadelphia newspapers. As of 2012, however, the project remained in startup mode, not hiring an executive director until February 2012.

Leaders at WHYY and the William Penn Foundation were quick to point out the differences they observed between their news initiatives. There are, indeed, important distinctions between the WHYY and Philadelphia Collaborative News Network projects. Against the past fourteen years of Philadelphia journalistic history, however, it is important to emphasize the similarities between the two organizations along with their differences. Citizens' participation in the news production process—conceived as a small component of a journalistic enterprise rather than as a replacement for professional news gathering—has been normalized to a degree that would have seemed surprising to the bloggers and Indymedia volunteers of the late 1990s. Both Newsworks and the collaborative journalism project emphasize the importance of networking the news, supplementing a core of targeted original reporting with the contributions of, and links to, other organizations. Most important, the primary drivers of this networked collaboration have been not local newspapers or websites but foundations and nonprofit organizations.

I will now turn my attention briefly to a final driver of journalistic change: the so-called hacker-journalists who make up a new generation of technologically oriented newsroom entrepreneurs. On April 30, 2010, more than 110 people filed into the all-day BarCamp News Innovation Philadelphia conference, which featured talks that ranged from "The Insight Graph: CRM [Customer Relationship Management] for Journalists" to discussions of business models being advanced by new news organization far from Philadelphia, including the startup news organization the Honolulu Civil Beat. Perhaps the most fascinating

BarCamp session was run by the self-identified hacker-journalist Greg Linch, who asked journalists to "rethink conventional newsroom thinking" in light of insights provided by hackers and computer programmers. "What are different types of thinking we use for journalism currently?" Linch asked BarCamp attendees over the course of his wide-ranging and insightful talk. "How should we be thinking in a way that informs our journalism better?"[89] And what is the relationship between this journalistic thinking, and other kinds of thinking, particularly the thinking of computer scientists? These types of questions and panels—practical yet esoteric at once—made up the bulk of the BarCamp sessions.

BarCamp Philadelphia was not a foundation-run meeting, although foundation officers were in attendance. Nor was it a meeting run by newspaper people or even by bloggers and tweeters. Bankruptcy judges were nowhere in sight. The web theorist Jack Lail actually called the attendees "edglings," drawing on a label first proffered by the future of news guru Stowe Boyd:

> [The BarCamp] was far from the hotel gatherings of American Society of News Editors, the Newspaper Association of America and the National Association of Broadcasters. . . . [The attendees] were eclectic: Young news and technology geeks, seasoned traditional journalists trying to refashion careers, software developers with visions of the future, mainstream journalists looking outside their box, enthusiastic journalism students full of hope and ambition and others just eager to carve a space in the media landscape.[90]

Taking place in the shadow of unfolding bankruptcies at Philadelphia Media Holdings, BarCamp Philadelphia was a reminder that the real future of journalism might be shaping itself at the edges of the news ecosystem. Chief among the groups pushing journalism in new directions is a rising cadre of technologically inclined journo-entrepreneurs. Included among these entrepreneurs were the young founders of a local journalism and consulting company Technically Philly, the organizers of Philadelphia BarCamp in 2010. Technically Philly was founded in February 2009, just as the Philadelphia newspapers were filing for bankruptcy, by Sean Blanda, Chris Wink, and Brian James Kirk, three recent journalism graduates from Temple University. "We graduated college, and we all had the chance to join what somebody called the 'traditional journalistic pipeline,' working our way up the ladder," Wink told me. "But newspapers were collapsing, and we all thought, 'Do we really want to do this?'" Wink recounted his thoughts about watching "amazing Philly journalists—reporters who had won Pulitzers and whose notebook I'm not even worthy of carrying"—struggle with layoffs and buyouts. And he watched reporters who had made the decision to go into journalism for themselves struggle with their lack of knowledge of the business side of the industry. "I realized that I didn't know reporting nearly as well as the people leaving the *Inquirer* and trying to strike out on their own," he said, "but I sure knew the business of where the industry was going a lot better than they did."[91]

Blanda, Kirk, and Wink described Technically Philly and its parent, Technically Media, as the journalistic equivalent of a catering business. Technically
Philly is a niche website that provides coverage of the Philadelphia technology
industry. "That's our retail business. But then you've got our catering business,
which is the consulting we do on how to build audiences for people like the
National Constitution Center," said Wink.[92] Blanda, Kirk, and Wink admitted
that it was probably the consulting arm of their company that would make the
bulk of their income but argued that the news had never been a money-making
product—that selling another product (historically, advertising) or, in their case,
technological and business know-how was always key to subsidizing the journalistic production. With its fusion of technological know-how, an entrepreneurial
spirit, and happiness with niche journalistic coverage of a small community,
Technically Philly represents an agglomeration of many of the trends discussed
in this chapter.

Just as these new journalism innovators busied themselves at the fringes of
the emerging local media ecosystem, Philadelphia's two major newspapers were
finally emerging from bankruptcy. In analyzing developments at the papers, the
contrast between the rapid pace of change outside Philadelphia's major news
institutions and the slow pace within them is stark.

Conclusion: Beyond Bankruptcy at Philly.com

Perhaps responding to a wave of post-bankruptcy criticism from the local owners of Philadelphia Media Holdings that Philadelphia's local newspapers would
soon be run by a consortium of bankers and journalistically ignorant hedge
fund managers, the Philadelphia newspapers' new owners wasted little time in
appointing a series of well-known journalists to management positions at the
Inquirer, Daily News, and Philly.com. Greg Osberg, a former president of *Newsweek,* was named publisher and chief executive of the reconstituted Philadelphia
Newspapers, along with Bob Hall, former publisher of the *Inquirer* and *Daily
News,* who was named chief operating officer. Osberg quickly replaced venerated
the *Inquirer* editor Bill Marimow with the veteran journalist Stan Wischnowski;
moved Michael Days, editor of the *Daily News,* over to the *Inquirer*; and named
Jim Brady, the highly regarded former head of Washington Post Digital and
TBD.com, as a consultant to Philly.com. Along with these personnel moves—
which seemed to promise a fresh start for the papers—came a series of logistical
changes. Philly.com abandoned its separate downtown offices, moving back into
the *Inquirer* building at 400 North Broad Street in 2010. Osberg promised readers a new focus on mobile news delivery and, perhaps most profound, hinted
that the days of entirely free newspaper content on the web were drawing to a
close.[93] At a speech at Temple University in late November 2010, Osberg highlighted the company's plans to launch "a media incubator inside the *Inquirer*
building, where small media companies can exist rent-free and [form] content
partnerships with universities and niche websites." But Osberg also noted, "It

would be a difficult transition. . . . [T]he papers had lost 25 percent of their readership over the past five years, and 50 percent of the advertising dollars has disappeared in those five years as well." In light of these financial difficulties, "there would likely be an online paywall established [in 2011]."[94]

Judging by speeches like that one, many changes appeared to be afoot as the primary local Philadelphia newspapers exited bankruptcy. A brief additional round of research in the winter of 2011, however, brought home the fact that (below the surface) Philadelphia's leading journalists continued to struggle to overcome legacy structures and their lack of adequate financial resources. While executives at Philly.com continued to speak gamely of external partnerships (and had, indeed, joined forces with the alternative weekly *City Paper* in a content-sharing agreement), most of the touted network partnerships remained in the planning stages or suffered from severe underdevelopment. The Philly.com web production team continued to suffer from a lack of resources and lack of integration with the rest of the organization; while producers at Philly.com had mastered the art of aggregating *Inquirer* and *Daily News* content, few members of the online staff had any input at all into coverage decisions made by the newspapers' news desks. Chief among Philly.com's accomplishments since the bankruptcy was the establishment of a breaking news coverage meeting that integrated the online staffs from Philly.com and both newspapers—a notable change, to be sure, but only a small step toward the level of integration needed to overcome the difficulties in collaboration discussed in Chapter 5. The absence of any sort of "digital-first" strategy also continued to plague the organization; while sitting in on a brief meeting at Philly.com in January 2011, I watched several web producers struggle to find a good way to migrate multistory newspaper "feature packages" onto the web. Standing in their way were such apparently banal issues as, first, trouble finding good feature artwork and, second, choosing appropriate headlines for stories that lacked descriptive titles outside the overall title of the package. What worked as a package when printed in the newspaper, in short, often made little sense when transferred to the web.[95] Discouragingly, these conversations still dominated newswork at Philly.com as late as the winter of 2011. Numerous editors and consultants I talked to spoke in despairing tones about these logistical snafus and about the absence of financial resources, problems that kept them from making the kinds of important changes they felt they needed to make to compete with emerging local competitors such as Patch.com and the reborn Journal Register Company.

These financial strains helped contribute to the most radical change at Philly.com, the *Inquirer,* and the *Daily News*: the decision to move their content behind a quasi-pay wall—a pay wall that was not really a pay wall at all. Inside the journalism world, Philly.com was not alone in its decision to charge for access to the news. The decision to take some content off the web and ask readers to pay for it—described by the news analyst Ken Doctor as the economics of "do-over"[96]—was a widespread trend at news organizations in 2010 and 2011; while the *Wall Street Journal* had charged for online access for years, metropolitan newspapers (led by the *Dallas Morning News*) and national newspapers (led by the *Times* of London and the *New York Times*) were increasingly embracing some variant of a hybrid pay-free revenue model.

The local website Phawker summarized the pay wall strategy of the post-bankruptcy Philly.com this way: "The virtual version of the print editions of both the *Inquirer* and *Daily News*—aka 'the *e-Inquirer*' and the soon-to-be unveiled '*e-Daily News*'—will go subscription, but Philly.com will not."[97] In other words, readers who want access to the content of both papers, complete with the look and feel of the print edition, will pay for an friendly e-reader, while web surfers will still be able to gain access to information for free on Philly.com. Of course, this strategy set up further logistical hurdles in coordinating the movement of content between the *Daily News*, the *Inquirer*, and the web of the kind already extensively chronicled in this book. When will a story be kept on an e-reader, and when will it become available for free? Perhaps even more profound: will anyone actually pay to gain access to journalism in Philadelphia? Will organizational investment in Philly.com decrease further? Will Philadelphia's legacy newspapers lose their place at the center of the local information ecosystem? What will partially pay-walled content do for the professional self-understanding of Philadelphia's journalists?

At the time of this writing, these questions, and many others, remain unresolved. Answering them will be among the many challenges Philadelphia news organizations face as they enter the second decade of the twenty-first century. The sale of the papers in 2012, combined with charges of political interference and concern that a new local ownership group will fundamentally alter the papers' culture of objectivity, also pose a number of questions that will be answered only in the passage of time.

Reporting and the Public in the Digital Age

In the dead of night on November 30, 2011, protesters affiliated with Occupy Philadelphia—the ideological grandchildren, perhaps, of the anti-globalization activists who stormed the Republican National Convention in 2000 with their protest banners and digital cameras—were evicted from Dilworth Plaza. Reporters with the *Philadelphia Daily News* and *Philadelphia Inquirer* were on the scene, transmitting developments to Twitter's live coverage platform Cover It Live. At the same time, the long-dormant Philly IMC had reawakened, providing a raft of participatory media coverage of the protest. Blogs and Twitter feeds sprang into action, some chronicling the midnight expulsion, and others weighing in with trenchant post-event analysis. Across the city, the networked news ecosystem pulsed with life, events translated into digital flows that raced across the Internet (see Figure C.1).

From the perspective of a decade, the two journalistic moments that open and close this book—the first citizen media coverage of the protests at the Republican National Convention and the expulsion of activists with Occupy Philadelphia—seem dramatically different. That a dramatic shift in how news coverage is provided to an always connected citizenry has taken place in ten years seems too obvious to even state. Simply look around. We live, it seems, in an information universe that is radically different from that of the year 2000. Along with the explosion of media sources and the ever faster pace of live event coverage, we have seen once powerful news institutions collapse, transform, or both. Everything, it appears, is different now. And yet the story in this book, if it can be said to have one, is a story of stasis. Or, perhaps more accurately, it is the story of a simultaneous vortex of external events and the complete lack of change of any kind. It may be time finally to apologize to my readers: there have been few moments of dramatic revolution in these pages. The story, perhaps, is more truthful: journalistic evolution as a long, slow, hard slog.

How can we reconcile these two seemingly incompatible perspectives? Everything seems different, and yet everything remains the same. Part of the explanation,

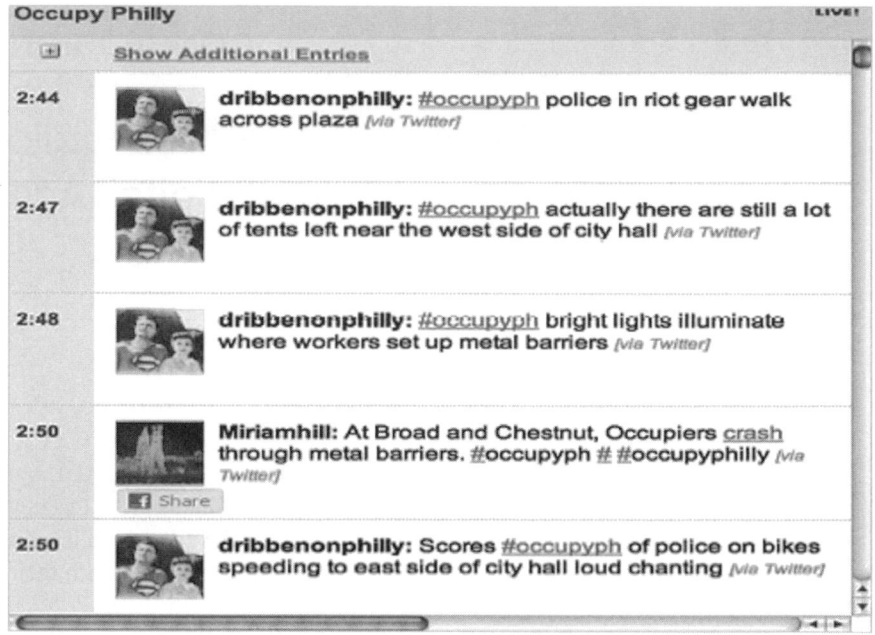

FIGURE C.1   Philly.com coverage of Occupy Philadelphia from the winter of 2012. *(Source: http://www.philly.com.)*

I argue, lies in themes that have run like red thread through this volume: the meaning of journalistic reporting, the complex nature of institutions in an era of apparently low-cost networking, and reporters' vision of "their" public under conditions of digitization.

Reporting

In the working paper "Making a Case for Open Journalism Now," Melanie Sill, an executive in residence at the University of Southern California's Annenberg School for Communication and Journalism, assembles an impressive list of open, networked journalism experiments, ranging from "digital-first" strategies at the Journal Register Corporation to the "mutualization of news" promoted by the British newspaper *The Guardian*.[1] To this impressive list of projects can be added even newer initiatives, such as the New York University–*Guardian* newspaper's "Citizens Agenda" brokered by Professor of Journalism Jay Rosen, and "Pipeline," the *Pittsburgh Post-Gazette*'s project on hydrofracking. Lists such as these will certainly continue to expand. Indeed, to read reports like Sill's is to come away with a sense of a news world in ferment and amid fundamental change.

Every time I visited Philadelphia, I arrived expecting to see the kind of brave new journalistic world reflected in Sill's report. And every time, I left disappointed. It is possible, of course, that my single-site research is an outlier, no matter how comprehensive it might be. But I do not think so. There is no reason to pick on Philadelphia; I would argue that the news ecosystem there is actually more like most emerging digital information networks than it is different. Indeed, I would even go as far as to say that, if one looks inside the larger organizational universes in which many new journalism experiments are embedded, one encounters a similar lack of revolutionary upheaval. Why? And does it matter?

For all of the fragmentation of journalism in Philadelphia, a distinct center of gravity remained, and that center was the *Inquirer* building at 400 North Broad Street. Indeed, one of the most interesting consequences of my ecosystemically oriented research was the fact that it often led me back, in the end, to the traditional media organizations I had left behind. It is hard to compare the amount of journalistic work that goes on at the *Inquirer,* the *Daily News,* and Philly.com to any other news organization in Philadelphia. Indeed, this is the very definition of a journalistic institution: a relatively stable pattern of workflows, organizational hierarchies, and technology that tends to produce a product called "news" at regular intervals and in large quantities.

In other words, the Philadelphia news ecosystem has a center; that center remained the traditional media organizations that historically have produced the news objects we call "newspapers"; and those dominant organizations were concerned with *reporting the news in a particularly traditionalist sense.* It is here that we can start to see the relationship between journalists' understanding of "reporting" as the central aspect of what they do and the slow pace of change in many media organizations. As long as the primary work task at the institutions that make up the news ecosystem remains reporting—defined conservatively as the routinized collection of evidence from traditional bureaucratic sources, packaged at a regular chronological intervals—most newswork in most places most of the time will struggle to be open and will struggle to be networked.

Is there anything that can and should be done to alter this dynamic? There are two possible alternatives. The first is for reporters to adjust their ingrained understandings of what reporting actually is and why it matters. Outside of the legacy Philadelphia media institutions I studied and even, in a fragmentary way, inside those organizations, there were a multitude of definitions and understandings of what reporting was. Aggregation, distributed reporting, computational journalism—all of these were names by which outside organizations seek to redefine the meaning of reporting in a digital age. To the degree that reporters begin to internalize these new concepts, the central tasks of news institutions will inevitably change.

This type of cultural evolution in a profession does not happen simply through working papers, seminars, and speeches, however. Indeed, another interesting research finding—and the type of insight that only long-term ethnographic research can provide—was the degree to which executives, editors, and reporters in Philadelphia were capable of talking about transformation and reinvention in their off-hours, in blog-post–type think pieces, and when they sat on "future of news" panels at conferences. When the panel was over, however, and the curtain came down, these reporters, editors, and executives usually returned to their newsrooms and did exactly what they had been doing before the speech began. My informants were not being disingenuous. It is simply that the gulf between the abstract understanding of what journalism must do to reinvent itself and the daily work of having a job in a newsroom is a wide one. In short, traditional news institutions remain far more central to the operation of a well-functioning news ecosystem than many digital media theorists might like to admit. They also, however, remain far less open to fundamental change than many optimistic industry analysts hope. Given the crisis inside the U.S. news industry, these conclusions are not reassuring.

Does any of this actually matter? Isn't change inevitable? If journalistic evolution is occurring in fits and starts, and if a number of exciting experiments *are* already under way, is it not possible that organizational evolution will inexorably create the kind of networked, open, collaborative news environment that many argue is essential for journalism in the twenty-first century? Possibly. Another alternative, however, is that the journalism industry will continue its current trajectory of fragmentation, in which a plethora of dynamic, temporary, widely publicized new media experiments will command a great deal of attention from commentators who specialize in punditry about the future of journalism as the vast bulk of the newsmaking machinery grinds on into oblivion. Whether this outcome is good, bad, or neither depends crucially on two other issues also discussed at length in this book: the nature and purpose of journalistic institutions and journalists' vision of the public.

Institutions

The dominant feature of newswork in the digital age is its increasing precariousness, a situation that is summed up in Chapter 6 with a quote from a former *Philadelphia Daily News* photographer: "My old medium is dying, and my new one doesn't pay." The organizational equivalent of this precariousness is institutional fragility, which can be attributed to the pulverized condition of traditional news institutions; the ad hoc, deinstitutionalized nature of many of the newer media organizations; and increasing organizational demands for content from fewer rationally managed or compensated workers. The conclusion to Chapter 6 discusses some of the ways that news institutions were attempting to rationalize news production by using web metrics and through other management strategies. The seeming irrationality of many traditional media institutions, combined with their increasingly fragile economic state, has led many theorists to advocate for a third form of journalistic organization that goes beyond traditional institutional forms. Much of this work, drawing on the work of the legal theorist Yochai Benkler, sees networked partnerships as they key to journalism's future.[2] Paradoxically, however, my research has shown that successful networked news ecosystems often depend on the presence of strong institutions dedicated to building networks. What is more, while the discussion of journalistic institutions is often dominated by a perspective that emphasizes the role played by falling information costs in the success of networked news projects, the empirical problems posed by the emerged networked news environment go far beyond these legal-economic perspectives.

I argue in Chapter 5 that news networks failed to emerge in Philadelphia between 2005 and 2010 because the local ecosystem lacked the *institutions* that could make *networks* possible. Instead, journalistic institutions remained dedicated to a particularly traditionalist form of reporting over and above all else. The point is even clearer when we see the outcome of the Philadelphia Enterprise Reporting project; ultimately, traditional institutions, such as local foundations, stepped up to the plate to turn networked collaboration into a reality. There is a hint of paradox here. For networked news to be possible, traditional institutions dedicated to collaborative production must *also* exist. News networks do not appear out of nowhere, emerging from a digital swamp of news ecosystems *in potentia*. Networks need dedicated institutions to help build them. In Philadelphia, there were no such institutions—at least, not during the initial phase of my research. That changed in 2010 with the launch of the Enterprise Reporting Awards. Until 2010, dominant institutions such as WHYY and Philadelphia Media Holdings remained dedicated to reporting the news in mostly traditional ways. Local foundations had not yet begun to invest in news production. And the organizations that seemed most interested in collaborative production (such as the Philly IMC and Philly Future) were weak outliers that lacked the long-term stability and cultural clout to bring about change.

Institutions, moreover, do more than simply manage resources and rationalize the behavior of recalcitrant members; their success or failure is more than simple a question of falling (or rising) "information costs." As Daniel Kreiss has argued in his work on the presidential campaigns of Howard Dean and Barack Obama, "Much of the information costs literature [on networked politics] has the wrong object of analysis in view. A singular focus on the informational affordances of digital technologies leads scholars to pose a very narrow set of questions of networked politics."[3] The same argument might be made about the world of networked journalism; the questions that have plagued the news organizations studied in this book include, but cannot be limited to, arguments about transaction costs. The scholars of informational costs have provided us with valuable insights about the changing roles of organizations, networks, and institutions in the digital age, but their questions are not the only ones, and their answers do not exhaust the scope of possible insights we might wish to gain.

In this book, a rational appraisal of transaction costs might have led organizational leaders to embrace more networked forms of journalistic work. Why report on every political development at City Hall when you can simply form a partnership with a local freelance journalist or media organization who can supplement that coverage? Why cover every development in Philadelphia sports when you can simply link to local sports blogs? On the one hand, the conservatism of institutional structure led organizations to neglect these and other seemingly rational options. Yet institutions played other roles in Philadelphia that went beyond simply blocking "rational" change. Institutions may provide their members with alternative forms of work-oriented rationality, and forms of purpose-oriented behavior that do not map easily onto the notion of transaction costs. The ability to manage both *news space* and *news time* through the place-based assemblage of actors was certainly emphasized by my Philadelphia informants, as shown in Chapters 3 and 4. And as described in Chapter 6, news institutions led their members to orient themselves toward value-centered notions of rationality, feelings of "purpose" and "belonging" that helped buffer against the effects of a purely market-oriented attitude toward journalistic work.[4] News institutions helped their members discover meaning and purpose to their working lives. Indeed, by 2008, feelings of precarity and institutional fragility, along with an increasingly market-oriented attitude toward newswork, were creating a corps of deeply disillusioned journalists in Philadelphia.

Institutions, in short, do not simply block innovative change—although that is certainly one of the things that they do. They also, paradoxically, enable change by directing fixed organizational resources toward innovative strategies. Moreover, it is wrong to think of institutions in terms of purely "ends-means" rationality.[5] To do so is to reduce organizations to monodimensional caricatures and thus to place the blame for "lack of change" in the news industry solely on the backs of misguided traditionalists.

The Public

What, finally, about the public? How has that vitally important concept figured in the shifting imaginary of twenty-first-century journalism? Over the course of this book, I have shown how journalists' visions of their public have played a key role in how they have understood their work, their profession, and their relationship to democracy. In Part I, traditional news reporters struggled to manage their understanding of their public during the digital transition; most often, they imagined that the news public could be transported, tout court, online. Alternative media makers, by contrast, articulated different understandings of what the public was online. In Part II, we began to see the emerging tensions in traditional journalists' understanding of the homogeneous public. In Part III, finally, journalists came face to face with their "actual" public as mediated through web metrics and an increasing understanding of the public as a fragmentary audience. In every case, confusion about the meaning of "the public" in the digital age blocked journalists from clearly considering alternatives to their existing organizational arrangements.

Scholarly interest in the relationship between journalism and the public has been long-standing, of course. In particular, concern with the public was a major topic of interest for theorists affiliated with the civic journalism movement.[6] For those scholars, a key normative dilemma lay in the fact that journalism had "abandoned" the public and was focusing its attention on the concerns of elites and political insiders. The argument of this book is slightly different. Rather than forgetting the public, the journalists I spoke to over the course of my research had a deep commitment to it; this commitment, however, was seen as eternal and timeless when in actuality it was provisional and historically contingent. My argument, in other words, is empirical rather than normative. Journalists' particular conception of the public as an aggregate, unified entity was rendered problematic by the Internet. Because Philadelphia journalism had not yet visualized an alternative conception of what the local public looked like, it remained locked in place and unable to change. As James Carey summarized in 1997:

> Insofar as journalism is grounded, it is grounded in the public. Insofar as journalism has a client, the client is the public. The press justifies itself in the name of the public; it exists—or so it is regularly said—to inform the public, to serve as the extended eyes and ears, to protect the public's right to know, to serve the public interest. The canons of journalism originate in and flow from the relationship of the press to public. The public is totem and talisman, and object of ritual homage.[7]

This invocation of the public is the bulwark on which a wide variety of journalists of all ideological and organizational stripes base their authority-making claims. I have documented Philly IMC's claims to represent the public through open publishing and universal access; Philly.com's notion that it represented "anything and everything Philly," even in the face of contradictory demographic evidence, and the desire, expressed over and over again, for Philly.com to be "the center" of the news network, to be "the one place everyone has to go on when they want to learn about this city"; Philly Future's desire to embody the public conversation of Philadelphia through a single website; and so on. The claim to embody the city of Philadelphia through reporting acted as the "totem and talisman, and object of ritual homage" for an array of media makers in Philadelphia.

As should be clear from the previous pages, the Internet has deeply problematized local journalism's vision of its public. While the philosophical status of the public sphere has long groaned under the weight of attacks from intellectuals and sociologists (there is no public sphere, it has long been argued; there are only "public sphericules," "sub-altern counter publics," "issue-publics," and so on)[8], only recently have journalists and journalistic institutions come face to face with the *materiality* of the public's uncapturability. Online, all publics appear fragmentary. There is always an element of the public that cannot be networked. There is always a fraction of this uncaptured public only a mouse click away. This is not just another argument about online polarization and fragmentation; it is not even an argument that mass, web-based aggregation is impossible. It is not a technologically deterministic argument; it makes no claims about the *actual* nature of the public and the impact of technology on that public. It is simply a contention that, insofar as journalistic authority rests on its claim to give the public flesh, such a claim is no longer tenable—if it ever was. Insofar as local journalism's image of the public is grounded in a vision that sees the public as a unitary, structural, or even interlocking entity that journalists can either confidently speak to or call into being, the authority of journalism has become deeply problematic.

According to the most hopeful advocates of networked journalism, the future of journalism—as a functioning business enterprise and as an occupation that possesses cultural authority—lies in deinstitutionalization, disaggregation, porousness, linking out, and collaboration. If various media workers and news organizations can actively work together, the theory goes, journalistic functions once housed in institutions can be dispersed outward. This book has demonstrated the very real difficulties inherent in collaborative solutions. It is ironic: newsworkers and journalism institutions are more entangled in local media ecosystems than ever before, as the various examples throughout this book have shown, but this entanglement is not the result of any deliberate collaborative strategy. Indeed, the mixing and mingling of various types of newsworkers and media organizations seems to have led to deliberate strategies of misrecognition and the erection of even higher rhetorical walls.

Bound by the demands of medium and time, this research is, in the end, only a snapshot of a particularly tumultuous moment in the history of news. Over the course of its writing, it became clear to me that this book was much a history as it was the story of online journalism in the early years of the twenty-first century. Perhaps this is the fate of all of us who hope to write about digital culture. The speed of that culture turns ethnographies into histories.

Despite all of the surface transformations in digital journalism, however, I hope that I have uncovered some of the deep structural questions that confront this journalism as it moves, pell-mell, into the future. As the news industry and the journalism profession begin to settle on new business and editorial models for the Internet age, they should not forget the deeper dilemmas brought to light in the early years of digital news. What kind of work constitutes legitimate journalism? Toward what kind of public does journalism direct its knowledge claims? And what role should stable, traditional institutions play in the new digital ecosystem? These are the questions I have tried to ask in these pages. For all the traumas of the past fifteen years—the jobs lost, the certainties shattered, the local news left unreported—metropolitan journalism has been given the chance to rethink many of its old practices and beliefs. Ultimately, scholars and pundits will not determine the course of digital journalism. Local reporters, editors, foundation heads, hackers, regulators, and media activists will. Given all of the pain journalism has experienced in the past decade and a half, it would be a shame to waste this moment.

Methodology

W e stand, I think, at the threshold of a second golden age in news ethnography.[1] Recently published work and additional research in various stages of production provide happy evidence of the fact that scholars are rising to the challenge posed by the empirical changes in the journalistic field over the past decade and a half.[2] There are many ways to understand the transformation of journalism being spurred on by the emergence of digital technology and transforming economic models of content production—content analysis, large-scale data collection and quantitative analysis, surveys, social network analysis, and critical theory. Ethnographic research is reassuming its pride of place on the list.

Ironically, however, just as ethnographic research is re-emerging as a preferred method for studying newsrooms, the walls of those newsrooms, both physical and literal, are shifting dramatically. The same developments that make newsrooms promising sites of fieldwork—the key role played by boundary-spanning devices and information flows, the professional challenges posed to traditional journalists by amateur bloggers and new news startups, and an economic crisis in journalistic business models that is driving more and more newswork outside formal organizations—make them problematic sites of fieldwork. In short, the classic "newsrooms" of Herbert Gans, Gaye Tuchman, and others cannot serve as our only model for fieldwork in a world in which our informants are daily contesting the very definition of journalism.[3]

In this Appendix, I suggest a model of research that not only holds on to what is valuable in most newsroom fieldwork but also opens both newsrooms and our imaginations to the larger journalistic "ecosystem" that is coalescing outside newsroom walls. It should be clear that I do not want to suggest that the newsroom has no role in contemporary journalistic production. Indeed, this book actually concludes the opposite: the newsroom's role remains central. However, we can no longer take its primacy for granted. The status of the traditional institutional newsroom must be continually problematized. I attempt that problematization in the pages that follow by drawing on a methodology of "networks," in two senses. First, I discuss my application of Philip N. Howard's notions of the "network ethnography" to the world of journalism and to the mapping of journalistic ecosystems.[4] Second, I discuss the many ways actor-network theory can help us follow journalistic "actants"—stories, facts, links, employees, technologies, work routines—across this suddenly wide-open communicative space. I conclude with a specific overview of the research found in this book.

Blowing Up the Newsroom:
From the News Desk to the News Ecosystem

Although the most influential micro-level accounts of journalistic behavior inside the newsroom were published within years of each other in the late 1970s and early 1980s, early examinations of "social control" in the newsroom were conducted as early as the mid-1950s and grew out of communications research on small-scale, location-specific subject interactions influenced by the so-called Chicago School.[5] Unlike David Manning White's psychologically grounded research on news gatekeeping, Warren Breed based his arguments about journalistic behavior on participant observation of the newsroom and imported his theoretical premises from the sociological literature on organizations and occupations.[6] While White's line of analysis would ultimately connect highly individual, possibly even idiosyncratic, opinions about news with large-scale political and ideological forces, Breed pitched his analytical tent in the newsroom itself. It was in the newsroom and, more important, from *within* the newsroom, according to Breed, that the forces that determined the production of news emerged and played themselves out. "While [Breed's analysis] suggested that journalists direct rewards and motivations toward colleagues rather than readers," Barbie Zelizer argues, "it also portrayed journalists acting only according to normative behavior and existing in a world populated exclusively by other journalists."[7] In the major ethnographic studies published in the 1970s, many of Breed's theoretical foci, original contributions, and blind spots would repeat themselves.

Today, the term "ethnography" is often applied as a generic label to a variety of qualitative methods. Originally, however, ethnography referred to a specific practice of participant observation originally pioneered by anthropological fieldworkers and usually conducted in non-Western areas after a period of deep cultural immersion.[8] "Ethnographers take a detailed look at what is going on in a social setting," notes one helpful online guide to the method. "A central aspect of ethnography is that it is interested in participants' perspectives.[9]

Zelizer has used the term "newsroom ethnography," in contrast to "qualitative fieldwork" and "participant observation," to describe the ethnomethodological studies carried out by Gans, Tuchman, and Mark Fishman in the late 1970s. Dividing her overview of the journalism studies literature into sociological, historical, linguistic, political, and cultural lenses, Zelizer further subdivides the sociological study of news into three periods, with ethnographic study occupying the middle period, preceded by the emergence of "journalists as sociological beings" and followed by the analysis of the institutions and ideology of journalism. These ethnographers, notes Zelizer, engaged in participant observation, examined newsrooms in large urban centers, used organizations to examine the relationships that determined journalistic praxis, and shared "one focal point of analysis—usually the newsroom—frozen in order to flesh out the practices by which it was inhabited."[10] The work of the late 1970s demonstrated the importance of news routines in determining journalistic behavior, the link between sources and journalists, the relevance of ideology, and the tight relationship between parallel bureaucratic structures in news organizations and the government. The ethnographies provided a detailed, empirically grounded corrective to sweeping theories about the media that usually operated without reference to actual processes of news production. By focusing scholarship on the point of production, moreover, ethnographers laid the early groundwork for a research alternative to media-consumption theories prevalent in the 1980s and 1990s.

Simon Cottle also provides a historical overview of the "ethnographic period" of journalism studies, outlining its strengths and weaknesses.[11] Ethnography makes the invisible visible, he argues, giving non-researchers access to the normally hidden, professionally bounded worlds of journalistic production. It "counters the problem of inference," correcting speculative generalizations (usually based almost entirely on content analysis) about the motivations behind the production of individual news items. It insists on the triangulation of empirical data, if possible, and consequently qualifies overly broad theoretical claims.[12] "This anthropological approach . . . has won important insights into the nature of news, its informing practices and culture," Cottle writes. "Participant observation, perhaps more than most other methods is destined to be reflexive, open to the contingencies of the field experience and therefore less than strictly linear in its execution or predictable in its findings."[13]

Nevertheless problems with the traditional ethnographic approach to the study of news production become increasingly apparent as we widen our analytical lens. Integrating these micro-studies of journalistic behavior into the standard approaches to the sociology of news production, first typologized in 1989 by Michael Schudson, points toward one particular difficulty. Schudson argues that there are four distinct approaches to explaining how news is produced: political, economic, social-organizational, and cultural. The newsroom ethnography would seem to fall into the category of social-organizational approaches—although, interestingly, the phrase is never used in any of the multiple versions of Schudson's important article. Instead, Schudson argues that scholars have paid the most attention to relationships between sources and reporters. In other words, they have focused on the gathering of news rather than on editor-reporter relations.[14] The problem of how "sources" (external, apparently non-journalistic actors connected to "the newsroom" primarily through the symbolic umbilical cord of a reporter's notes) can be analyzed through the newsroom ethnography already draws attention to the deeper question of how, given that news is a "manufactured good," one can analyze the place of non intraorganizational factors in that manufacturing process. Are sources equivalent to iron ore in a steel plant? How do reporter-source relations embed themselves within the physical newsroom? Ironically, the overwhelming tendency of most early media sociologists to emphasize the *manufactured* nature of the news tended to diminish the attention paid to the raw materials involved in that manufacture and increased the focus on the process of manufacturing itself.[15]

Perhaps more important, Cottle has noted that the digitization of news content and the rapid creation of an "interpenetrating communications environment" means that the production of news no longer occurs at single central site. Instead, it "has become increasingly dispersed across multiple sites, different platforms, and can be contributed to by journalists based in different locations around the world. This clearly poses challenges for today's ethnographer." Echoing comments made above, however, Cottle argues that news production has always been a networked activity "in the sense of being plugged into incoming sources of news, engaging in relations of mutual benefit with competitor colleagues, and monitoring avidly the wider outpouring if news from different news outlets."[16] The obvious solution to the problems posed by digitization, Cottle argues, is to conduct a multisite ethnography. I return to this notion of the multisite ethnography, as well as to some of the logistical difficulties posed by such an endeavor, below.

Zelizer summarizes the general scholarly consensus regarding the ethnographic approach to the study of news production:

> The ethnographies set in place certain—by now—overused frames for thinking about journalistic practice. Perhaps nowhere is this as evident as in the lingering currency of "the newsroom" as a metaphor for journalistic practice, a currency largely due to the studies that used newsrooms as stand-ins for the broader picture of journalism. While emphasis on the newsroom as a research setting made sense for ethnographers, it has since been generalized far beyond its relevance to news making. Few, if any, news organizations operate with the same degree of dependence on "classic" newsrooms that they displayed in earlier decades, and decisions taken at a far more diverse set of venues—in the field, internet or telephone exchanges, social gatherings, publishing conventions—should not be left out of the picture. In so privileging certain settings over others, what counts as evidence has here been narrowed.[17]

In other words, as news production decentralizes, traditional methods of exploring the behavior of journalists "at work" grow ever more problematic. This is not an argument that examining journalists at work is methodologically meaningless; rather, it merely points out that the question of where journalistic work occurs is a difficult one. If this has always been true for journalism, it is now doubly so, as the Internet and assorted types of digital technology flatten and disperse the (post)modern work space. To overcome these difficulties, Howard argues that two strands of research— the traditional, ethnography and social network analysis—can, be combined as a *network ethnography* to analyze online "communities of practice."[18] Howard's research was on the e-politics community, but his methods can be adapted to examine new forms of journalistic production.

Ethnographic analysis has long been part of the repertoire of communications research. Social-network analysis, however, may be less familiar. Social-network analysis "is the mapping and measuring of relationships and flows between people, groups, organizations, animals, computers or other information/knowledge processing entities. The nodes in the network are the people and groups while the links show relationships or flows between the nodes. [Social-network analysis] provides both a visual and a mathematical analysis of human relationships."[19] Social-network analysis ignores the traditional sociological focus on self-defined, close-knit groups and concentrates instead on links—on a node's "centrality," a network's periphery, "bridges," "clusters," "connectors," and so on. Often, the strongest ties of various network nodes span boundaries between apparently separate groups; in Howard's study of the e-politics community, for instance, a strong link emerges between political consultants and open-source technology activists, a connection that might have been ignored through an exclusive focus on one group or the other.

At the same time, Howard criticizes the "un-grounded" nature of social-network analysis. While almost no researcher using social-network analysis adopts it as his or her only methodological tool, the fairly unsystematic follow-up interviews or questionnaires submitted to key network nodes often fail to provide the kind of deep, rich empirical detail provided by ethnographic study. For this reason, Howard advocates the use of the "network ethnography" to analyze the new hypermedia organization. The network ethnography uses ethnographic field methods to analyze field sites chosen via social-network analysis. "Active or passive observation," writes Howard, "extended immersion, or in-depth interviews are conducted at multiple sites or with interesting subgroups that have been purposively sampled after comparison through social network analysis."[20]

In conducting a network ethnography, Howard concludes, the meaning of "field sites" is expanded; the researcher gains new tools through which to manage sample bias; and initial ethnographic work can improve the construction of social-network analysis, which then "loops back" on further ethnographic work. While Howard's method would need to be altered somewhat to examine the twenty-first-century networked newsroom—which continues to be geographically centered in a way that many other hypermedia organizations are not—his paper can serve as a series of rough guidelines to help facilitate the study of journalistic work in a local news community.

Visualizing the Emerging News Ecosystem

In *Rebuilding the News,* my goal has been to determine how the production routines of journalism, the organizational structure of journalism, and the authority of journalism changed under the impact of economic crises and digital newsgathering techniques. All three of these rather disparate interests were united in a focus on the actualities of newswork and the day-to-day practices by which journalistic identity was affirmed. To investigate these questions, my research methodology first and foremost was ethnographic, and the study summarized in these pages is based on long-term participant observation in Philadelphia. In that vein, I spent three years engaged in the qualitative research of news in Philadelphia, with a period of extensive ethnographic immersion in March–August 2008. In that time, I conducted more than sixty semi-structured interviews with journalists, editors, activists, bloggers, and media executives and more than three hundred hours of participant observation. This immersive period was marked by a further period of follow-up research and secondary site visits that lasted from the fall of 2008 until 2010. The interviews and ethnographic notes were then coded manually, following the general model of "grounded theory," with early observations used to determine initial categories, then iteratively revised after several cycles of additional fieldwork and coding.

One major difference between *Rebuilding the News* and earlier sociology of news studies is that it marks the first in-depth ethnographic study of an entire local news ecosystem, as opposed to a few key, usually traditional and large-scale journalistic institutions. Since the cultural, economic, and technological challenges to journalism were both extra- and intra-institutional, I resolved early on that I could not simply study the *Philadelphia Inquirer* or Philly.com. I wanted to study the entire news system—what I called the Philadelphia blogosphere when I began the study and now refer to as the Philadelphia news ecosystem. An important aspect in this process of studying the Philadelphia news ecosystem (as opposed to the institutions within it) was the adoption of the network ethnography as a methodological perspective. In other words, I used quantitative social-network mapping to help me initially draw the boundaries of my study—boundaries that were nevertheless permeable enough to be supplemented by more traditional procedures of ethnographic analysis.

A key step in formulating my network ethnography of Philadelphia journalism was this the creation of social-network maps of the online Philadelphia media sphere, which themselves drew on data compiled through both IssueCrawler and Morningside Analytics. The methods of Morningside Analytics "draw on social network analysis . . . to uncover Attentive Clusters—communities, large or small—that share knowledge and focus attention on particular sources of information and opinion."[21] IssueCrawler, a project of Govcom, a foundation based in Amsterdam that is "dedicated to . . . mapping issue networks on the Web," is web network location software that consists of a crawler, a co-link analysis engine, and three visualization modules.[22] It is server-side software that crawls specified sites, captures the outlinks from the specified sites, performs co-link analysis on the outlinks, returns densely interlinked networks, and visualizes them in circle, cluster and geographical maps."[23] Both of these maps of the Philadelphia blogosphere gave me clues regarding the local news networks' "central nodes," periphery, "bridges," "clusters," and "connectors," to quote Howard.[24] The maps gave me a very early, very rough sense of which newsrooms I should observe, which bloggers I should interview, and so on.

It is important to note, at this point, that these network maps functioned as only a general guide and starting point for my research. To avoid the kind of schematization and structuring that would result from overdependence on social-network analysis, I wanted to focus not only on the actors and institutions in the Philadelphia media ecosystem but also on how these actors interacted and networked across that ecosystem. In that vein, I turn to a second "theory of networks"—one that was more focused on action and assemblage than on structural mapping.

Journalism as Assemblage, or
What It Means to Rebuild the News

The methodological skeleton of this book also intersects with a basic theoretical argument: the work of journalism on an organizational, institutional, and normative level can usefully be thought of as the *work of assemblage.*[25] Journalism, in other words, can be envisioned and described as the continuous process of networking the news. This notion of journalism as assemblage guides the methodology of my research, the concepts used to organize the narrative, and the general structure of the book itself. It also distinguishes the book conceptually from other approaches to studying news, among them organizational approaches and field approaches, both of which have been among the dominant frameworks for studying news production. Finally, within this operating framework, news can be seen as networked either well or badly, concepts that carry within them an implicit normative judgment about how journalism ought to function in a democracy. In journalism studies, this assemblage perspective is only now beginning to take on aspects of an actual theoretical frame—encouraged, in part, by two decades of remarkably productive work in science and technology studies. Within science and technology studies., the variant of the assemblage theory I adopt here is also known as actor-network theory.

Having originated in the 1980s as an insurgent movement within the sociology of science, the actor-network theory of Bruno Latour, Michael Callon, and John Law makes several noteworthy claims. First, it argues that social categories (science, journalism, or anything else) should not be approached as obdurate macro-structures; rather, they should be seen as the contingent assemblage of networks. Through this theoretical lens, journalism is thought of less as a finished product than as a continual process of assemblage. Second, actor-network theory emphasizes the radical heterogeneity of both humans and non-humans in the makeup of these social assemblages; this argument—that "objects have agency"—is perhaps the best-known feature of actor-network theory. Drawing on this perspective, this book treats all social and technological objects as potential news objects. Finally, actor-network theory contends that the creation of "social solidity" must been seen as a process of "black boxing," the "weaving together human and non-human actors into relatively stable network nodes, or 'black boxes.'"[26] As Law argues about science:

> "[Scientific] knowledge" then, is embodied in a variety of material forms. But where does it come from? The actor-network answer is that it is the end product of a lot of hard work in which heterogeneous bits and pieces—test tubes, reagents, organisms, skilled hands, scanning electron microscopes, radiation monitors, other scientists, articles, computer terminals, and all the rest—that would like to make off on their own are juxtaposed into a patterned network which overcomes their resistance. In short, it is a material matter but also a matter of organizing and ordering those materials.

Modifying Law's concluding statement about science, we can see how this book applies assemblage theory to journalism:

> So this is the actor-network diagnosis of ~~science~~ journalism: that it is a process of "heterogeneous engineering" in which bits and pieces from the social, the technical, the conceptual, and the textual are fitted together, and so converted (or "translated") into a set of equally heterogeneous ~~scientific~~ journalistic products.[27]

Applications of assemblage and actor-network theory to non-science domains are increasingly coming from the fields of political communication and media sociology. In a pair of remarkably creative works, Daniel Kreiss and Rasmus Kleis Nielsen have analyzed the machinery of the modern political campaign as a socio-technical assemblage leveraging both "networked social relationships" and "mundane tools."[28] Andrew Chadwick has extended these arguments in his analysis of political information systems.[29] Journalism researchers have also begun to use an actor-network approach in their analyses of the manner by which journalists and journalistic *technology* construct news facts and news actors over the course of their daily work routines. Emma Hemmingway's groundbreaking ethnographic research analyzes the processes of video news production in a single regional newsroom of the BBC, using actor-network theory as both a theoretical resource and a methodological guide.[30]

David Domingo, Amy Schmitz Weiss, Pablo Boczkowski, and Fred Turner have likewise taken an assemblage-oriented approach to their analysis news production, although in different ways and with different emphases.[31] My research builds on this earlier scholarship while sharpening the methodological, organizational, and normative implications of an assemblage theory of journalism.

This notion of journalism as assemblage guides the methodology of this volume insofar as it encourages an ecosystemic analysis of journalism in Philadelphia. In other words, because *Rebuilding the News* takes the cross-institutional processes of journalistic assemblage seriously and because it was written in a moment in which the actual structure of the journalistic field was so underdetermined, its analytical lens goes beyond the work practices and journalistic outputs of stable, long-existing news institutions like the *Philadelphia Inquirer* and the *Philadelphia Daily News*. It also details the institutional histories and work practices of neighborhood blogs, radical "citizen media" organizations, local foundations, and other participants in the metropolitan news network. It analyzes how these heterogeneous organizations work together (or fail to do so), diffuse different patterns of innovation, and "network the news" in Philadelphia. An ecosystemic analysis studies how different people and groups interact across the boundaries of the wider local news network. Understanding journalism as assemblage also provides insight into the major concepts—news objects, news networks, and newswork—that populate this book. Law's analysis of all social production (including journalism) as a heterogeneous but patterned network of objects is echoed in Graham Harman's description of the flat ontology of actor-network theory:

> The world is made up of actors or actants (which I also call "objects"). Atoms and molecules are actants, as are children, raindrops, bullet trains, politicians, and numerals. All entities are on exactly the same ontological footing. An atom is no more real than Deutsche Bank or the 1976 Winter Olympics, even if one is likely to endure much longer than the others.[32]

When this book discusses news objects, it means them in precisely this way: as material things—documents, links, websites, blogs, interviews, reader metric reports, stories, tweets, Facebook pages, and news organizations—that may all be potentially networked together into larger assemblages. Newswork refers to this process of assembling (and not assembling) particular objects. None of these concepts—news objects, newswork, and news networks—is new, of course. Ethnographers of news have been discussing the laborious work of journalism for decades, even though they have not used the terms "actants" and "assemblage," and field theorists and news institutionalists have contributed remarkable insights into the structure of and relationship between different news organizations. Rather than a radical new theory providing unheard-of insight into journalistic processes, my use of assemblage concepts in this volume indicates a certain degree of empirical emphasis and an affinity with other, similar emphases in political communication, science and technology studies, and organizational theory.

The link between organizational theory—the study of how institutions grow, succeed, and fail—and notions of the actor-network mark the third use of assemblage theory in this book. Drawing on the neo-institutionalism of Paul DiMaggio and Walter Powell and the actor-network concepts of Latour, Callon, Law, and others,[33] this book looks at how actors assemble the daily news but also how they assemble news organizations. This is the link between the book's focus on the work of journalism (in Part II) and the work of building news organizations (in Part III). It is one of the arguments of the volume that there is no difference—at least, in the first instance—between assembling the news and assembling the organizations that produce the news. There actually are substantive differences, of course. But these differences should not be assumed as an analytical starting point inasmuch as both processes are driven fundamentally by the weaving together of diverse and often recalcitrant human and non-human materials, and both processes rely heavily on what actor-network theorists call punctualization or black boxing. These punctualizations—"network packages, routines, that can . . . be more or less taken for granted in the process of heterogeneous engineering"[34]—encompass news routines, as well as explicit managerial agreements for partnerships between different local journalism organizations. One hinge between the shop floor–level assemblages discussed in Part II and the managerial-level assemblage of Part III was the *hyperlink,* a complex socio-technical artifact that mediates both work routines and institutions' understanding of their relationship with other institutions.

Finally, within this larger framework of "networked news," news can be judged as networked well or networked badly, and these judgments carry within them an implicit normative argument about how journalism ought to function vis-à-vis the democratic public. The key point is this: empirical evidence presented in this book shows that journalists imagine that they assemble in a particular way not only the news but also, through their assemblage of the news, the *public.* The cultural imaginary of journalism, in other words, draws heavily on a particular vision of the public that is constituted and informed in the act of reporting itself. Journalism, in short, *makes things public* and possesses a particular internal occupational narrative about how it does so. In the past decade and a half, this occupational self-conception has been disrupted. How journalism as a profession dedicated to serving the public has dealt with this disruption has been one of the major narrative threads of this book.

The Research

To conclude, I will outline in a little more detail the process by which the theories and methods described above were applied in actual research. Remember the three questions that animated this project from the beginning:

- How is the work of journalism changing?
- How is journalistic collaboration changing?
- How is the authority of journalism being reimagined?

These questions ultimately guided the research method adopted here.

Throughout the 2000s, I conducted a hybrid mix of participant observation and full-fledged participation in various independent media projects around the country, particularly in New York. My affiliation with the New York City Independent Media Center in 2001–2008 gave me a very early sense of how the media ecosystem was changing, how citizens were (and were not) involving themselves in the news process, and how important it was to consider a multitude of institutional actors when thinking about news in the twenty-first century. At the same time, however, I wanted to study local, urban news, and it always seemed to me that New York City was a particularly bad place to conduct such research. New York is a city, for sure, with some of the greatest newspapers in the world, but the line between local and global news is hard to draw in the media capital of the world. Philadelphia struck me as a far more representative example of how news practices were changing in the early twenty-first century. My complex involvement with the New York IMC also rendered it a problematic site for scholarly research.

In 2005, I began to reach out to independent media makers and journalists in Philadelphia, particularly those affiliated with the IMC there. That connection led me to former IMC volunteers who had gone on to other types of newswork, as well as to various city bloggers. Perhaps the most important contacts I made in these early days were with Karl Martino of Philly Future and Susan Philips of WHYY, a former IMC volunteer. My big break came in the spring of 2006, when I was invited to attend the Norgs conference discussed in Chapter 5. It was there that I made nearly all of my key contacts and met many of Philadelphia's most important journalistic actors. Also in March 2006, I obtained initial permission from Wendy Warren, then of the *Philadelphia Daily News,* to observe the *Daily News* newsroom.

About this time, I began to systematize my ecosystemic approach to ethnographic analysis, working with John Kelly of Morningside Analytics to construct a network of the Philadelphia media ecosystem. This map, when combined with my deliberately catholic approach of following the journalistic actors across the media ecosystem, was of great assistance when I finally arrived in the Philadelphia newsrooms for a spring and summer of fieldwork in 2008. The quantitative picture of journalism in Philadelphia helped me structure the research I did outside the traditional newsrooms and yet would have been worthless without a more qualitative, snowball sample–based approach. In addition, Wendy Warren moved to Philly.com from the *Daily News* between 2006 and 2008, which provided additional ethnographic access. As I note above, my time inside and outside the Philadelphia newsrooms resulted in more than three hundred hours of participant observation and more than sixty interviews. From the fall of 2008 until the winter of 2011, I conducted a number of follow-up visits, returning to my field site to observe important events as well as simply to keep tabs on the various changes that were (and were not) occurring in the city. More recently, I have been able to present my findings to my informants in a variety of public and private venues, and this triangulation has served me well in gaining a more nuanced understanding of journalistic change and stasis in Philadelphia. Finally, I made extensive use of the "Wayback Machine" at the Internet Archive (www.archive.org) to gain information about the history of the different digital organizations I was studying. In all cases, this historical research was supplemented by interviews with founders of and participants in key sites.

While this research cannot be generalized (generalizability ultimately is not the goal of ethnographic research), I hope its unique approach and ecosystemic focus have uncovered enough interesting material and have raised enough interesting questions that the findings can serve as a provocation for other quantitative and qualitative scholars to conduct similar research. The transformation of digital journalism obviously has just begun. Only further study will help us glimpse the contours of the new news ecosystem.

Notes

INTRODUCTION

1. Dennis Roddy, "Police, Protesters Battle in the Streets," *Pittsburgh Post-Gazette,* August 2, 2000.

2. Norgs Working Group, "The Norgs Unconference Statement of Principles," *Norgs—the New News Organization Wiki,* May 9, 2007, available at http://norgs.pbwiki.com/The+Norgs+Unconference+Statement+Of+Principles.

3. William Densmore, Media Giraffe Teleconference, University of Massachusetts, Amherst, 2006, available at www.mediagiraffe.org/wiki/index.php/Mgp2006-video (accessed January 11, 2010).

4. Joey Sweeney, "Breaking: Worst Monday Ever at Broad and Whatever as Philly Newspapers File Chapter 11," Philebrity, February 22, 2009, available at http://www.philebrity.com/2009/02/22/breaking-worst-monday-ever-at-broad-whatever (accessed February 10, 2009).

5. Christopher Wink, "BarCamp NewsInnovation 2.0: My Take Aways and Experience," May 5, 2010, available at http://christopherwink.com/2010/05/05/barcamp-news innovation-2-0-my-take-aways-and-experience (accessed May 5, 2010).

6. Jan Schaffer, "Exploring a Networked Journalism Collaborative in Philadelphia," JLab.org, April 2010, available at http://www.j-lab.org/publications/philadelphia_media _project (accessed April 11, 2010).

7. Philip N. Howard, "Network Ethnography and the Hypermedia Organization: New Media, New Organizations, New Methods," *New Media and Society* 4, no. 4 (2002): 550.

8. Graham Harman, "The Importance of Bruno Latour for Philosophy," *Cultural Studies Review* 13, no. 1 (2007): 33. In linking the notion of assemblage with actor-network theory, I primarily refer to the idea that both social and natural objects are ontologically flat compounds that cannot be reduced to either their "larger" or causal components. As Harman makes clear, in most others respects the assemblage theory of DeLanda and the actor-network theory of Brumo Latour, Michel Callon, and John Law are actually quite different.

9. For recent uses of the term "assemblage" in social science research, see esp. Rasmus Kleis Nielsen, *Ground Wars: Personalized Communication in Political Campaigns*

(Princeton, NJ: Princeton University Press, 2012); Daniel Kreiss, *Taking Our Country Back: The Crafting of Networked Politics from Howard Dean to Barack Obama* (New York: Oxford University Press, 2012).

10. Herbert J. Gans, *Deciding What's News: A Study of CBS Evening News, NBC Nightly News, Newsweek and Time* (Chicago: Northwestern University Press, 2004), 84.

11. Joseph Turow, "Audience Construction and Culture Production: Marketing Surveillance in the Digital Age," *Annals of the American Academy of Political and Social Science* 597, no. 1 (2005): 103–121.

CHAPTER 1

1. Mark Bowden, "Sources Say: Journalism's Future Is in Global Dialogue," Pop Matters website, June 19, 2007, available at http://www.popmatters.com/pm/post/journalisms -future-is-in-global-dialogue.

2. Phyllis Kaniss, *Making Local News* (Chicago: University of Chicago Press, 1991), 13.

3. For a history of the early Internet and its relationship to the rise of the "network society," see Manuel Castells, *The Rise of the Network Society* (New York: Blackwell, 2000).

4. Benjamin Hill, "Software (,) Politics and Indymedia," March 11, 2003, available at http://mako.cc/writing/mute-indymedia_software.html.

5. Joey Sweeney, "Philly Internet History Week," Philebrity, September 1, 2008, available at http://www.philebrity.com/category/philly-internet-history-week.

6. Project for Excellence in Journalism, "The State of the News Media 2008," Journalism.org, 2008, available at http://www.stateofthenewsmedia.org/2008.

7. Janice Castro, "Last Rites for a Proud Paper," *Time*, February 8, 1982, available at http://www.time.com/time/magazine/article/0,9171,953344-2,00.html.

8. John Morton, "Forty Years of Death in the Afternoon," *American Journalism Review*, November 1991, available at http://www.ajr.org/article.asp?id=73.

9. Michael Shapiro, "Looking for Light," *Columbia Journalism Review Online*, April 2006, available at http://cjrarchives.org/issues/2006/2/shapiro.asp.

10. National editor, *Inquirer*, interview by the author, July 17, 2008.

11. Felicity Barringer, "Philadelphia Inquirer Editor Is Forced Out," *New York Times*, November 7, 2001, sec. C.

12. William Glaberson, "Another City Faces Cuts at Its Papers," *New York Times*, November 6, 2008, available at http://query.nytimes.com/gst/fullpage.html?res=9B06E4D 81739F935A35752C1A963958260.

13. Jennifer Musser-Metz, "Case Study: Design Evolution," paper presented at the International Digital Media Arts Conference, Philadelphia, November 7, 2007.

14. Jennifer Musser-Metz, interview by the author, June 15, 2008.

15. Ibid.

16. Ibid.

17. Steve Outing, "Philadelphia Online Goes on a Home Page Diet," *Editor and Publisher*, June 26, 1998, available at http://www.allbusiness.com/services/business-services -miscellaneous-business/4670478-1.html.

18. Ibid.

19. Steve Outing, "Philadelphia Online Goes on a Home Page Diet.

20. Bowden, "Sources Say."

21. Ibid.

22. Staff members, Philly.com, interview by the author, June 15, 2008.

23. "KR Launches Philly.com Site," *News and Tech.com,* May 1999, available at http://www.newsandtech.com/issues/1999/05-99/ot/05-99_phillycom.htm.

24. Mel Taylor, "Personal History: I Used to Love Her (the Radio, That Is), But I Had to Kill Her (with the Internet)," Philebrity, August 26, 2008, available at http://www.philebrity.com/2008/08/26/personal-history-i-used-to-love-her-the-radio-that-is-but-i-had-to-kill-her-with-the-internet.

25. Janelle Brown, "Local Explosion," *Salon,* October 25, 1999, available at http://www.salon.com/tech/view/1999/10/25/dan_finnigan.

26. "Knight Ridder Site Gains Another News Provider," *Editor and Publisher,* September 1, 2000, available at http://www.allbusiness.com/services/business-services-miscellaneous-business/4677474-1.html.

27. Rajiv Pant, "About PhillyFinder," available at http://www.rajiv.com/work/com/phillyfinder/toc.htm.

28. Programmer, Philly.com, interview by the author, June 15, 2008.

29. Musser-Metz interview.

30. Ibid.

31. Field notes, June 2008.

32. Musser-Metz interview.

33. Ibid.

34. Designer, Philly.com, interview by the author, June 15, 2008

35. Derek, "Un-Real Cities," This Is Blandiose.org, April 12, 2002, available at http://www.blandiose.org/2002/04/12/un-real-cities.

36. Steve Outing, "Knight Ridder Digital Cedes Some Control," *Editor and Publisher,* July 17, 2002, available at http://www.allbusiness.com/services/business-services-miscellaneous-business/4693261-1.html.

37. Jennifer Musser-Metz, interview by the author, June 15, 2008.

38. Staff member, Philly.com, interview by the author, June 15, 2008.

39. Director, Avenue A Razorfish, interview by the author, May 30, 2008.

40. Ibid.

41. Ibid.

42. "The New Philly.com," May 11, 2008, available at http://www.philly.com/philly/hp/news_update/The_New_Phillycom.html.

43. Former executive in charge of website redesign, Philly.com, interview by the author, June 4, 2008.

44. Staff member, Philly.com, interview by the author, June 15, 2008.

45. Kevin G. Barnhurst and John Nerone, *The Form of News: A History* (New York: Guilford, 2001).

CHAPTER 2

1. Axel Bruns, "Gatewatching, Gatecrashing: Futures for Tactical News Media," in *Gatewatching: Collaborative Online News Production,* Digital Formations (New York: Peter Lang, 2005).

2. Gal Beckerman, "Inside the Indymedia Collective, Passion versus Pragmatism," *Columbia Journalism Review* 5 (2003), available at http://www.cjr.org/issues/2003/5/anarchy-beckerman.asp; Dorothy Kidd, "The Independent Media Center: A New Model," *Media Development* 50, no. 4 (2003): 7–10; Victor W. Pickard, "United Yet Autonomous:

Indymedia and the Struggle to Sustain a Radical Democratic Network," *Media, Culture, and Society* 28, no. 3 (2006): 315; Sara Platon and Mark Deuze, "Indymedia Journalism: A Radical Way of Making, Selecting and Sharing News?" *Journalism* 4, no. 3 (2003): 336.

3. Indybay, "Indymedia and Indybay History," May 11, 2005, available at http://www.indybay.org/newsitems/2005/03/11/17262451.php; emphasis added.

4. Tom Regan, "News You Can Use from the Little Guys," *Christian Science Monitor,* December 9, 1999, available at http://docs.indymedia.org/view/Global/CsmArticle.

5. Lynn Owens and L. Kendall Palmer, "Making the News: Anarchist Counter-Public Relations on the World Wide Web," *Critical Studies in Media Communication* 20, no. 4 (2003): 335–361.

6. Grassroots Media Network, "Homeless People's Network: GMC Organizers Update: Progress in Austin," letter, October 20, 1999, available at http://hpn.asu.edu/archives/Oct99/0185.html (emphasis added).

7. Gene Hyde, "Independent Media Centers: Cyber-Subversion and the Alternative Press," First Monday website, March 25, 2002, available at http://firstmonday.org/issues/issue7_4/hyde/index.html.

8. Matthew Arnison, "A Guide to the Active Software," Active: Stuff for Social Change website, July 2000, available at http://web.archive.org/web/20000816125945/http://active.org.au/doc.

9. Gabriella Coleman, "Indymedia's Independence: From Activist Media to Free Software" (English version of "Los Temps d'Indymedia"), *Multitudes* 21 (May 2005): 41–48.

10. Naomi Klein, *Fences and Windows: Dispatches from the Front Lines of the Globalization Debate* (New York: Picador, 2002).

11. Miguel Bocanegra, "Indymedia: Precursors and Birth," in *We Are Everywhere: The Irresistible Rise of Global Anticapitalism,* ed. Notes from Nowhere (London: Verso 2003).

12. Aaron Couch, "PhillyIMCHistory," Indymedia Documentation Project, January 14, 2005, available at http://docs.indymedia.org/view/Main/PhillyIMCHistory.

13. Bruns, "Gatewatching, Gatecrashing."

14. Seattle organizer, interview by the author, December 4, 2008.

15. Couch, "PhillyIMCHistory."

16. Karl Martino, founder, Philly Future, interview by the author, May 27, 2008.

17. Karl Martino, "Site News," *Philly Future—the Philadelphia Region Weblog,* June 11, 2000, available at http://web.archive.org/web/20001212202200/phillyfuture.editthispage.com/newsItems/viewDepartment$Site+News.

18. Ed Cone, "Karl Martino/Philly Future," Edcone.com, December 30, 2004, available at http://radio.weblogs.com/0107946/stories/2004/12/30/karlMartinophillyFuture.html.

19. Martino, "Site News"; emphasis added.

20. Martino interview.

21. Alexis Layton, Justin Scott, and Mariusz Zydyk, "What Is a Bulletin Board System?" in Whatis.com, 2005, available at http://searchcio-midmarket.techtarget.com/sDefinition/0,,sid183_gci213807,00.html.

22. Jen Oliver, "Fear, Loathing and Anal Sex . . . on a Dial-Up: The Other Side of CPCN's First Philly Internet Community," *Philebrity,* August 29, 2008, available at http://www.philebrity.com/2008/08/29/fear-loathing-and-anal-sex-on-a-dial-up-the-other-side-of-cpcns-first-philly-internet-community.

23. Trishy Gdowik, "GrooveLingo: Philly's Premiere Local Music Proto-Blog," *Phi-*

lebrity, August 27, 2008, available at http://www.philebrity.com/2008/08/27/groovelingo
-phillys-premiere-local-music-proto-blog.

24. W. Caleb McDaniel, "Common-Place: Blogging in the Early Republic," *Common-Place* 5, no. 4 (July 2005), available at http://www.historycooperative.org/journals/cp/vol-05/no-04/mcdaniel/index.shtml.

25. Rebecca Blood, "Weblogs: A History and Perspective," *Rebecca's Pocket,* September 7, 2000, available at http://www.rebeccablood.net/essays/weblog_history.html; Jesse James Garrett, "The Page of Only Weblogs," jjg.net, April 10, 2002, available at http://www.jjg.net/retired/portal/tpoowl.html.

26. Susan C. Herring, Inna Kouper, John C. Paolillo, Lois Ann Scheidt, Michael Tyworth, Peter Welsch, Elijah Wright, and Ning Yu, "Conversations in the Blogosphere: An Analysis 'From the Bottom Up,'" in *Proceedings of the 38th Hawaii International Conference on System Sciences (HICSS-38),* ed. Hawaii International Conference on System Sciences (Los Alamitos, CA: IEEE Press, 2005).

27. Blood, "Weblogs."

28. Scott Rosenberg, *Say Everything: How Blogging Began, What It's Becoming, and Why It Matters* (New York: Crown, 2009).

29. Scott Rosenberg, "Question about the History of Blogging" (via Wordyard contact form), letter, December 8, 2008.

30. David Sifry, "State of the Blogosphere, April 2006, Part 1: On Blogosphere Growth," Sifry's Alerts website, April 17, 2006, available at http://www.sifry.com/alerts/archives/000432.html.

31. Amy Z. Quinn, interview by the author, July 9, 2008.

32. Joey Sweeney, "About Us," *Philebrity,* December 4, 2004, available at http://web.archive.org/web/20041204072729/www.philebrity.com/about.html.

33. Field notes, April 2008.

34. Founder, Beerleaguer blog, interview by the author, July 23, 2008.

35. Tony Green, interview by the author, December 28, 2008.

36. Evidence that the vast majority of blogging is personal rather than political can be found in Amanda Lenhart and Susannah Fox, "Bloggers: A Portrait of the Internet's New Storytellers," Pew Internet and American Life Project, July 19, 2006, available at http://www.pewinternet.org/PPF/r/186/report_display.asp.

37. Green interview.

38. Joseph Turow and Lokman Tsui, *The Hyperlinked Society: Questioning Connections in the Digital Age* (Ann Arbor: University of Michigan Press, 2008).

39. Vance Lehmkuhl, interview by the author, June 15, 2008.

40. Manager, TechLife section, *Philadelphia Inquirer,* interview by the author, June 15, 2008.

41. Dan Gilmor, interview by the author, June 2, 2008.

42. Matthew Gold, "An Interview with Will Bunch of Attytood," Tattered Coat website, May 28, 2005, available at http://web.archive.org/web/20050314084956/http://tatteredcoat.com/.

43. Top editor, Philly.com, interview by the author, June 15, 2008.

44. Indymedia Documentation Project, "Philly IMC Strategizing Session," *Indymedia Documentation Project,* available at https://docs.indymedia.org/Local/PhillyIMCmeeting Strat1.

45. Stephen Lacy, Daniel Riffe, Esther Thorson, and Margaret Duffy, "PEJ Report on Citizen Journalism Sites," *PEJ State of the News Media Report,* 2008, available at http://www.stateofthemedia.org/files/2008/01/citizenmediafinal.pdf.

CHAPTER 3

1. Sam Wood, e-mail correspondence, July 16, 2008.
2. Field notes, July 14, 2008.
3. Julie Busby, interview by the author, June 26, 2008.
4. Reporter, *Philadelphia Daily News,* interview by the author, June 5, 2008.
5. Field notes, July 17, 2008.
6. Tom Fitzgerald, "Rendell Named Head of National Governors Association," Philly.com, July 14, 2008, available at http://www.philly.com/philly/news/breaking/25336124.html.
7. Angela Couloumbis, "Director of Pa. Gaming Board Resigns," Philly.com, May 29, 2008, available at http://www.philly.com/philly/news/breaking/19357249.html; Angela Couloumbis, interview by the author, July 15, 2008.
8. Field notes, July 15, 2008.
9. Reporter, *Philadelphia Inquirer,* interview by the author, July 14, 2008.
10. Field notes, October 2001–August 2008.
11. Ibid., July 16, 2008.
12. Ibid., July 16, 2008.
13. Bob Moran, interview by the author, July 16, 2008.
14. Ibid., July 16, 2008.
15. Ibid.
16. Ibid., July 14, 2008.
17. Ibid., April 1–August 1, 2008.
18. After the bankruptcy of Philadelphia Media Holdings, Philly.com was moved back into the *Inquirer* building in 2010. I discuss the implications of this move in Chapter 6.
19. Field notes, June 23, 2008.
20. Moran interview.
21. Reporter, *Philadelphia Daily News,* interview by the author, July 17, 2008.
22. Dee Dee Halleck, *The IMC: A New Model* (Walcot-upon-Avon: Hedonist Press, 2004), available at http://www.hedonistpress.com/indymedia/IMC.txt.
23. Karl Martino, e-mail correspondence, May 27, 2008.
24. Moderator, Young Philly Politics, interview by the author, July 9, 2008.
25. Field notes, June 2, 2008.
26. Amy Z. Quinn, interview by the author, July 9, 2008.
27. Sports blogger, *Philadelphia Daily News,* interview by the author, June 12, 2008.
28. "Blog," *Wikipedia—the Free Encyclopedia,* available at http://en.wikipedia.org/wiki/Weblog.
29. Field notes, June 2008–July 2008.
30. Dan Gross, interview by the author, June 3, 2008.
31. Ibid.
32. Editor, *Philadelphia Daily News,* interview by the author, June 12, 2008.
33. Field notes, June 19, 2008.
34. Ibid.
35. Reporter, interview by the author, June 11, 2008.
36. David O'Reilly, interview by the author, June 11, 2008.
37. Jason Weitzel, interview by the author, July 24, 2008.
38. Amy Z. Quinn, interview by the author, July 24, 2008.
39. Will Bunch, interview by the author, June 30, 2008.
40. Jason Weitzel, interview by the author, July 23, 2008.

41. Ed Barkowitz, interview by the author, June 14, 2008.

42. Ed Barkowitz, "Rams Update," Bark's Bytes, November 30, 2002, available at http://web.archive.org/web/20021204205005/http://www.pnionline.com/dnblog/eagles.

43. Ibid.

44. Barkowitz interview.

45. Field notes, April 2008.

46. Bunch interview.

47. Weitzel interview (July 23, 2008).

CHAPTER 4

1. Pete Tridish, "Police Critics Arrested, Home Seized in Police Raid!" Independent Media Center of Philadelphia, June 13, 2008, available at http://www.phillyimc.org/en/node/68912.

2. Christina Dunbar-Hester, "Propagating Technology, Propagating Community? Low Power Radio Activism and Technological Negotiation in the U.S., 1996–2006" (Ph.D. diss., 2008).

3. Hans Bennett, "PROPOSED FEATURE: Police Critics Arrested, Home Seized in Police Raid," message posted on Philadelphia Independent Media Center listserv, June 13, 2008.

4. Tridish, "Police Critics Arrested."

5. journalists4mumia, "Police Critics Arrested, Home Seized in Police Raid," Young Philly Politics, June 13, 2008, available at http://youngphillypolitics.com/police_critics_arrested_home_seized_police_raid.

6. MrLuigi, "Can You Back Up the 'Community Meetings' a Little?" Young Philly Politics, June 13, 2008, available at http://youngphillypolitics.com/police_critics_arrested_home_seized_police_raid#comment-25948.

7. journalists4mumia, "Good Point on Ramsey, but They Can Still Be Better," Young Philly Politics, June 13, 2008, available at http://youngphillypolitics.com/police_critics_arrested_home_seized_police_raid#comment-25949; emphasis added.

8. Dan U-A, "YPP Standards," Young Philly Politics, June 14, 2008, available at http://youngphillypolitics.com/police_critics_arrested_home_seized_police_raid#comment-25952.

9. journalists4mumia, "There Is a Clear Source," Young Philly Politics, June 14, 2008, available at http://youngphillypolitics.com/police_critics_arrested_home_seized_police_raid#comment-25957.

10. Dan U-A, "Sure, You Can Stand Behind," Young Philly Politics website, June 14, 2008, available at http://youngphillypolitics.com/police_critics_arrested_home_seized_police_raid#comment-25958.

11. jennifer, "So Wait," posted on journalists4mumia's blog, Young Philly Politics, June 14, 2008, available at http://youngphillypolitics.com/police_critics_arrested_home_seized_police_raid#comment-25961; emphasis added.

12. Dan U-A, "Sure, You Can Stand Behind."

13. Dan Urevick-Ackelsberg, interview by the author, July 9, 2008.

14. Isaiah Thompson, interview by the author, June 17, 2008.

15. Isaiah Thompson, interview by the author, June 17, 2008.

16. Available at http://www.citypaper.net/blogs/clog.

17. The quotation marks around "investigation" are from The Clog's online photo caption.

18. Isaiah Thompson, "There's Something Fishy in Francisville," The Clog, June 14, 2008, available at http://www.citypaper.net/blogs/clog/2008/06/14/theres-something-fishy-in-francisville.

19. Ibid.

20. Thompson interview.

21. Field notes, June 18, 2008.

22. Ibid., June 17, 2008.

23. Hannahjs, "Release: Homeowners Fighting Police Brutality Illegally Arrested, Never Charged," Young Philly Politics, June 16, 2008, available at http://youngphilly politics.com/release_homeowners_fighting_police_brutality_illegally_arrested_never _charged.

24. City editor, Daily News, interview by the author, June 17, 2008.

25. Ibid.

26. Gar Joseph, interview by the author, June 19, 2008.

27. Ibid.

28. Dave Davies, interview by the author, June 17, 2008.

29. Ibid.

30. Daniel Rubin, "17th and Ridge Story," email to the author, June 17, 2008.

31. Field notes, June 24, 2008.

32. Ibid.

33. Field notes, June 17, 2008.

34. Dave Davies, "The Cops Came, Searched and Left a Mess for Puzzled Home-owner," Philadelphia Daily News, June 17, 2008, available at http://www.philly.com/philly/hp/news_update/20006679.html.

35. Daniel Rubin, "Who Wrote 'Kill the Pigs' at 17th and Ridge?" Blinq, June 17, 2008, available at http://www.philly.com/philly/blogs/inq-blinq/20009829.html.

36. Davies, "The Cops Came"; Rubin, "Who Wrote 'Kill the Pigs'?"

37. Rubin, "Who Wrote 'Kill the Pigs'?"

38. Field notes, May–August 2008.

39. Daily News editor, interview by the author, June 17, 2008.

40. Kia Gregory, "At City Hall Rally, Police Raid Is Questioned," Philadelphia Inquirer, June 18, 2008, available at http://www.philly.com/philly/news/local/20250159.html.

41. Kia Gregory, interview by the author, July 14, 2008.

42. "It Would Be Hilarious if It Weren't True: Philly Cops Mistake Hipsters for M.O.V.E.-esque Hate Group," Philebrity.com, June 17, 2008, available at http://www.philebrity.com/2008/06/17/it-would-be-hilarious-if-it-werent-true-philly-cops-mistake-hipsters-for-move-esque-hate-group.

43. D-Mac, "Cops Raid Dreamboat Terrorist's House," Philadelphia Will Do, June 17, 2008, available at http://willdo.philadelphiaweekly.com/archives/2008/06/cops_raid _dream.html.

44. Jeff Deeney, "Fear and Loathing in Francisville," Phawker, June 17, 2008, available at http://www.phawker.com/2008/06/17/valley-of-shadow-fear-loathing-francisville.

45. D-Mac, "Cops Raid Dreamboat Terrorist's House."

46. "It Would Be Hilarious if It Weren't True."

47. Will Bunch, "Moscow on the Schuylkill: Philly Cops Bust Activists . . . for What?" Attytood, June 17, 2008, available at http://www.philly.com/philly/blogs/attytood/Moscow _on_the_Schuylkill_Cops_bust_anti-camera_activists.html.

48. Will Bunch, "Re 17th and Ridge Story," email to the author, June 17, 2008.

49. Deeney, "Fear and Loathing in Francisville."

50. Ibid.

51. Ibid.

52. Bunch, "Re 17th and Ridge Story."

53. Corey Doctorow, "Philly Cops Raids [*sic*] Activists Who Circulated Anti-CCTV Petition," Boing Boing, June 17, 2008, available at http://www.boingboing.net/2008/06/17/ philly-cops-raids-ac.html.

54. Bunch, "Re 17th and Ridge Story."

55. The entire text of the post reads, "I do not think that phrase means what 9th District Police Capt. Dennis Wilson thinks it means": Atrios [Duncan Black], "Hate Group," Eschaton, June 17, 2008, available at http://www.eschatonblog.com/2008_06_15_archive .html#4206074044172460609. Tom Marcinko, "Question Surveillance, Go to Jail," Futurismic, June 17, 2008, available at http://futurismic.com/2008/06/17/it-cant-happen-here-in -philadelphia-on-the-other-hand.

56. Doctorow, "Philly Cops Raids Activists."

57. "Boing Boing on Technorati," Technorati, 2007, available at http://technorati.com/ blogs/www.boingboing.net.

58. Davies, interview by the author, June 17, 2008.

59. Ibid.

60. *Daily News* editor, interview by the author, June 17, 2008.

61. Jill Porter (pseudonym), interview by the author, June 20, 2008.

62. Field notes, June 19, 2008.

63. Ibid.

64. Ibid.

65. "Report: Top PC Articles_may29#94BC3," Philly.com, June 29, 2008.

66. Will Bunch, "Alycia Tells Her Side—in Suit," *Philadelphia Daily News,* June 20, 2008, available at http://www.philly.com/philly/hp/news_update/20593889.html.

67. Porter interview.

68. Jeff Rousset and Jen Rock, "Philadelphia Activists Still Homeless after Arrests and Seizure of Home," Philadelphia IMC, June 22, 2008, available at http://www.phillyimc .org/en/node/69583.

69. Philly Clout, "Clout: This Is How City Hall Treats Citizens with No Record," June 27, 2007, available at http://www.philly.com/philly/hp/news_update/21930154.html.

70. Gregory interview.

CHAPTER 5

1. Field notes, June 2, 2008.

2. Pablo J. Boczkowski, "When More Media Equals Less News: Patterns of Content Homogenization in Argentina's Leading Print and Online Newspapers," *Political Communication* 24, no. 2 (2007); Pablo J. Boczkowski, *News at Work: Imitation in an Age of Information Abundance* (Chicago: University of Chicago Press, 2011).

3. Wendy Warren, interview by the author, June 4, 2008.

4. Field notes, June 3, 2008.

5. Josh Braun, "Electronic Components and Human Interventions: Distributing Television News Online" (Ph.D. diss., Cornell University, Ithaca, NY, 2011).

6. Jeff Jarvis, "Networked Journalism," BuzzMachine website, July 5, 2006, available at http://www.buzzmachine.com/2006/07/05/networked-journalism.

7. Charlie Beckett, *Supermedia: Saving Journalism So It Can Save the World* (Hoboken, NJ: Wiley-Blackwell, 2008).

8. Josh Stearns, "A Growing Inventory of Journalism Collaborations," Groundswell, April 22, 2010, available at http://stearns.wordpress.com/2010/04/22/indexing-journalism-collaboration.

9. Ibid.

10. Ibid.

11. Braun, "Electronic Components and Human Interventions."

12. Ibid.

13. Fred Turner, "Actor-Networking the News," *Social Epistemology* 19, no. 4 (2005): 321–324; Fred Turner, *From Counterculture to Cyberculture: Stewart Brand, the Whole Earth Network, and the Rise of Digital Utopianism* (Chicago: University of Chicago Press, 2006), 12.

14. Editor, *Daily News,* interview by the author, June 10, 2008.

15. Will Bunch, "The Philadelphia Experiment," Attytood, October 25, 2005, available at http://www.pnionline.com/dnblog/attytood/archives/002437.html.

16. Ibid.

17. Ibid.

18. Jeff Jarvis, "Saving Journalism Isn't about Saving Jobs," BuzzMachine website, November 3, 2005, available at http://www.buzzmachine.com/2005/11/03/saving-journalism-isnt-about-saving-jobs.

19. Karl Martino, interview by the author, May 27, 2008.

20. Susan Leigh Star and James R. Griesemer, "Institutional Ecology, 'Translations' and Boundary Objects: Amateurs and Professionals in Berkeley's Museum of Vertebrate Zoology," 1907–39," *Social Studies of Science* 19, no. 3 (1989): 393.

21. Bruno Latour, "On Recalling ANT," in *Actor Network Theory and After,* ed. John Law and John Hassard (Malden, MA: Blackwell, 1999), 16.

22. Karl Martino, "Saving Journalism Isn't about Saving Jobs," Philly Future, November 4, 2005, available at http://phillyfuture.org/node/1998.

23. Field notes, March 26, 2006.

24. William Densmore, "Media Giraffe Teleconference," University of Massachusetts, Amherst, 2006, available at http://www.mediagiraffe.org/wiki/index.php/Mgp2006-video.

25. Amy Dalton, interview by the author, May 9, 2008.

26. Howard Hall, "After the Unconference," Smedley Log, March 25, 2006, available at http://www.thesmedleylog.com/archives/632.

27. Field notes, March 26, 2006.

28. Wendy Warren, "Norgs: What We Did Saturday," *Norgs: News Organizations and the Future—an Ongoing Conversation,* March 25, 2006, available at http://blogs.phillynews.com/dailynews/norg/archives/002988.html.

29. Wendy Warren, "Norgs: Norgs Whiteboards," *Norgs: News Organizations and the Future—an Ongoing Conversation,* March 25, 2006, available at http://blogs.phillynews.com/dailynews/norg/archives/002984.html.

30. Ibid.

31. Norgs Working Group, "The Norgs Unconference Statement of Principles," *Norgs—the New News Organization Wiki,* May 9, 2007, available at http://norgs.pbwiki.com/The+Norgs+Unconference+Statement+Of+Principles.

32. Warren, "Norgs: What We Did Saturday."

33. Densmore, "Media Giraffe Teleconference."

34. Ibid.

35. See posts about the Norgs Unconference at, among other blogs, http://www
.paradox1x.org, http://philadelphia.metblogs.com, http://www.attytood.com, http://my
digimedia.com, http://blogs.philly.com/blinq, http://www.thesmedleylog.com, http://
dragonballyee.blogs.com, and http://indypendent.typepad.com.

36. Will Bunch, "Re: A Thanksgiving Wish," November 11, 2008, available at http://
groups.yahoo.com/group/Norgs/message/1468.

37. Wendy Warren, "Re: A Thanksgiving Wish," letter, November 28, 2008, available
at http://groups.yahoo.com/group/Norgs/message/1469.

38. Bruno Latour, *The Pasteurization of France* (Cambridge, MA: Harvard University
Press, 1988); Turner, *From Counterculture to Cyberculture.*

39. Daniel Mazone, Wendy Warren, and Fatima Nelson, "WHYY, the *Philadelphia
Daily News,* and the Committee of Seventy Launch 'The Next Mayor Project,'" press
release, December 5, 2005, in my possession.

40. Art Howe, "He Didn't Have To," *Philadelphia City Paper,* December 9, 1999,
available at http://www.citypaper.net/articles/120999/feat.slant.shtml.

41. Mazone et al., "WHYY."

42. Tanni Haas, "From 'Public Journalism' to the 'Public's Journalism'? Rhetoric and
Reality in the Discourse on Weblogs," *Journalism Studies* 6, no. 3 (2005): 387–396; Jay
Rosen, *What Are Journalists For?* (New Haven, CT: Yale University Press, 2001); Theo-
dore L. Glasser, *The Idea of Public Journalism* (New York: Guilford, 1999).

43. Alicia C. Shepard, "Yo! Read This!" *American Journalism Review* (November 2000),
available at http://www.ajr.org/Article.asp?id=538.

44. Wendy Warren, interview by the author, January 14, 2009.

45. Ibid.

46. Ibid.

47. Wendy Warren, "If You Don't Vote, You've Lost Already," TheNextMayor.com,
March 28, 2007, available at http://blogs.phillynews.com/dailynews/nextmayor/2007/03/
if_you_dont_vote_youve_lost_al.html.

48. Jeff Bundy, "The Next Mayor Project Announces Community Network," press
release, 2007, available at www.whyy.org/about/pressroom/nm_network_release_000.doc.

49. Wendy Warren, interview by the author, January 18, 2009.

50. Participant, Philly IMC, e-mail correspondence with the author, May 1, 2005.

51. Warren interview (January 18, 2009).

52. Jeff Bundy, "The Next Mayor Project and WHYY to Provide Unmatched Coverage of the Philadelphia Mayoral Primary," press release, 2007, available at http://www
.whyy.org/about/pressroom/primaryelection.doc.

53. Wendy Warren, interview by the author, January 18, 2009.

54. Dave, "What Makes a Weblog a Weblog?" Weblogs at Harvard Law website, May
23, 2003, available at http://blogs.law.harvard.edu/whatmakesaweblogaweblog.html; Jay
Rosen, "Jay Rosen of NYU on the Ethic of the Link," YouTube, April 8, 2008, available
at http://www.youtube.com/watch?v=RIMB9Kx18hw; Jeff Jarvis, "The Ethic of the Link
Layer on News," BuzzMachine website, June 2, 2008, available at http://www.buzz
machine.com/2008/06/02/the-ethic-of-the-link-layer-on-news.

55. Joseph Turow and Lokman Tsui, *The Hyperlinked Society: Questioning Connections in the Digital Age* (Ann Arbor: University of Michigan Press, 2008).

56. Madeleine Akrich, "The De-scription of Technical Objects," in *Shaping Technol-
ogy/Building Society: Studies in Sociotechnical Change,* ed. Wiebe E. Bijker and John Law
(Boston: MIT Press, 1992), 205–224.

57. Wendy Warren, interview by the author, June 4, 2008.

58. Ed Cone, "Karl Martino/Philly Future." Edcone.com, December 30, 2004, available at http://radio.weblogs.com/0107946/stories/2004/12/30/karlMartinophillyFuture.html.

59. "Introduction to RSS," WebReference.com, 2005, available at http://www.webreference.com/authoring/languages/xml/rss/intro.

60. Karl Martino, "Philly Future: It's Alive!" February 1, 2004, available at http://paradox1x.org/2004/02/philly-future-i; emphasis added.

61. Karl Martino, interview by the author, August 3, 2008.

62. Cone, "Karl Martino/Philly Future."

63. Aaron Couch, interview by the author, May 8, 2008; Amy L. Dalton, interview, May 30, 2008.

64. Organizer, Philly IMC, interview by the author, May 30, 2008.

65. "PhillyIMC Strategizing Session," Indymedia Documentation Project, available at https://docs.indymedia.org/Local/PhillyIMCmeetingStrat1.

66. Volunteer, Philly IMC, interview by the author, June 5, 2008.

67. "PhillyIMC Strategizing Session."

68. Bob Hanke, "For a Political Economy of Indymedia Practice," *Canadian Journal of Communication* 30, no. 1 (2005), available at http://www.cjc-online.ca/index.php/journal/article/view/1479/1595.

69. Former volunteer, Philly IMC, interview by the author, May 8, 2008.

70. "PhillyIMC Strategizing Session."

71. Organizer, Philly IMC, interview by the author, June 5, 2008.

72. Herbert J. Gans, *Deciding What's News: A Study of CBS Evening News, NBC Nightly News, Newsweek and Time* (Chicago: Northwestern University Press, 1979).

73. Dean Starkman, "The Hamster Wheel," *Columbia Journalism Review* 49, no. 3 (September–October 2010), available at http://www.cjr.org/cover_story/the_hamster_wheel.php?page=all.

74. Karl Martino, interview by the author, October 12, 2008.

75. Available at http://newsworks.org.

76. Megan Garber, "Journal Register Company Joins with Outside.in for a Hyperlocal News/Ad Portal in Philadelphia," Nieman Journalism Lab, Harvard University, available at http://www.niemanlab.org/2010/09/journal-register-company-joins-with-outside-in-for-a-hyperlocal-newsad-portal-in-philadelphia.

CHAPTER 6

1. Andrew Abbott, *The System of Professions: An Essay on the Division of Expert Labor* (Chicago: University of Chicago Press, 1989).

2. D. Lucas Graves, "The Affordances of Blogging: A Case Study in Culture and Technological Effects," *Journal of Communication Inquiry* 31, no. 4 (2007): 331.

3. Consultant, Avenue A Razorfish, interview by the author, May 30, 2008.

4. Newsroom manager, Philly.com, interview by the author, June 23, 2008.

5. Chris Brennan, interview by the author, June 19, 2008.

6. Field notes, June 26, 2008.

7. Wendy Warren, interview by the author, June 25, 2008.

8. Reporter, *Philadelphia Inquirer,* interview by the author, June 11, 2008.

9. Producer, Philly.com, interview by the author, July 23, 2008.

10. Executive, Philly.com, interview by the author, June 26, 2008.

11. Field notes, June 25, 2008.

12. Ibid., June 23, 2008.

13. Web producer, Philly.com, interview by the author, June 30, 2008.

14. Phil MacGregor, "Tracking the Online Audience," *Journalism Studies* 8, no. 2 (2007): 287.

15. Field notes, July 2, 2008.

16. Ibid., July 9, 2009.

17. Ibid., July 22, 2009.

18. Yoni Greenbaum, interview by the author, July 12, 2008.

19. Brett Neilson and Ned Rossiter, "From Precarity to Precariousness and Back Again: Labour, Life and Unstable Networks," *Fibreculture Journal,* no. 5 (September 2005), available at http://journal.fibreculture.org/issue5/neilson_rossiter.htm.

20. David Hesmondhalgh and Sarah Baker, "Creative Work and Emotional Labour in the Television Industry," *Theory, Culture, and Society* 25, nos. 7–8 (December 2008): 97–118.

21. Field notes, April 2008.

22. Ibid., May 2008–August 2008.

23. Reporter, *Daily News,* interview by the author, June 3, 2008.

24. Field notes, June 10, 2008.

25. Mark Potts, "Bubble, Bubble, Toil and Trouble," Recovering Journalist website, June 17, 2008, available at http://recoveringjournalist.typepad.com/recovering_journalist/ 2008/06/bubble-bubble-toil-and-trouble.html; "Philly the First to Fall?" Newspaper Biz website, June 6, 2008, available at http://www.newspaperbiz.com/2008/06/philly-first-to -fall.html.

26. "Papers Name a Manager to Look into Consolidation," *Philadelphia Inquirer,* July 9, 2008, available at http://www.philly.com/philly/business/20080709_Papers_name _a_manager_to_look_into_consolidation.html.

27. Daniel McQuade, "Inquirer Wackiness Continues," Philadelphia Will Do (blog), July 2, 2008, available at http://willdo.philadelphiaweekly.com/archives/2008/07/inquirer _wackin.html.

28. Steve Volk, "*Inquirer, Daily News* to Shed More Staff," *Philly Mag,* August 25, 2008, available at http://www.phillymag.com/news/2008/08/25/inquirer-daily-news-to-shed -more-staff.

29. Sam Wood, interview by the author, July 14, 2008.

30. Chris Brennan, interview by the author, June 19, 2008.

31. Marcelo Duran, "Philly.com Gears Up for Local Content Dominance," *International Journal of Newspaper Technology* 7 (2008), available at http://www.newsandtech .com/issues/2008/July/ot/07-08_websiteprofile-philly.htm.

32. Field notes, July 10, 2008.

33. Ibid., May 2008–August 2008.

34. Newspaper Guild member, interview by the author, June 5, 2008. I should note that the Philly.com's employees were unionized in the fall of 2010, when Philly.com moved back into the *Inquirer*'s offices.

35. Field notes, June 4, 2008.

36. Ibid.

37. Will Bunch, "Disconnected," *American Journalism Review,* September 2008, available at http://www.ajr.org/Article.asp?id=4584.

38. Senior web producer, Philly.com, interview by the author, June 25, 2008.

39. Reporter, *Philadelphia Inquirer,* interview by the author, July 17, 2008.

40. Field notes, May 2008–August 2008.

41. Ibid., July 18, 2008.

42. Ibid., July 15, 2008.

43. Columnist, *Daily News,* interview by the author, June 4, 2008.

44. Field notes, May 2008–August 2008.

45. Reporter-blogger, *Daily News,* interview by the author, June 19, 2008.

46. Field notes, April 23, 2008.

47. Ibid., July 10, 2008.

48. Volunteer, Philly IMC, interview by the author, May 9, 2008.

49. Ibid., May 15, 2008.

50. Bruce Arnold, "Blogging: Statistics and Demographics," Carlson Analytics website, 2007, available at http://www.caslon.com.au/weblogprofile1.htm.

51. Dan Urevick-Ackelsberg, interview by the author, July 9, 2008.

52. Yochai Benkler, "Coase's Penguin, or, Linux and the Nature of the Firm," *Yale Law Journal* 112 (2002): 369.

53. Karl Martino, e-mail interview by the author, August 5, 2008.

54. Field notes, July 17, 2008.

55. Reporter, *Daily News,* e-mail interview by the author, August 15, 2008.

56. Herbert J. Gans, *Deciding What's News: A Study of CBS Evening News, NBC Nightly News, Newsweek and Time* (Chicago: Northwestern University Press, 1979); Robert Darnton, "Writing News and Telling Stories," *Daedalus* 104, no. 2 (1975): 175–194.

57. Dean Starkman, "The Hamster Wheel," *Columbia Journalism Review* 49, no. 3 (September–October 2010), available at http://www.cjr.org/cover_story/the_hamster_wheel.php?page=all.

58. Yoni Greenbaum, interview by the author, June 23, 2008.

59. Reporter, *Daily News,* interview by the author, July 14, 2008.

60. Field notes, June 23, 2008.

61. Benkler, "Coase's Penguin"; Clay Shirky, *Here Comes Everybody: The Power of Organizing without Organizations* (New York: Penguin, 2008).

62. "Not that long ago, owning a metropolitan newspaper guaranteed a seat at the civic table, immediate respectability and, given that many papers were almost monopolies, a press practically capable of printing money": *New York Times,* June 15, 2009.

63. David Folkenflik, "Major U.S. Newspapers Announce Staff Cuts," *All Things Considered,* National Public Radio, September 21, 2005, available at http://www.npr.org/templates/story/story.php?storyId=4857927; Jay Rosen, "A Prayer for the Philly Papers," PressThink website, June 2, 2006, available at http://journalism.nyu.edu/pubzone/weblogs/pressthink/2006/06/02/pray_phl.html; Michael Shapiro, "Looking for Light," *Columbia Journalism Review Online,* April 2006, available at http://cjrarchives.org/issues/2006/2/shapiro.asp; field notes, May 2008–August 2008.

64. Rosen, "A Prayer for the Philly Papers."

65. Joe Strupp, "Guild Asks for Volunteers to Ease Sting of Philly Layoffs," *Editor and Publisher,* January 3, 2007, available at http://www.editorandpublisher.com/eandp/article_brief/eandp/1/1003527084.

66. Will Bunch, "No Blood in Ants," Attytood, August 19, 2008, available at http://www.philly.com/philly/blogs/attytood/No_blood_in_ants4.html?text=lg&month=&main=&year=&cat=&page=9&c=y.

67. The newspapers were purchased for $562 million in 2006; $412 million of that was borrowed, and by the time of the Chapter 11 filing, the papers remained $390 million in debt.

68. Chris Nolter, "Philly's Full Court Press," 2010, available at http://www.thedeal.com/magazine/ID/034427/features/philly-full-court-press.php.

69. Susie Madrak, "*Philadelphia Daily News* Wins Pulitzer—and the Paper Gets Auctioned Off April 27," Crooks and Liars (blog), April 14, 2010, available at http://crooksandliars.com/susie-madrak/philadelphia-daily-news-wins-pulitzer.

70. Field notes, January 21, 2011.

71. Ken Doctor, "Smelling New Value in Old Philly Newspapers," Ken Doctor's Instablog, April 28, 2010, available at http://newsonomics.com/smelling-new-value-in-old-philly.

72. Nolter, "Philly's Full Court Press."

73. Martin Langeveld, "Who Owns Newspaper Companies? The Banks, Funds, and Investors and Their (Big) Slices of the Industry," Nieman Journalism Lab website, March 7, 2011, available http://www.niemanlab.org/2011/03/who-owns-newspaper-companies-the-banks-funds-and-investors-and-their-big-slices-of-the-industry.

74. J-Lab, "2010 Enterprise Reporting Awards," available at http://www.j-lab.org/about/press-releases/2010_enterprise_reporting_awards.

75. C. W. Anderson. "A Critical Approach to Computational Journalism," *New Media and Society,* forthcoming.

76. Seth Lewis, "From Journalism to Information: The Transformation of the Knight Foundation and News Innovation," *Mass Communication and Society* 15 (2012): 309–334.

77. Clay Shirky, "News Papers and Thinking the Unthinkable," 2009, available at http://www.shirky.com/weblog/2009/03/newspapers-and-thinking-the-unthinkable.

78. John Thornton, "Nonprofit News Outlets Will Be a Bigger Part of Our Future than Alan Mutter Thinks," 2010, available at http://www.niemanlab.org/2010/03/john-thornton-nonprofit-news-outlets-will-be-a-bigger-part-of-our-future-than-alan-mutter-thinks.

79. Indeed, the quote from Thornton came in response to an earlier post by the news analyst Alan Mutter: Alan Mutter, "Non-Profits Can't Possibly Save the News," 2010, available at http://newsosaur.blogspot.com/2010/03/non-profits-cant-possibly-save-news.html.

80. Lewis, "From Journalism to Information."

81. Although the history of the public journalism movement and its relationship to current media reform efforts lies outside the scope of this book, it would be fascinating to compare "civic" and "citizen" journalism reform using an institutional analytical frame.

82. Steve Volk, "Dead Air," *Philadelphia Magazine,* October 2007, available at http://www.phillymag.com/articles/dead_air.

83. Field notes, January 18, 2011.

84. Ibid. See also Christopher Wink, "Newsworks: WHYY Online News Brand Launching Means a Lot to These Legacies," ChristopherWink.com, November 11, 2010, available at http://christopherwink.com/2010/11/22/newsworks-whyy-online-news-brand-launching-means-a-lot-to-these-legacies; Bruce Schimmel, "Journalists Wanted," *City Paper,* January 1, 2009, available at http://citypaper.net/articles/2009/01/01/journalists-needed.

85. Newsworks actually made use of a system in which a link to an internal URL would immediately be followed by a redirect to the outside partner's website, allowing the site, in Satullo's words, to capture page views while sharing traffic with its partners.

86. Chris Satullo, interview by the author, January 18, 2011.

87. Available at http://www.j-lab.org/publications/philadelphia_media_project.

88. Joshua Breitbart, "Toward a Healthy Media Ecosystem For Philadelphia." New America Foundation blog, 2010, available online at http://mediapolicy.newamerica.net/blogposts/2010/towards_a_healthy_media_ecosystem_for_philadelphia-32202.

89. Greg Linch, quoted in Lauren Rabaino, "Notes from BCNI: Greg Linch on 'Rethinking our Thinking,'" 2010, available online at http://laurenmichell.com.

90. Jack Lail, "Where Journalism Gets Reinvented," Jacklail.com, 2010, available at http://www.jacklail.com/2010/04/-a-group-of-what.html.

91. Christopher Wink, interview with the author, February 8, 2011.

92. Ibid.

93. Jim MacMillan, "Greg Osberg: It's Going to Take a Couple of Years to Achieve This Miracle," Philadelphia Initiative for Journalistic Innovation website, 2010, available at http://phiji.org/2010/11/21/greg-osberg-its-going-to-take-a-couple-of-years-to-achieve -this-miracle.

94. "Greg Osberg: "It's Going to Take a Couple of Years to Achieve This Miracle," Entrepreneurial Journalists of Philadelphia, 2010, available at http://diyphiladelphia.blog spot.com/2010/11/greg-osberg-its-going-to-take-couple-of.html.

95. Field notes, January 21, 2011.

96. Ken Doctor, "The Newsonomics of Do-Over," Nieman Journalism Lab website, 2010, available at http://www.niemanlab.org/2011/01/the-newsonomics-of-do-over.

97. "Debunked: The Great Philadelphia Paywall Scare," Phawker, 2011, available at http://www.phawker.com/2011/01/05/reality-check-correcting-fact-errors-in-philebritys -reporting-on-phillycom-going-paywall.

CONCLUSION

1. Melanie Sill, "The Case for Open Journalism Now: A New Framework for Inform- ing Communities," Annenberg Innovation Lab website, December 5, 2011, available at http://www.annenberginnovationlab.org/OpenJournalism.

2. See, e.g., Yochai Benkler, "Coase's Penguin, or, Linux and the Nature of the Firm." *Yale Law Journal* 112 (2002): 369.

3. Daniel Kreiss, *Taking Our Country Back: Political Consultants and the Crafting of Networked Politics from Howard Dean to Barack Obama* (New York: Oxford University Press).

4. For other work in this vein, see esp. David Stark, *The Sense of Dissonance: Accounts of Worth in Economic Life* (Princeton, NJ: Princeton University Press, 2010).

5. For the previous section, I am obviously indebted to Max Weber, *Economy and Society* (Berkeley: University of California Press, 1978), whose writings on rationality provide a rich set of alternatives to purely transactional analyses of the impact of digital technology.

6. See esp. James W. Carey, "The Press and Public Discourse," *Center Magazine* 20, no. 2, 1987, 5; Jay Rosen, *What Are Journalists For?* (New Haven, CT: Yale University Press, 2001); Theodore L. Glasser, *The Idea of Public Journalism* (New York: Guilford, 1999).

7. Carey, "The Press and Public Discourse."

8. Todd Gitlin, "Public Sphere or Public Sphericules?" in *Media, Ritual and Identity,* ed. Tamar Liebes, James Curran, and Elihu Katz (London: Routledge, 1998), 168–174;

Nancy Fraser, "Rethinking the Public Sphere: A Contribution to the Critique of Actually Existing Democracy," *Social Text*, nos. 5–6 (1990): 56–80; Noortje Marres, "Issues Spark a Public into Being," in *Making Things Public: Atmospheres of Democracy*, ed. Bruno Latour and Peter Weibel (Karlsruhe: MIT Press, 2005).

APPENDIX

1. Simon Cottle, "Ethnography and News Production: New(s) Developments in the Field." *Sociology Compass* 1, no. 1 (2007): 1–16.

2. Pablo J. Boczkowski, "When More Media Equals Less News: Patterns of Content Homogenization in Argentina's Leading Print and Online Newspapers." *Political Communication* 24, no. 2 (2007): 167–180; David Domingo, "Interactivity in the Daily Routines of Online Newsrooms: Dealing with an Uncomfortable Myth," *Journal of Computer-Mediated Communication* 13, no. 3 (2008): 680–704; Emma Hemmingway, "PDP, the News Production Network and the Transformation of News," *Convergence* 11, no. 3 (2005): 8; Eric Klinenberg, "Convergence: News Production in a Digital Age," *Annals of the American Academy of Political and Social Science* 597, no. 1 (2005): 48.

See also Seth C. Lewis, "From Journalism to Information: The Transformation of the Knight Foundation and News Innovation," *Mass Communication and Society* 15, no. 3 (2012): 309–334; Nikki Usher, "Making Business News" (Ph.D. diss., University of Southern California, Los Angeles, 2011); Josh A. Braun, "Electronic Components and Human Interventions: Distributing Television News Online" (Ph.D. diss., Cornell University, Ithaca, NY, 2011).

3. Edward J. Epstein, *News from Nowhere: Television and the News* (Chicago: I. R. Dee, 1973); Mark Fishman, *Manufacturing the News* (Austin: University of Texas Press, 1980); Herbert J. Gans, *Deciding What's News: A Study of CBS Evening News, NBC Nightly News, Newsweek and Time* (Chicago: Northwestern University Press, 1979); Gaye Tuchman, *Making News: A Study in the Construction of Reality* (New York: Free Press, 1979); Nina Eliasoph, "Routines and the Making of Oppositional News," in *Social Meanings of News: A Text-Reader*, ed. Dan Berkowitz (Thousand Oaks, CA: Sage, 1997): 230–254.

4. Philip N. Howard "Network Ethnography and the Hypermedia Organization: New Media, New Organizations, New Methods," *New Media and Society* 4, no. 4 (2002): 550.

5. Warren Breed, "Social Control in the Newsroom: A Functional Analysis," *Social Forces* 33 (1954): 326.

6. Ibid.; David Manning White, "The 'Gate Keeper,'" in *Social Meanings of News: A Text-Reader*, ed. Dan Berkowitz (Thousand Oaks, CA: Sage, 1997), 63–71.

7. Barbie Zelizer, *Taking Journalism Seriously: News and the Academy* (Thousand Oaks, CA: Sage, 2004), 54.

8. Barbara Tedlock, "Ethnography and Ethnographic Representation," in *Handbook of Qualitative Research*, 2d ed., ed. Norman K. Denzin and Yvonna S. Lincoln (Thousand Oaks, CA: Sage, 2003), 455–486.

9. David Barton, "What Is Ethnography?" *Reflect Online Magazine*, vol. 1, October 2004, available at http://www.nrdc.org.uk/content.asp?CategoryID=607.

10. Zelizer, *Taking Journalism Seriously*, 68.

11. Cottle, "Ethnography and News Production."

12. Ibid., 6–7.

13. Ibid., 7.

14. Michael Schudson, "Four Approaches to the Sociology of News Production," in *Mass Media and Society,* 5th ed., James Curran and Michael Gurevitch (London: Hodder Arnold, 2005), 183.

15. Ibid.

16. Cottle, "Ethnography and News Production," 9.

17. Zelizer, *Taking Journalism Seriously,* 68.

18. Howard, "Network Ethnography."

19. Valdis Krebs, "Social Network Analysis," Org.net, 2008, available at http://www.orgnet.com/sna.html.

20. Howard, "Network Ethnography," 560.

21. John Kelly, "About Morningside Analytics," Morningside Analytics website, available at http://morningside-analytics.com/aboutus.php (accessed November 20, 2008).

22. "About Govcom.org," Govcom.org, 2009, available at http://www.govcom.org/about_us.html.

23. "IssueCrawler: Instructions of Use," Govcom.org, 2009, available at http://www.govcom.org/Issuecrawler_instructions.htm.

24. Howard, "Network Ethnography," 570.

25. Bruno Latour, *Reassembling the Social: An Introduction to Actor-Network Theory* (New York: Oxford University Press, 2007); Manuel DeLanda, *A New Philosophy of Society: Assemblage Theory and Social Complexity* (London: Continuum, 2006); Graham Harman, *Prince of Networks: Bruno Latour and Metaphysics* (Melbourne: Re:press, 2009).

26. Geoffrey Bowker, "Actor-Network Theory," in *Blackwell Encyclopedia of Sociology,* ed. George Ritzer (Malden, MA: Blackwell, 2007), available at http://www.blackwellreference.com/public/tocnode?id=g9781405124331_chunk_g97814051243317_ss1-9.

27. John Law, "Notes on the Theory of the Actor-Network: Ordering, Strategy, and Heterogeneity," *Systemic Practice and Action Research* 5, no. 4 (1992): 381.

28. Daniel Kreiss, *Taking Our Country Back: The Crafting of Networked Politics from Howard Dean to Barack Obama* (New York: Oxford University Press, 2012); Rasmus Kleis Nielsen, *Ground Wars: Personalized Communication in Political Campaigns* (Princeton, NJ: Princeton University Press, 2012).

29. Andrew Chadwick, "The Political Information Cycle in a Hybrid News System: The British Prime Minister and the 'Bullygate' Affair," *International Journal of Press/Politics* 16, no. 1 (2011): 3–29.

30. Emma Hemmingway, *Into the Newsroom: Exploring the Digital Production of Regional Television News* (New York: Routledge, 2008).

31. See Domingo, "Interactivity in the Daily Routines of Online Newsrooms"; Amy Schmitz Weiss and David Domingo, "Innovation Processes in Online Newsrooms as Actor-Networks and Communities of Practice," *New Media and Society* 12, no. 7 (2010): 1156–1171; Pablo J. Boczkowski, "The Processes of Adopting Multimedia and Interactivity in Three Online Newsrooms," *Journal of Communication* 54, no. 2 (2004): 197–213; Fred Turner, "Actor-Networking the News," Social Epistemology 19, no. 4 (2005): 321–324.

32. Harman, *Prince of Networks,* 14.

33. Paul DiMaggio and Walter Powell, "The 'Iron Cage' Revisited: Institutional Isomorphism and Collective Rationality in Organizational Fields," *American Sociological Review* 48 (1983): 147–160.

34. Law, "Notes on the Theory of the Actor-Network," 385.

Selected Bibliography

SCHOLARLY ARTICLES, BOOKS, AND DOCTORAL THESES

Abbott, Andrew D. *The System of Professions: An Essay on the Division of Expert Labor.* Chicago: University of Chicago Press, 1988.

Adorno, Theodor W., and Max Horkheimer. "The Culture Industry: Enlightenment as Mass Deception" (1944). In *Dialectic of Enlightenment,* trans. Edmund Jephcott, 94–136. Stanford, CA: Stanford University Press, 2002.

Akrich, Madeleine. "The De-Scription of Technical Objects." In *Shaping Technology/ Building Society: Studies in Sociotechnical Change,* ed. Wiebe E. Bijker and John Law, 205–224. Boston: MIT Press, 1992.

Anderson, C. W. "A Critical Approach to Computational Journalism." *New Media and Society* (forthcoming).

———. "Journalism: Expertise, Authority, and Power in Democratic Life." In *The Media and Social Theory,* ed. David Hesmondhalgh and Jason Toynbee, 248–264. London: Routledge, 2008.

Anderson, Rob, Robert Dardenne, and George M. Killenberg. *The Conversation of Journalism: Communication, Community, and News.* Santa Barbara, CA: Praeger, 1994.

Arnold, Bruce. "Blog Statistics and Demographics." Caslon Analytics website, 2007. Available at http://www.caslon.com.au/weblogprofile1.htm.

Banks, Mark. *The Politics of Cultural Work.* New York: Palgrave Macmillan, 2007.

Barnhurst, Kevin G., and John Nerone. *The Form of News: A History.* New York: Guilford, 2001.

Barton, David. "What Is Ethnography?" *Reflect Online Magazine,* vol. 1, October 2004. Available at http://www.nrdc.org.uk/content.asp?CategoryID=607.

Beckerman, Gal. "Edging Away from Anarchy: Inside the Indymedia Collective, Passion versus Pragmatism." *Columbia Journalism Review* 5 (2003). Available at http://www.cjr.org/issues/2003/5/anarchy-beckerman.asp.

Beckett, Charlie. *Supermedia: Saving Journalism So It Can Save the World.* Hoboken, NJ: Wiley-Blackwell, 2008.

Benkler, Yochai. "Coase's Penguin, or, Linux and the Nature of the Firm." *Yale Law Journal* 112 (2002): 369–446.

———. *The Wealth of Networks: How Social Production Transforms Markets and Freedom.* New Haven, CT: Yale University Press, 2006.

Benson, Rodney. "Commercialism and Critique: California's Alternative Weeklies." In *Contesting Media Power: Alternative Media in a Networked World,* ed. Nick Couldry and James Curran, 111–128. Oxford: Rowman and Littlefield, 2003.

Benson, Rodney, and Erik Neveu. "Bourdieu and the Journalistic Field." *Journal of Communication Inquiry* 30, no. 3 (2006): 276–279.

Bocanegra, Miguel. "Indymedia: Precursors and Birth." In *We Are Everywhere: The Irresistible Rise of Global Anticapitalism,* ed. Notes from Nowhere. London: Verso, 2003.

Boczkowski, Pablo J. *Digitizing the News: Innovation in Online Newspapers.* Boston: MIT Press, 2004.

———. *News at Work: Imitation in an Age of Information Abundance* Chicago: University of Chicago Press, 2011.

———. "The Processes of Adopting Multimedia and Interactivity in Three Online Newsrooms." *Journal of Communication* 54, no. 2 (2004): 197–213.

———. "When More Media Equals Less News: Patterns of Content Homogenization in Argentina's Leading Print and Online Newspapers." *Political Communication* 24, no. 2 (2007): 167–180.

Bourdieu, Pierre, and Priscilla P. Ferguson. *On Television and Journalism.* London: Pluto, 1998.

Bowker, Geoffrey. "Actor-Network Theory." In *Blackwell Encyclopedia of Sociology,* ed. George Ritzer. London: Blackwell, 2007. Available at http://www.blackwellreference.com/public/tocnode?id=g9781405124331_chunk_g97814051243317_ss1-9.

Braun, Josh A. "Electronic Components and Human Interventions: Distributing Television News Online." Ph.D. diss., Cornell University, Ithaca, NY, 2011.

Breed, Warren. "Social Control in the Newsroom: A Functional Analysis." *Social Forces* 33 (1954): 326–335.

Brown, Janelle. "Local Explosion." *Salon,* October 25, 1999. Available at http://www.salon.com/tech/view/1999/10/25/dan_finnigan.

Bruns, Axel. "Gatewatching, Gatecrashing: Futures for Tactical News Media." In *Gatewatching: Collaborative Online News Production.* New York: Peter Lang, 2005.

Bunch, Will. "Disconnected." *American Journalism Review,* September 2008. Available at http://www.ajr.org/Article.asp?id=4584.

Callon, Michel. *The Laws of the Markets.* Sociological Review Monograph no. 4. Malden, MA: Blackwell, 1998.

Carey, James W. *Communication as Culture: Essays on Media and Society.* New York: Routledge, 1989.

———. "The Press and Public Discourse." *Center Magazine* 20, no. 2 (1987): 4–32.

Cassidy, William P. "Online News Credibility: An Examination of the Perceptions of Newspaper Journalists." *Journal of Computer-Mediated Communication* 12, no. 2 (2007): 478–498.

Castells, Manuel. *The Rise of the Network Society.* New York: Blackwell, 2000.

Chadwick, Andrew. "The Political Information Cycle in a Hybrid News System: The British Prime Minister and the 'Bullygate' Affair." *International Journal of Press/Politics* 16, no. 1 (2011): 3–29.

Champagne, Patrick. "The 'Double Dependency': The Journalistic Field between Politics and Markets." In *Bourdieu and the Journalistic Field,* ed. Rodney Benson and Erik Neveu, 48–63. Cambridge, MA: Polity, 2005.

Coleman, Gabriella. "Indymedia's Independence: From Activist Media to Free Software" (English version of "Los Temps d'Indymedia"). *Multitudes* 21 (May 2005): 41–48.

Cottle, Simon. "Ethnography and News Production: New(s) Developments in the Field." *Sociology Compass* 1, no. 1 (2007): 1–16.

Couldry, Nick. "Actor Network Theory and Media: Do They Connect and on What Terms?" 2004. Available at http://www.andredeak.com.br/pdf/Couldry_ActorNetworkTheory Media.pdf.

Darnton, Robert. "An Early Information Society: News and the Media in Eighteenth-Century Paris." *American Historical Review* 105, no. 1 (2004): 1–35.

———. "Writing News and Telling Stories." *Daedalus* 104, no. 2 (1975): 175–194.

DeLanda, Miguel. *A New Philosophy of Society: Assemblage Theory and Social Complexity.* London: Continuum, 2006.

Deuze, Mark. *Media Work.* Cambridge: Polity, 2007.

———. "Understanding Journalism as Newswork: How It Changes, and How It Remains the Same," 2007. Available at http://www.wmin.ac.uk/mad/pdf/WPCC-Vol5-No2 -Mark_Deuze.pdf.

Deuze, Mark, and Christina Dimoudi. "Online Journalists in the Netherlands: Towards a Profile of a New Profession." *Journalism* 3, no. 1 (2002): 85–100.

de Vries, Gerard. "Should We Send Collins and Latour to Dayton, Ohio?" Paper presented at the European Association for the Study of Science and Technology, 1995. Available at http://documents.stanford.edu/67/382.

Dewey, John. *The Public and Its Problems.* New York: Henry Holt, 1927.

DiMaggio, Paul, and Walter Powell. "The 'Iron Cage' Revisited: Institutional Isomorphism and Collective Rationality in Organizational Fields." *American Sociological Review* 48 (1983): 147–160.

Domingo, David. "Interactivity in the Daily Routines of Online Newsrooms: Dealing with an Uncomfortable Myth." *Journal of Computer-Mediated Communication* 13, no. 3 (2008): 680–704.

———. "Inventing Online Journalism: Development of the Internet as a News Medium in Four Catalan Online Newsrooms." Ph.D. diss., Universitat Rovira I Virgili, Tarragona, Spain, 2006.

Domingo, David, Thorsten Quandt, Ari Heinonen, Steve Paulussen, Jane B. Singer, and Marina Vujnovic. "Participatory Journalism Practices in the Media and Beyond." *Journalism Practice* 2, no. 3 (2008): 326–342.

Dunbar-Hester, Christina. "Propagating Technology, Propagating Community? Low Power Radio Activism and Technological Negotiation in the U.S., 1996–2006." Ph.D. diss. Cornell University, Ithaca, NY, 2008.

Duran, Marcelo. "Philly.com Gears Up for Local Content Dominance." *International Journal of Newspaper Technology* 7 (2008). Available at http://www.newsandtech.com/ issues/2008/July/ot/07-08_websiteprofile-philly.htm.

Eliasoph, Nina. "Routines and the Making of Oppositional News." In *Social Meanings of News: A Text-Reader,* ed. Dan Berkowitz, 230–254. Thousand Oaks, CA: Sage, 1997.

Epstein, Edward J. *News from Nowhere: Television and the News.* Chicago: I. R. Dee, 1973.

Farmer, James, and Anne Bartlett-Bragg. "Blogs@ Anywhere: High Fidelity Online Communication." *Balance, Fidelity, Mobility: Maintaining the Momentum,* ed. Halima Goss, 197–203. Sydney: Australasian Society for Computers in Learning in Tertiary Education, 2005.

Fishman, Mark. *Manufacturing the News.* Austin: University of Texas Press, 1980.

Florida, Richard. *The Rise of the Creative Class: And How It's Transforming Work, Leisure, Community and Everyday Life*. New York: Basic, 2002.

Fraser, Nancy. "Rethinking the Public Sphere: A Contribution to the Critique of Actually Existing Democracy." *Social Text*, nos. 5–6 (1990): 56–80.

Freidson, Eliot. *Profession of Medicine: A Study of the Sociology of Applied Knowledge*. Chicago: University of Chicago Press, 1988.

Gans, Herbert J. *Deciding What's News: A Study of CBS Evening News, NBC Nightly News, Newsweek and Time*. Chicago: Northwestern University Press, 1979.

Gilbert, Clark G. "Unbundling the Structure of Inertia: Resource versus Routine Rigidity." *Academy of Management Journal* 48, no. 5 (2005): 741–763.

Gill, Kathy E. "Blogging, RSS, and the Information Landscape: A Look at Online News." In *WWW 2005 Workshop on the Weblogging Ecosystem*, 2005. Available at http://www-idl.hpl.hp.com/blogworkshop2005/gill.pdf.

Gitlin, Todd. *Media Unlimited: How the Torrent of Images and Sounds Overwhelms Our Lives*. New York: Holt Paperbacks, 2002.

———. "Public Sphere or Public Sphericules?" In *Media, Ritual and Identity*, ed. Tamar Liebes, James Curran, and Elihu Katz, 168–174. London: Routledge, 1998.

———. *The Whole World Is Watching: Mass Media in the Making and Unmaking of the New Left*. Berkeley: University of California Press, 1980.

Glasser, Theodore L. *The Idea of Public Journalism*. New York: Guilford, 1999.

Graves, Lucas. "The Affordances of Blogging: A Case Study in Culture and Technological Effects." *Journal of Communication Inquiry* 31, no. 4 (2007): 331–346.

Haas, Tanni. "From 'Public Journalism' to the 'Public's Journalism'? Rhetoric and Reality in the Discourse on Weblogs." *Journalism Studies* 6, no. 3 (2005): 387–396.

Hall, Stuart. "Encoding/Decoding." In *Media and Cultural Studies: Keyworks*, ed. Meenakshi Gigi Durham and Douglas Kellner, 166–176. Malden, MA: Blackwell, 2001.

———. "The Rediscovery of 'Ideology': Return of the Repressed in Media Studies." *Culture, Society and the Media*, ed. Michael Gurevitch, Tony Bennett, James Curran, and Janet Woolacott, 56–90. London: Methuen, 1982.

Halleck, Dee Dee. *The IMC: A New Model*. Walcot-upon-Avon: Hedonist Press, 2004. Available at http://www.hedonistpress.com/indymedia/IMC.txt.

Hallin, Daniel C., and Paolo Mancini. *Comparing Media Systems: Three Models of Media and Politics*. New York: Cambridge University Press, 2004.

Hanke, Bob. "For a Political Economy of Indymedia Practice." *Canadian Journal of Communication* 30, no. 1 (2005): 41–64.

Hardt, Michael, and Antonio Negri. *Multitude: War and Democracy in the Age of Empire*. New York: Penguin, 2004.

Harman, Graham. "The Importance of Bruno Latour for Philosophy." *Cultural Studies Review* 13, no. 1 (March 2007): 31–49.

———. *Prince of Networks: Bruno Latour and Metaphysics*. Melbourne: Re:press, 2009.

Hemmingway, Emma. *Into the Newsroom: Exploring the Digital Production of Regional Television News*. New York: Routledge, 2008.

———. "PDP, the News Production Network and the Transformation of News." *Convergence* 11, no. 3 (2005): 8–27.

Hermida, Alfred, and Neil Thurman. "Comments Please: How the British News Media Is Struggling with User-Generated Content." Paper presented at the Eighth International Symposium on Online Journalism, University of Texas, Austin, 2007. Available at http://online.journalism.utexas.edu/2007/papers/Hermida.pdf.

Herring, Susan C., Inna Kouper, John C. Paolillo, Lois Ann Scheidt, Michael Tyworth, Peter Welsch, Elijah Wright, and Ning Yu. "Conversations in the Blogosphere: An Analysis 'From the Bottom Up.'" In *Proceedings of the 38th Hawaii International Conference on System Sciences (HICSS-38)*, ed. Hawaii International Conference on System Sciences, 1–11. Los Alamitos, CA: IEEE Press, 2005.

Herring, Susan C., Lois Ann Scheidt, Inna Kouper, and Elijah Wright. "A Longitudinal Content Analysis of Weblogs: 2003–2004." In *Blogging, Citizenship, and the Future of Media*, ed. Mark Tremayne, 3–20. New York: Routledge, 2007.

Hesmondhalgh, David, and Sarah Baker. "Creative Work and Emotional Labour in the Television Industry." *Theory, Culture, and Society* 25, nos. 7–8 (December 2008): 97–118.

Hine, Christine, and R. Shields. *Virtual Ethnography.* Thousand Oaks, CA: Sage, 2000.

Howard, Philip N. "Network Ethnography and the Hypermedia Organization: New Media, New Organizations, New Methods." *New Media and Society* 4, no. 4 (2002): 550–574.

Howe, Art. "He Didn't Have To." *Philadelphia City Paper,* December 9, 1999. Available at http://www.citypaper.net/articles/120999/feat.slant.shtml.

Howkins, John. *The Creative Economy: How People Make Money from Ideas.* New York: Penguin, 2002.

Jones, Julie M., and Itai Himelboim. "Just a Guy in Pajamas? Framing the Blogs: Emergence of the Blogosphere in Mainstream U.S. Newspaper Coverage (1999–2005)." Paper presented at the 58th Annual Convention of the Association for Education in Journalism and Mass Communication, San Francisco, August 9–13, 2007.

Kaniss, Phyllis. *Making Local News.* Chicago: University of Chicago Press, 1991.

Katz, Elihu. "Journalists as Scientists." *American Behavioral Scientist* 33, no. 2 (1989): 238–246.

Kidd, Dorothy. "The Independent Media Center: A New Model." *Media Development* 50, no. 4 (2003): 7–10.

Klein, Naomi. *Fences and Windows: Dispatches from the Front Lines of the Globalization Debate.* New York: Picador, 2002.

Klinenberg, Eric. "Convergence: News Production in a Digital Age." *Annals of the American Academy of Political and Social Science* 597, no. 1 (2005): 48–65.

Kreiss, Daniel. *Taking Our Country Back: The Crafting of Networked Politics from Howard Dean to Barack Obama.* New York: Oxford University Press, 2012.

Lacy, Stephen, Daniel Riffe, Esther Thorson, and Margaret Duffy. "PEJ Report on Citizen Journalism Sites." *PEJ State of the News Media Report,* 2008. Available at http://www.stateofthemedia.org/files/2008/01/citizenmediafinal.pdf.

Larson, Margali S. *The Rise of Professionalism: A Sociological Analysis.* Berkeley: University of California Press, 1997.

Latour, Bruno. "On Recalling ANT." In *Actor Network Theory and After,* ed. John Law and John Hassard, 15–25. Malden, MA: Blackwell, 1999.

———. *The Pasteurization of France.* Cambridge, MA: Harvard University Press, 1998.

———. *Reassembling the Social: An Introduction to Actor-Network Theory.* New York: Oxford University Press, 2005.

———. *Science in Action.* London: Open University Press, 1987.

Law, John. "Notes on the Theory of the Actor-Network: Ordering, Strategy, and Heterogeneity." *Systemic Practice and Action Research* 5, no. 4 (1992): 379–393.

———. "Traduction/Trahision: Notes on ANT," 2003. Available at http://cseweb.ucsd.edu/~goguen/courses/175/stslaw.html.

Lewis, Seth C. "From Journalism to Information: The Transformation of the Knight Foundation and News Innovation." *Mass Communication and Society* 15, no. 3 (2012): 309–334.

Lippmann, Walter. *Public Opinion.* Edison, NJ: Transaction, 1922.

Lowrey, Wilson. "Journalism and Blogging." *Journalism Practice* 2, no. 1 (2008): 64–81.

———. "Mapping the Journalism–Blogging Relationship." *Journalism: Theory, Practice, and Criticism* 7, no. 4 (2006): 477–500.

Lowrey, Wilson, and William Anderson. "The Journalist behind the Curtain: Participatory Functions on the Internet and Their Impact on Perceptions of the Work of Journalism." *Journal of Computer-Mediated Communication* 10, no. 3 (2005). Available at http://jcmc.indiana.edu/vol10/issue3/lowrey.html.

MacDonald, Keith M. *The Sociology of the Professions.* New York: Sage, 1995.

MacGregor, Phil. "Tracking the Online Audience." *Journalism Studies* 8, no. 2 (2007): 280–298.

Marres, Noortje. "Issues Spark a Public into Being." In *Making Things Public: Atmospheres of Democracy,* ed. Bruno Latour and Peter Weibel, 208–218. Karlsruhe: MIT Press, 2005.

McChesney, Robert. *The Political Economy of Media: Enduring Issues, Emerging Dilemmas.* New York: Monthly Review Press, 2008.

McDaniel, W. Caleb. "Common-Place: Blogging in the Early Republic." *Common-Place* 5, no. 4 (July 2005). Available at http://www.historycooperative.org/journals/cp/vol-05/no-04/mcdaniel/index.shtml.

McGill, Douglas. "Largemouth: A Citizen Journalism Syllabus." McGill Report website, 2007. Available at http://www.mcgillreport.org/largemouthsyllabus.htm.

McRobbie, Angela. "Clubs to Companies: Notes on the Decline of Political Culture in Speeded Up Creative Worlds." *Cultural Studies* 16, no. 4 (2002): 516–531.

Merritt, Davis. *Knightfall: Knight Ridder and How the Erosion of Newspaper Journalism Is Putting Democracy at Risk.* New York: AMACOM Books, 2005.

Morton, John. "Forty Years of Death in the Afternoon." *American Journalism Review,* November 1991. Available at http://www.ajr.org/article.asp?id=73.

Murley, Bryan, and Chris Roberts. "Biting the Hand That Feeds: Blogs and Second-Level Agenda Setting." Unpublished ms., Brigham Young University, 2005. Available at http://bryanmurley.com/site/wp-content/uploads/2007/01/Murley_Roberts12-05.pdf.

Musser-Metz, Jennifer. "Case Study: Design Evolution." Paper presented at the International Digital Media Arts Conference, Philadelphia, November 7, 2007.

Nardi, Bonnie A., Diane J. Schiano, and Michelle Gumbrecht. "Blogging as Social Activity, or, Would You Let 900 Million People Read Your Diary?" *Proceedings of the 2004 ACM Conference on Computer Supported Cooperative Work* 6, no. 3 (2004): 222–231.

Neilson, Brett, and Ned Rossiter. "From Precarity to Precariousness and Back Again: Labour, Life and Unstable Networks." *Fibreculture Journal,* no. 5 (September 2005). Available at http://journal.fibreculture.org/issue5/neilson_rossiter.html.

Nerone, John, and Kevin G. Barnhurst. "U.S. Newspaper Types, the Newsroom, and the Division of Labor, 1750–2000." *Journalism Studies* 4, no. 4 (2003): 435–449.

Nielsen, Rasmus Kleis. *Ground Wars: Personalized Communication in Political Campaigns.* Princeton, NJ: Princeton University Press, 2012.

Niles, Robert. "Are Blogs a 'Parasitic' Medium?" *Online Journalism Review,* March 2, 2007. Available at http://www.ojr.org/ojr/stories/070301niles.

———. "How to Report a News Story Online." *Online Journalism Review,* June 8, 2006. Available at http://www.ojr.org/ojr/wiki/reporting.

Noam, Eli. *Media Ownership and Concentration in America.* New York: Oxford University Press, 2007.

Nolter, Chris. "Philly's Full Court Press." *The Deal,* May 14, 2010. Available at http://www.thedeal.com/magazine/ID/034427/features/philly-full-court-press.php.

Orita, Hiroharu. "What Are Incunabula?" In *Incunabula—Dawn of Western Printing,* online exhibition catalogue, National Diet Library, Tokyo, 2004. Available at http://www.ndl.go.jp/incunabula/e/chapter1/chapter1_04.html.

Outing, Steve. "Knight Ridder Digital Cedes Some Control." *Editor and Publisher,* July 17, 2002. Available at http://www.editorandpublisher.com/PrintArticle/Knight-Ridder-Digital-Cedes-Some-Control.

———. "Philadelphia Online Goes on a Home Page Diet." *Editor and Publisher,* June 26, 1998. Available at http://www.editorandpublisher.com/PrintArticle/Philadelphia-Online-Goes-on-a-Home-Page-Diet.

———. "Sophisticated Web Stats Give Editors Better Idea of Reader Interests." *Editor and Publisher,* July 26, 2005. Available at http://www.editorandpublisher.com/Article/Sophisticated-Web-Stats-Give-Editors-Better-Idea-of-Reader-Interests.

Owens, Lynn, and L. Kendall Palmer. "Making the News: Anarchist Counter-Public Relations on the World Wide Web." *Critical Studies in Media Communication* 20, no. 4 (2003): 335–361.

"Parting Thoughts: An Invitation." *Columbia Journalism Review Online,* July 17, 2008. Available at http://www.cjr.org/parting_thoughts/parting_thoughts_an_invitation_1.php.

Paterson, Chris A., and David Domingo. *Making Online News: The Ethnography of New Media Production.* New York: Peter Lang, 2008.

Pickard, Victor W. "United Yet Autonomous: Indymedia and the Struggle to Sustain a Radical Democratic Network." *Media, Culture, and Society* 28, no. 3 (2006): 315–336.

Pinch, Trevor J., and Richard Swedberg, eds. *Living in a Material World: Economic Sociology Meets Science and Technology Studies.* Boston: MIT Press, 2008.

Platon, Sara, and Mark Deuze. "Indymedia Journalism: A Radical Way of Making, Selecting and Sharing News?" *Journalism* 4, no. 3 (2003): 336–355.

Powell, Walter W. "The Capitalist Firm in the Twenty-First Century: Emerging Patterns." *The Twenty-First Century Firm: Changing Economic Organization in International Perspective,* ed. Paul DiMaggio, 33–68. Princeton, NJ: Princeton University Press, 2001.

Project for Excellence in Journalism. "The Changing Newsroom." Project for Excellence in Journalism website, Pew Research Center, July 21, 2008. Available at http://www.journalism.org/node/11961.

———. "The State of the News Media 2006." Project for Excellence in Journalism website, Pew Research Center, 2006. Available at http://www.stateofthenewsmedia.org/2006.

———. "The State of the News Media 2008." Project for Excellence in Journalism website, Pew Research Center, 2008. Available at http://www.stateofthenewsmedia.org/2008.

Reese, Stephen D. "The Media Sociology of Herbert Gans: A Chicago Functionalist." Paper presented to the International Communication Association, Sydney, 1994.

Reese, Stephen D., Lou Rutigliano, Kideuk Hyun, and Jaekwan Jeong. "Mapping the Blogosphere: Professional and Citizen-Based Media in the Global News Arena." *Journalism: Theory, Practice, Criticism* 8, no. 3 (2007): 235–262.

Robinson, Susan. "The Mission of the J-Blog: Recapturing Journalistic Authority Online." *Journalism* 7, no. 1 (2006): 65–83.

Rosen, Jay. *What Are Journalists For?* New Haven, CT: Yale University Press, 2001.

Rosenberg, Scott. *Say Everything: How Blogging Began, What It's Becoming, and Why It Matters.* New York: Crown, 2009.

Roth, Marci McCoy. "How Journalists See the Blogosphere." Unpublished manuscript, Annenberg School for Communication, University of Pennsylvania, December 2004. Available at http://www.glog.nl/wiki/upload/docs/how_journalists_see_the_blogosphere.pdf.

Ryan, Bill. *Making Capital from Culture: The Corporate Form of Capitalist Production.* Berlin: Walter de Gruyter, 1992.

Ryfe, David Michael. "Guest Editor's Introduction: New Institutionalism and the News." *Political Communication* 23, no. 2 (2006): 135–144.

Schudson, Michael. *Discovering the News.* New York: Basic Books, 1981.

———. "Four Approaches to the Sociology of News." In *Mass Media and Society,* 5th ed., ed. James Curran and Michael Gurevitch, 172–197. London: Hodder Arnold, 2005.

Schudson, Michael, and C. W. Anderson,. "Objectivity, Professionalism, and Truth Seeking." In *The Handbook of Journalism Studies,* ed. Karin Wahl-Jorgensen and Thomas Hanitzsch, 88–101. Mahwah, NJ: Lawrence Erlbaum, 2008.

Scott, Esther. "'Big Media' Meets the 'Bloggers': Coverage of Trent Lott's Remarks at Strom Thurmond's Birthday Party." Case study C14-04-1731.0, Kennedy School of Government, Harvard University, 2004.

Seidman, Steven, and Michael Gruber. "Capitalism and Individuation in the Sociology of Max Weber." *British Journal of Sociology* 28, no. 4 (1997): 498–508.

Seltzer, Kimberley, and Tom Bentley. *The Creative Age: Knowledge and Skills for the New Economy.* London: Demos, 1999.

Shapiro, Michael. "Looking for Light." *Columbia Journalism Review Online,* April 2006. Available at http://cjrarchives.org/issues/2006/2/shapiro.asp.

Shepard, Alicia C. "The Inquirer's Midlife Crisis." *American Journalism Review,* January–February 1995. Available at http://www.ajr.org/article.asp?id=1600.

———. "Yo! Read This!" *American Journalism Review* (November 2000). Available at http://www.ajr.org/Article.asp?id=538.

Shirky, Clay. *Here Comes Everybody: The Power of Organizing without Organizations.* New York: Penguin, 2008.

Sill, Melanie. "The Case for Open Journalism Now: A New Framework for Informing Communities," Annenberg Innovation Lab website, December 5, 2011. Available at http://www.annenberginnovationlab.org/OpenJournalism.

Singer, Jane B. "The Political J-blogger: 'Normalizing' a New Media Form to Fit Old Norms and Practices." *Journalism* 6, no. 2 (2005): 173–198.

———. "Strange Bedfellows? The Diffusion of Convergence in Four News Organizations." *Journalism Studies* 5, no. 1 (2004): 3–18.

Star, Susan Leigh, and James R. Griesemer. "Institutional Ecology, 'Translations' and Boundary Objects: Amateurs and Professionals in Berkeley's Museum of Vertebrate Zoology, 1907–39." *Social Studies of Science* 19, no. 3 (1989): 387–420.

Stark, David. "Ambiguous Assets for Uncertain Environments: Heterarchy in Postsocialist Firms." In *The Twenty-First Century Firm: Changing Economic Organization in International Perspective,* ed. Paul DiMaggio, 69–104. Princeton, NJ: Princeton University Press, 2001.

Starkman, Dean. "The Hamster Wheel." *Columbia Journalism Review* 49, no. 3 (September–October 2010). Available at http://www.cjr.org/cover_story/the_hamster_wheel.php ?page=all.

Starr, Paul. *The Social Transformation of American Medicine.* New York: Basic Books, 1982.

Tedlock, Barbara. "Ethnography and Ethnographic Representation." In *Handbook of Qualitative Research,* 2d ed., ed. Norman K. Denzin and Yvonna S. Lincoln, 455–486. Thousand Oaks, CA: Sage, 2003.

Tuchman, Gaye. *Making News: A Study in the Construction of Reality.* New York: Free Press, 1979.

———. "Objectivity as Strategic Ritual: An Examination of Newsmen's Notions of Objectivity." *American Journal of Sociology* 77, no. 4 (1972): 660–679.

———. "The Production of News." In *A Handbook of Media and Communication Research: Qualitative and Quantitative Methodologies,* ed. Klaus Bruhn Jensen, 78–90. New York: Routledge, 2003.

Turner, Fred. "Actor-Networking the News." *Social Epistemology* 19, no. 4 (2005): 321–324.

———. *From Counterculture to Cyberculture: Stewart Brand, the Whole Earth Network, and the Rise of Digital Utopianism.* Chicago: University of Chicago Press, 2006.

Turow, Joseph. "Audience Construction and Culture Production: Marketing Surveillance in the Digital Age." *Annals of the American Academy of Political and Social Science* 597, no. 1 (2005): 103–121.

Turow, Joseph, and Lokman Tsui. *The Hyperlinked Society: Questioning Connections in the Digital Age.* Ann Arbor: University of Michigan Press, 2008.

Usher, Nikki. "Making Business News." Ph.D. diss., University of Southern California, Los Angeles, 2011.

van Loon, Joost, and Emma Hemmingway. "Organisations, Identities and Technologies in Innovation Management: The Rise and Fall of Bi-media in the BBC East Midlands." *Intervention Research* 1, no. 2 (2005): 125–147.

Wall, Melissa. "'Blogs of War': Weblogs as News." *Journalism* 6, no. 2 (2005): 153–172.

Weaver, David Hugh, Randal Beam, Bonnie Brownlee, Paul Voakes, and G. Cleveland Wilhoit. *The American Journalist in the 21st Century: U.S. News People at the Dawn of a New Millennium.* Englewood Cliffs, NJ: Lawrence Erlbaum Associates, 2006.

Weber, Max. *Economy and Society.* Berkeley: University of California Press, 1978.

———. *General Economic History.* Piscataway, NJ: Transaction, 1981.

Weiss, Amy Schmitz, and David Domingo. "Innovation Processes in Online Newsrooms as Actor-Networks and Communities of Practice." *New Media and Society* 12, no. 7 (2010): 1156–1171.

White, David Manning. "The 'Gate Keeper.'" In *Social Meanings of News: A Text-Reader,* ed. Dan Berkowitz, 63–71. Thousand Oaks, CA: Sage, 1997.

Winer, Dave. "What Makes a Weblog a Weblog?" Weblogs at Harvard Law website, May 23, 2003. Available at http://blogs.law.harvard.edu/whatmakesaweblogaweblog .html.

Zelizer, Barbie. *Covering the Body: The Kennedy Assassination, the Media, and the Shaping of Collective Memory.* Chicago: University of Chicago Press, 1992.

———. *Taking Journalism Seriously: News and the Academy.* Thousand Oaks, CA: Sage, 2004.

NEWS ARTICLES, BLOG POSTS, E-MAILS, AND LISTSERV RECORDS

"About Govcom.org," Govcom.org, 2009. Available at http://www.govcom.org/about_us .html.

Arnison, Matthew. "A Guide to the Active Software." Active: Stuff for Social Change website, July 2000. Available at http://web.archive.org/web/20000816125945/http://active .org.au/doc.

———. "Why Open Publishing Is the Same as Free Software." Catalyst website, 2001. Available at http://www.purplebark.net/maffew/cat/openpub.html.

Atrios [Duncan Black]. "Hate Group." Eschaton, June 17, 2008. Available at http://www .eschatonblog.com/2008_06_15_archive.html#4206074044172460609.

Barkowitz, Ed. "Crystal Balls." Bark's Bytes, November 28, 2002. Available at http://web .archive.org/web/20021204205005/http://www.pnionline.com/dnblog/eagles.

———. "Rams Update." Bark's Bytes, November 30, 2002. Available at http://web.archive .org/web/20021204205005/http://www.pnionline.com/dnblog/eagles.

Barringer, Felicity. "Fear of Cutbacks Rattles Papers in Philadelphia." *New York Times,* October 23, 2000. Available at http://query.nytimes.com/gst/fullpage.html?res=9F0 DE0DF1631F930A15753C1A9669C8B63.

———. "Philadelphia Inquirer Editor Is Forced Out." *New York Times,* November 7, 2001, sec. C.

Blood, Rebecca. "Weblogs: A History and Perspective." Rebecca's Pocket, September 7, 2000. Available at http://www.rebeccablood.net/essays/weblog_history.html.

"Boing Boing on Technorati." Technorati, 2007. Available at http://technorati.com/blogs/ www.boingboing.net.

Bowden, Mark. "Sources Say: Journalism's Future Is in Global Dialogue." PopMatters, June 19, 2007. Available at http://www.popmatters.com/pm/post/journalisms-future -is-in-global-dialogue.

Breitbart, Joshua. (2010). "Toward a Healthy Media Ecosystem For Philadelphia." Available at http://mediapolicy.newamerica.net/blogposts/2010/towards_a_healthy_media _ecosystem_for_philadelphia-32202.

Bunch, Will. "Alycia Tells Her Side—in Suit." *Philadelphia Daily News,* June 20, 2008. Available at http://www.philly.com/philly/hp/news_update/20593889.html.

———. "Moscow on the Schuylkill: Philly Cops Bust Activists . . . For What?" Attytood, June 17, 2008. Available at http://www.philly.com/philly/blogs/attytood/Moscow_on _the_Schuylkill_Cops_bust_anti-camera_activists.html.

———. "No Blood in Ants." Attytood, August 19, 2008. Available at http://www.philly .com/philly/blogs/attytood/No_blood_in_ants4.html?text=lg&month=&main=&year =&cat=&page=9&c=y.

———. "The Philadelphia Experiment." Attytood, October 25, 2005. Available at http:// www.pnionline.com/dnblog/attytood/archives/002437.html.

———. "RE: [Norgs] Re: A Thanksgiving Wish," November 11, 2008. Available at http:// groups.yahoo.com/group/norgs/message/1468.

Bundy, Jeff. "The Next Mayor Project and WHYY to Provide Unmatched Coverage of the Philadelphia Mayoral Primary." Press release, 2007. Available at http://www.whyy .org/about/pressroom/primaryelection.doc.

———. "The Next Mayor Project Announces Community Network." Press release, 2007. Available at www.whyy.org/about/pressroom/nm_network_release_000.doc.

Castro, Janice. "Last Rites for a Proud Paper." *Time Magazine,* February 8, 1982. Available at http://www.time.com/time/magazine/article/0,9171,953344-2,00.html.

Cone, Ed. "Karl Martino/Philly Future." Edcone.com, December 30, 2004. Available at http://radio.weblogs.com/0107946/stories/2004/12/30/karlMartinophillyFuture.html.

Couch, Aaron. "PhillyIMCHistory." Indymedia Documentation Project, January 14, 2005. Available at http://docs.indymedia.org/view/Main/PhillyIMCHistory.

Couloumbis, Angela. "Director of Pa. Gaming Board Resigns." Philly.com, May 29, 2008. Available at http://www.philly.com/philly/news/breaking/19357249.html.

Dan U-A. "Sure, You Can Stand Behind." Young Philly Politics, June 14, 2008. Available at http://youngphillypolitics.com/police_critics_arrested_home_seized_police_raid#comment-25958.

———. "YPP Standards." Young Philly Politics, June 14, 2008. Available at http://young phillypolitics.com/police_critics_arrested_home_seized_police_raid#comment-25952.

Davies, Dave. "The Cops Came, Searched and Left a Mess for Puzzled Homeowner." *Philadelphia Daily News,* June 17, 2008. Available at http://www.philly.com/philly/hp/news_update/20006679.html.

Deeney, Jeff. "Fear and Loathing in Francisville." Phawker, June 17, 2008. Available at http://www.phawker.com/2008/06/17/valley-of-shadow-fear-loathing-francisville.

Densmore, William. "Media Giraffe Teleconference." University of Massachusetts, Amherst, 2006. Available at www.mediagiraffe.org/wiki/index.php/Mgp2006-video.

Derek. " Un-Real Cities." This Is Blandiose.org, April 12, 2002. Available at http://www .blandiose.org/2002/04/12/un-real-cities.

D-Mac. "Cops Raid Dreamboat Terrorist's House." Philadelphia Will Do, June 17, 2008. Available at http://willdo.philadelphiaweekly.com/archives/2008/06/cops_raid_dream .html.

Doctor, Ken. "The Newsonomics of Do-Over." Nieman Journalism Lab website, January 2011. Available at http://www.niemanlab.org/2011/01/the-newsonomics-of-do-over.

———. "Smelling New Value in Old Philly Newspapers." Ken Doctor's Instablog, April 28, 2010. Available at http://newsonomics.com/smelling-new-value-in-old-philly.

Doctorow, Corey. "Philly Cops Raids [*sic*] Activists Who Circulated Anti-CCTV Petition." Boing Boing, June 17, 2008. Available at http://www.boingboing.net/2008/06/17/philly-cops-raids-ac.html.

Doran, James. "Besieged U.S. Newspaper Journalists Face Final Deadline." *Observer,* June 29, 2008.

Fitzgerald, Tom. "Rendell Named Head of Nat[iona]l Governors Association." Philly.com, July 14, 2008. Available at http://www.philly.com/philly/news/breaking/25336124.html.

Folkenflik, David. "Major U.S. Newspapers Announce Staff Cuts." *All Things Considered,* National Public Radio, September 21, 2005. Available at http://www.npr.org/templates/story/story.php?storyId=4857927.

Garber, Megan. "Journal Register Company Joins with Outside.in for a Hyperlocal News/Ad Portal in Philadelphia," Nieman Journalism Lab, Harvard University, 2009. Available at http://www.niemanlab.org/2010/09/journal-register-company-joins-with-outside-in-for-a-hyperlocal-newsad-portal-in-philadelphia.

Garrett, Jesse James. "The Page of Only Weblogs." Jjg.net, April 10, 2002. Available at http://www.jjg.net/retired/portal/tpoowl.html.

Gdowik, Trishy. "GrooveLingo: Philly's Premiere Local Music Proto-Blog." Philebrity, August 27, 2008. Available at http://www.philebrity.com/2008/08/27/groovelingo -phillys-premiere-local-music-proto-blog.

Glaberson, William. "Another City Faces Cuts at Its Papers." *New York Times,* November 6, 2008. Available at http://query.nytimes.com/gst/fullpage.html?res=9B06E4D81739 F935A35752C1A963958260.

Gold, Matthew. "An Interview with Will Bunch of Attytood." Tattered Coat website, May 28, 2005. Available at http://www.tatteredcoat.com/archives/2005/05/28/an-interview -with-will-bunch-of-attytood.

Grassroots Media Network. "Homeless People's Network: GMC Organizers Update: Progress in Austin." Letter, October 20, 1999. Available at http://hpn.asu.edu/archives/ Oct99/0185.html.

Gregory, Kia. "At City Hall Rally, Police Raid Is Questioned." *Philadelphia Inquirer,* June 18, 2008. Available at http://www.philly.com/philly/news/local/20250159.html.

Hall, Howard. "After the Unconference." Smedley Log, March 25, 2006. Available at http://www.thesmedleylog.com/archives/632.

Hill, Benjamin Mako. "Software (,) Politics and Indymedia." March 11, 2003. Available at http://mako.cc/writing/mute-indymedia_software.html.

Hyde, Gene. "Independent Media Centers: Cyber-Subversion and the Alternative Press." First Monday, March 25, 2002. Available at http://firstmonday.org/issues/issue7_4/ hyde/index.html.

"Indymedia and Indybay History." Indybay website, May 11, 2005. Available at http:// www.indybay.org/newsitems/2005/03/11/17262451.php.

"Introduction to RSS." WebReference.com, 2005. Available at http://www.webreference .com/authoring/languages/xml/rss/intro.

"Issuecrawler: Instructions of Use." Govcom.org, 2009. Available at http://www.govcom .org/Issuecrawler_instructions.htm.

"It Would Be Hilarious if It Weren't True: Philly Cops Mistake Hipsters for M.O.V.E.- esque Hate Group." Philebrity, June 17, 2008. Available at http://www.philebrity .com/2008/06/17/it-would-be-hilarious-if-it-werent-true-philly-cops-mistake -hipsters-for-move-esque-hate-group.

Jarvis, Jeff. "The Ethic of the Link Layer on News." BuzzMachine website, June 2, 2008. Available at http://www.buzzmachine.com/2008/06/02/the-ethic-of-the-link-layer-on -news.

———. "Networked Journalism." BuzzMachine website, July 5, 2006. Available at http:// www.buzzmachine.com/2006/07/05/networked-journalism.

———. "New Rule: Cover What You Do Best: Link to the Rest." BuzzMachine website, July 22, 2007. Available at http://www.buzzmachine.com/2007/02/22/new-rule-cover -what-you-do-best-link-to-the-rest.

———. "Saving Journalism Isn't about Saving Jobs." BuzzMachine website, November 3, 2005. Available at http://www.buzzmachine.com/2005/11/03/saving-journalism-isnt -about-saving-jobs.

jennifer. "So Wait." Young Philly Politics, June 14, 2008. Available at http://youngphilly politics.com/police_critics_arrested_home_seized_police_raid#comment-25961.

J-Lab. "2010 Enterprise Reporting Awards." *J-Lab,* August 2010. Available at http:// www.j-lab.org/about/press-releases/2010_enterprise_reporting_awards.

journalists4mumia. "Good Point on Ramsey, but They Can Still Be Better." Young Philly Politics, June 13, 2008. Available at http://youngphillypolitics.com/police_critics _arrested_home_seized_police_raid#comment-25949.

———. "Police Critics Arrested, Home Seized in Police Raid." Young Philly Politics, June 13, 2008. Available at http://youngphillypolitics.com/police_critics_arrested_home _seized_police_raid.

———. "There Is a Clear Source." Young Philly Politics, June 14, 2008. Available at http://youngphillypolitics.com/police_critics_arrested_home_seized_police_raid#comment-25957.

Kelly, John. "About Morningside Analytics." Morningside Analytics website, 2007. Available at http://morningside-analytics.com/aboutus.php.

Kennedy, Dan. "Pro-am Journalism," 2006. Available at http://journalismofweb.blogspot.com/2006/09/pro-am-journalism.html.

"Knight Ridder Site Gains Another News Provider." *Editor and Publisher,* September 1, 2000. Available at http://www.allbusiness.com/services/business-services-miscellaneous-business/4677474-1.html.

Krebs, Valdis. "Social Network Analysis." Org.net, 2008. Available at http://www.orgnet.com/sna.html.

"KR Launches Philly.com Site." News and Tech.com, May 1999. Available at http://www.newsandtech.com/issues/1999/05-99/ot/05-99_phillycom.htm.

Lail, Jack. "Where Journalism Gets Reinvented." Jacklail.com, 2010. Available at http://www.jacklail.com/2010/04/-a-group-of-what.html.

Langeveld, Martin. "Who Owns Newspaper Companies? The Banks, Funds, and Investors and Their (Big) Slices of the Industry." Nieman Journalism Lab website, March 7, 2011. Available at http://www.niemanlab.org/2011/03/who-owns-newspaper-companies-the-banks-funds-and-investors-and-their-big-slices-of-the-industry.

Layton, Alexis, Justin Scott, and Mariusz Zydyk. "What Is a Bulletin Board System?" In Whatis.com, 2005. Available at http://searchcio-midmarket.techtarget.com/sDefinition/0,,sid183_gci213807,00.html.

Lenhart, Amanda, and Susannah Fox. "Bloggers: A Portrait of the Internet's New Storytellers." Pew Internet and American Life Project website, July 19, 2006. Available at http://www.pewinternet.org/PPF/r/186/report_display.asp.

MacMillan, Jim. "Greg Osberg: It's Going to Take a Couple of Years to Achieve This Miracle." Philadelphia Initiative for Journalistic Innovation website, 2010. Available at http://phiji.org/2010/11/21/greg-osberg-its-going-to-take-a-couple-of-years-to-achieve-this-miracle.

Madrak, Susie. "Philadelphia Daily News Wins Pulitzer—and the Paper Gets Auctioned Off April 27." Crooks and Liars, April 14, 2010. Available at http://crooksandliars.com/susie-madrak/philadelphia-daily-news-wins-pulitzer.

Manyank. "Why Professional Bloggers Suggest to Post Regularly?" Blog Design Studio, July 10, 2008. Available at http://blogdesignstudio.com/blogging-tips/why-professional-bloggers-suggest-to-post-regularly.

Marcinko, Tom. "Question Surveillance, Go to Jail." Futurismic, June 17, 2008. Available at http://futurismic.com/2008/06/17/it-cant-happen-here-in-philadelphia-on-the-other-hand.

Martino, Karl. "Saving Journalism Isn't about Saving Jobs." Philly Future, November 4, 2005. Available at http://phillyfuture.org/node/1998.

———. "Site News." Philly Future, June 11, 2000. Available at http://web.archive.org/web/20001212202200/phillyfuture.editthispage.com/newsItems/viewDepartment$Site+News.

Mazone, Daniel, Wendy Warren, and Fatima Nelson. "WHYY, the *Philadelphia Daily News,* and the Committee of Seventy Launch 'The Next Mayor Project.'" Press release, December 5, 2005. Available at http://www.prnewswire.com/news-releases/whyy-the-philadelphia-daily-news-and-the-committee-of-seventy-launch-the-next-mayor-project-67503772.html.

McQuade, Daniel. "Inquirer Wackiness Continues." Philadelphia Will Do, July 2, 2008. Available at http://willdo.philadelphiaweekly.com/archives/2008/07/inquirer_wackin .html.

Miller, G. W. "Stop the Presses." *Philadelphia Weekly Online,* September 3, 2008. Available at http://www.philadelphiaweekly.com/articles/17593/cover-story.

MrLuigi. "Can You Back Up the 'Community Meetings' a Little?" Young Philly Politics, June 13, 2008. Available at http://youngphillypolitics.com/police_critics_arrested_home _seized_police_raid#comment-25948.

Netanel, Neil. "The Demise of Newspapers: Economics, Copyright, Free Speech." Balkin .com website, May 5, 2008. Available at http://balkin.blogspot.com/2008/05/demise -of-newspapers-economics.html.

"The New Philly.com." Philly.com, May 11, 2008. Available at http://www.philly.com/ philly/hp/news_update/The_New_Phillycom.html.

Nolter, Chris. "Philly's Full Court Press." Available at http://www.thedeal.com/magazine/ ID/034427/features/philly-full-court-press.php.

Norgs Working Group. "The Norgs Unconference Statement of Principles." *Norgs—the New News Organization Wiki,* May 9, 2007. Available at http://norgs.pbwiki.com/ The+Norgs+Unconference+Statement+Of+Principles.

Oliver, Jen. "Fear, Loathing and Anal Sex . . . on a Dial-Up: The Other Side of CPCN's First Philly Internet Community." Philebrity, August 29, 2008. Available at http:// www.philebrity.com/2008/08/29/fear-loathing-and-anal-sex-on-a-dial-up-the-other -side-of-cpcns-first-philly-internet-community.

Pant, Rajiv. "About PhillyFinder." Rajiv Pant website. Available at http://www.rajiv.com/ work/com/phillyfinder/toc.htm.

"Papers Name a Manager to Look into Consolidation." *Philadelphia Inquirer,* July 9, 2008. Available at http://www.philly.com/philly/business/20080709_Papers_name_a_mana ger_to_look_into_consolidation.html.

Phawker. "Debunked: The Great Philadelphia Paywall Scare," January 5, 2011. Available at http://www.phawker.com/2011/01/05/reality-check-correcting-fact-errors-in -philebritys-reporting-on-phillycom-going-paywall.

Philly Clout. "Clout: This Is How City Hall Treats Citizens with No Record," June 27, 2007. Available at http://www.philly.com/philly/hp/news_update/21930154.html.

"Philly the First to Fall?" Newspaper Biz website, June 6, 2008. Available at http://www .newspaperbiz.com/2008/06/philly-first-to-fall.html.

Potts, Mark. "Bubble, Bubble, Toil and Trouble." Recovering Journalist website, June 17, 2008. Available at http://recoveringjournalist.typepad.com/recovering_journalist/ 2008/06/bubble-bubble-toil-and-trouble.html.

Quinn, Amy. "Whither the Feminist Housewife?" Citizen Mom, April 13, 2005. Available at http://www.citizenmom.net/2005/04/page/2.

Rabaino, Lauren. "Notes from BCNI: Greg Linch on 'Rethinking Our Thinking,' 2010. Available at http://laurenmichell.com.

Regan, Tom. "News You Can Use from the Little Guys." *Christian Science Monitor,* December 9, 1999. Available at http://docs.indymedia.org/view/Global/CsmArticle.

"Report: Pop PC Articles_May29#94BC3." Philly.com, June 29, 2008.

Roddy, Dennis. "Police, Protesters Battle in the Streets; Attempt to Disrupt Convention Results in 282 Arrests, Injury to Five Police." *Pittsburgh Post-Gazette,* August 2, 2000.

Rosen, Jay. "Jay Rosen of NYU on the Ethic of the Link." YouTube, April 8, 2008. Available at http://www.youtube.com/watch?v=RIMB9Kx18hw.

———. "Journalism Goes Pro-Am." *Guardian,* September 20, 2006. Available at http://www.guardian.co.uk/commentisfree/2006/sep/20/post394.

———. "A Prayer for the Philly Papers." PressThink website, June 2, 2006. Available at http://journalism.nyu.edu/pubzone/weblogs/pressthink/2006/06/02/pray_phl.html.

Rosenberg, Scott. "Question about the History of Blogging." [Via Wordyard contact form.] Letter, December 8, 2008.

Rousset, Jeff, and Jen Rock. "Philadelphia Activists Still Homeless after Arrests and Seizure of Home." Philadelphia Independent Media Center, June 22, 2008. Available at http://www.phillyimc.org/en/node/69583.

Rubin, Daniel "Who Wrote 'Kill the Pigs' at 17th and Ridge?" Blinq, June 17, 2008. Available at http://www.philly.com/philly/blogs/inq-blinq/20009829.html.

Sassaman, Hannah. "Release: Homeowners Fighting Police Brutality Illegally Arrested, Never Charged." Young Philly Politics, June 16, 2008. Available at http://young phillypolitics.com/release_homeowners_fighting_police_brutality_illegally_arrested _never_charged.

Schaffer, Jan. "Exploring a Networked Journalism Collaborative in Philadelphia," JLab .org, April 2010, available at http://www.j-lab.org/publications/philadelphia_media _project.

Schimmel, Bruce. "Journalists Wanted." *Philadelphia City Paper,* January 1, 2009. Available at http://citypaper.net/articles/2009/01/01/journalists-needed.

Shirky, Clay. "News Papers and Thinking the Unthinkable." March 2009. Available at http://www.shirky.com/weblog/2009/03/newspapers-and-thinking-the-unthinkable.

Sifry, David. "State of the Blogosphere, April 2006, Part 1: On Blogosphere Growth." Sifry's Alerts, April 17, 2006. Available at http://www.sifry.com/alerts/archives/ 000432.html.

Smith, Erica. "Paper Cuts." Paper Cuts, 2008. Available at http://graphicdesignr.net/ papercuts.

Socco, Daniel. "How Often Should I Blog?" DailyBlogTips, November 12, 2006. Available at http://www.dailyblogtips.com/how-often-should-i-blog.

Strupp, Joe. "Guild Asks for Volunteers to Ease Sting of Philly Layoffs." *Editor and Publisher,* January 3, 2007. Available at http://www.editorandpublisher.com/eandp/ article_brief/eandp/1/1003527084.

Sweeney, Joey. "About Us." Philebrity, December 4, 2004. Available at http://web.archive .org/web/20041204072729/www.philebrity.com/about.html.

———. "Breaking: Worst Monday Ever at Broad and Whatever as Philly Newspapers File Chapter 11." Philebrity, February 22, 2009. Available at http://www.philebrity.com/ 2009/02/22/breaking-worst-monday-ever-at-broad-whatever.

———. "Call for Volunteers: We Demand the New Style." Philebrity, March 28, 2007. Available at http://www.philebrity.com/2007/03/28/call-for-volunteers-we-demand -the-new-style.

———. "Philly Internet History Week." Philebrity, September 1, 2008. Available at http:// www.philebrity.com/category/philly-internet-history-week.

Taylor, Mel. "Personal History: I Used to Love Her (the Radio, That Is), But I Had to Kill Her (with the Internet)." Philebrity, August 26, 2008. Available at http://www .philebrity.com/2008/08/26/personal-history-i-used-to-love-her-the-radio-that-is -but-i-had-to-kill-her-with-the-internet.

Thompson, Isaiah. "There's Something Fishy in Francisville." The Clog, June 14, 2008. Available at http://www.citypaper.net/blogs/clog/2008/06/14/theres-something-fishy -in-francisville.

Thornton, John. "Nonprofit News Outlets Will Be a Bigger Part of Our Future than Alan Mutter Thinks," 2010. Available at http://www.niemanlab.org/2010/03/john-thornton -nonprofit-news-outlets-will-be-a-bigger-part-of-our-future-than-alan-mutter -thinks.

Tridish, Pete. "Police Critics Arrested, Home Seized in Police Raid!" Philly IMC, June 13, 2008. Available at http://www.phillyimc.org/en/node/68912.

Volk, Steve. "Dead Air." *Philadelphia Magazine,* October 2007. Available at http://www .phillymag.com/articles/dead_air.

———. "Inquirer, Daily News to Shed More Staff." *Philadelphia Magazine,* August 25, 2008. Available at http://www.phillymag.com/news/2008/08/25/inquirer-daily-news -to-shed-more-staff.

Warren, Wendy. "If You Don't Vote, You've Lost Already." TheNextMayor.com, March 28, 2007. Available at http://blogs.phillynews.com/dailynews/nextmayor/2007/03/ if_you_dont_vote_youve_lost_al.html.

———. "Norgs: Norgs Whiteboards." *Norgs: News Organizations and the Future—an Ongoing Conversation,* March 25, 2006. Available at http://blogs.phillynews.com/ dailynews/norg/archives/002984.html.

———. "Norgs: What We Did Saturday." *Norgs: News Organizations and the Future—an Ongoing Conversation,* March 25, 2006. Available at http://blogs.phillynews.com/ dailynews/norg/archives/002988.html.

———. "Re: A Thanksgiving Wish." Letter, November 28, 2008. Available at http://groups .yahoo.com/group/norgs/message/1469.

Wikipedia. "Blog." *Wikipedia—the Free Encyclopedia,* 2003. Available at http://en.wiki pedia.org/wiki/Weblog.

Wink, Christopher. "BarCamp NewsInnovation 2.0: My Take Aways and Experience," May 5, 2010, available at http://christopherwink.com/2010/05/05/barcamp-news innovation-2-0-my-take-aways-and-experience.

———. "Newsworks: WHYY Online News Brand Launching Means a Lot to These Legacies." ChristopherWink.com. November 11, 2010. Available at http://christopher wink.com/2010/11/22/newsworks-whyy-online-news-brand-launching-means-a-lot -to-these-legacies.

Index

C. W. Anderson is an Assistant Professor of Media Culture at the College of Staten Island (City University of New York). He has published in numerous academic journals and occasionally writes for the Nieman Journalism Lab and *The Atlantic* online. He has contributed chapters to various edited volumes, including *The Social Media Reader, Making Our Media, Making Online News,* and *The Handbook of Journalism Studies.*

DATE DUE

2/28/13 9977 3856 URS

PRINTED IN U.S.A.